S0-BRU-840

# T.L.S.

ESSAYS AND REVIEWS FROM

*The Times Literary Supplement · 1971*

# 10

# T.L.S.

## ESSAYS AND REVIEWS FROM

*The Times Literary Supplement · 1971*

# IO

*London*
OXFORD UNIVERSITY PRESS
1972

*Oxford University Press, Ely House, London W. 1*

GLASGOW NEW YORK TORONTO MELBOURNE WELLINGTON
CAPE TOWN IBADAN NAIROBI DAR ES SALAAM LUSAKA ADDIS ABABA
DELHI BOMBAY CALCUTTA MADRAS KARACHI LAHORE DACCA
KUALA LUMPUR SINGAPORE HONG KONG TOKYO

ISBN 0 19 211551 0



Printed in Great Britain by
Alden & Mowbray Ltd
at the Alden Press, Oxford

# CONTENTS

# NOTE

*TLS 10* is an anthology of the more significant reviews printed in the *Times Literary Supplement* during 1971. Some of the books discussed—E. M. Forster's *Maurice*, Solzhenitsyn's *August 1914*—were literary events of the year, others are convenient excuses for a full and stringent survey of particular fields of scholarship. The subjects covered in *TLS 10* range from politics to child psychotherapy, and there is also a selection of the year's new novels and collections of poetry.

# NOTE

# I

# VIEWS FROM THE TOP

## (*a*) A KHRUSHCHEV ANTHOLOGY

THIS VOLUME CONTAINS, besides the purported reminiscences of N. S. Khrushchev, a short publisher's note concerning the provenance of the material; a similar note by Strobe Talbott about his part in the preparation of the book; a twenty-two page introduction by Edward Crankshaw; four appendixes comprising a chronology of Khrushchev's career, an explanatory comment on Soviet institutions and terminology, potted biographies of nine of Khrushchev's former Kremlin colleagues and the text of Khrushchev's notorious 'de-Stalinization' speech at a closed session of the Twentieth Congress of the Soviet Communist Party in 1956; and seventy-one illustrations. In addition, Khrushchev's contribution is liberally interlarded with glosses and scene-setting commentary.

With all these aids to comprehension it is a fairly safe assumption that the volume is intended for general, even popular, consumption rather than for the specialist in Soviet affairs.

The specialist, in fact, is likely to be considerably exasperated by the book. He would presumably relish nothing better than a candid account of Kremlin politics over a period of several decades by a central participant recollecting his own experiences in tranquillity—which is what the advance publicity for these 'memoirs' may well have led him to expect. But any such hopes are dispelled immediately by the publisher's note with which the book opens. This affirms that the book is 'an authentic record of Nikita Khrushchev's words', but qualifies the claim with the statement that it 'is made up of material emanating from various sources at various times and in various circumstances'. Mr. Talbott confirms the patchwork nature of the

---

(*a*) *Khrushchev Remembers*. Translated and edited by Strobe Talbott. Introduction, Commentary and Notes by Edward Crankshaw. 639 pp. André Deutsch. £3.50.

(*b*) HAROLD WILSON: *The Labour Government 1964–1970: A Personal Record*. 836 pp. Weidenfeld and Nicolson/Michael Joseph. £4.80.

exercise with his observations that 'the original material, when it came into my hands, was quite disorganized' and that 'in trying to turn it into a readable English book, I have had to take certain liberties with the structure'. He too, however, insists that 'except for an occasional paraphrase or improvised transitional sentence, Khrushchev has said everything attributed to him in his book'.

The Russian reaction to Western reports of the imminent publication of *Khrushchev Remembers* was predictable. Khrushchev himself formally denounced assertions that he had ever passed on 'memoirs or materials of this nature to either a foreign or a Soviet publishing house' as 'a fabrication' typical of 'the venal bourgeois press', though it is perhaps noteworthy that his statement did not categorically deny that he had ever compiled such reminiscences.

*Izvestiya*, in an article characteristically loaded with virtuous indignation and cheap innuendo, elaborated the repudiation by declaring the 'memoirs' to be the fruits of a collaboration between the United States and British secret services. According to this account, Mr. Talbott is a neophyte member of the C.I.A. who retired to the cloistered peace of Oxford in order to work on the fabrication of Khrushchev's reminiscences under the wing of the British secret service. The association of Mr. Crankshaw with the project is accepted by *Izvestiya* as clinching proof of its spuriousness. Mr. Crankshaw is credited with being a long-time member of the 'Secret Intelligence Service' with a record of subversive activity so black that the Soviet Union has been obliged to close its frontiers to him.

Nothing in the narrative itself nullifies the claims of the publisher and editor that it is a true record of Khrushchev's words. Almost all of it is old hat, having been more or less publicly related by Khrushchev in his free-wheeling heyday, either when holding court among foreign journalists or diplomats, or during the long audiences he was wont to vouchsafe to foreign representatives in his pursuance of a new style of Soviet leadership; and even those passages which do not immediately recall previously published utterances by Khrushchev might conceivably derive from remarks made by him in circumstances which precluded their publication but which did not mean that records were not made.

On the most cynical interpretation, this reasoning would lend credibility to the theory that these 'reminiscences' are, in fact, a compilation of views expressed by Khrushchev, on or off the record, in the course of his public life and now extracted from some painstaking memory bank and skilfully pieced together to form a running narrative. This theory is consistent with the publisher's statement that the material emanated 'from various sources at various times and in various circumstances' and with the editor-translator's comment that the material he received was 'quite disorganized'. It does not, however, accord well with the enthusiasm with which Mr. Crankshaw in his introduction hails this 'voice from limbo'. Mr. Crankshaw seems to accept wholeheartedly that Khrushchev in retirement betook himself to his study and recorded his memoirs after the manner of a Harold Macmillan or a George Brown. But the only evidence he adduces in support of his conviction that the reminiscences are 'the real thing' is the assertion that 'to anyone who had listened to him [Khrushchev] in the days of his prime, or read his speeches in Russian, there was no mistaking the authentic tone'—an argument which, in the circumstances, will scarcely command universal acceptance.

Mr. Crankshaw remarks, incidentally, that his own decision about the authenticity of 'this remarkable document' had to be based on the evidence of 'a Russian typescript and nothing else at all'. One would like to know more about that typescript. Was it a complete Russian-language text of the reminiscences as now published in English translation? Or was it a series of instalments as received from various sources at various times? In plain fact, before either endorsing Mr. Crankshaw's opinion or taking issue with him on the point of authenticity one would require to see the original text oneself.

Meanwhile, if compelled to gamble on one theory or another to account for this assemblage of Khrushchev's recollections, one would be inclined to guess that they contain a certain number of reminiscences genuinely recorded by Khrushchev himself since his removal from the leadership, and that these have been padded out by a far greater quantity of much older material deriving from his undammable loquacity while in power.

The genesis of the material incorporated in *Khrushchev Remembers* will probably provide the experts with bones of kremlinological contention for a long time to come. To the general reader, however, this is of minor importance. What will matter to him is that the recollections now conveniently assembled in a single volume, whenever and however they may have been recorded, genuinely reflect the experiences and opinions on a vast number of fascinating topics of a man who for almost a decade wielded virtually autocratic authority in one of the world's two super-powers. As such, they help enormously to put the picture of the man in focus, to illuminate the dim corridors of the Kremlin and to fill out the rationale of post-war Russian policies and actions.

Khrushchev emerges from his own protestations as a man notably well-equipped to climb the political ladder in the circumstances which prevailed between the wars. His education was sketchy, he was no ideologist, and he was quick and shrewd rather than profound. But he was tough and courageous, hard-working and resourceful, self-confident and ambitious. Moreover, he was able to make himself liked by his superiors and his equals (including such as Kaganovich and Stalin, for whom in these pages he expresses an intemperate detestation), and he was very successful by one means or another in stimulating those under him to great effort (as in the building of the Moscow Metro). He also had a marked talent for survival, which he himself calls luck, though his emergence unscathed from the internal party struggles of the 1920s and 1930s was evidently not unconnected with the fact that he avowedly hitched his wagon to Stalin's star. For his part, Stalin trusted him and, as Khrushchev puts it, 'to the last day of his life he liked me'.

More than half the book is devoted to the internal political scene as Khrushchev progressed, surprisingly smoothly, from the Donbas, via Kharkov and Kiev, to the Kremlin itself. We are given glimpses of conditions during the Civil War, the forced collectivization, the great purges, the war with Finland and the 'Great Patriotic War'; and there are sidelights on the K.G.B., Soviet antisemitism, particular industrial problems, the atmosphere of fear and plotting which surrounded Stalin, and the manner in which government policies were determined. Almost all of this stands out in stark contrast to the unflawed and universal nobility and perfection customarily portrayed by official Soviet publicity.

Khrushchev also expresses frank opinions about a whole range of personalities in the upper reaches of the Communist Party hierarchy, including Beria, Bulganin, Malenkov, Mikoyan and Molotov (but nobody still active in the present leadership), about notable military leaders, including Marshals Zhukov, Malinovsky and Rokossovsky, and about Stalin's wife, Nadezhda Alliluyeva, and their daughter Svetlana. All these opinions are highly subjective, and many of Khrushchev's judgments call for a pinch of salt, but they are none the less readable for that and they undoubtedly contribute to the reader's understanding of the picture in general and of Khrushchev's own character and personality in particular.

There are glaring gaps in Khrushchev's narrative. He provides no account of his own assumption and consolidation of supreme power in the years following the death of Stalin, makes no mention of the 'anti-Party' group and the dramatic clash of 1957, and ignores the circumstances of his removal from power in 1964. He explains his own and other people's attitudes towards his proposal to destroy the image of Stalin as 'The People's Father and Friend' at the Twentieth Party Congress, but says nothing about his possibly even more pregnant 'general report' to the same Congress, which ushered in Khrushchev's version of 'peaceful coexistence' and brought in its train intellectual indiscipline at home, physical rebellion within the East European block, polycentrism within the world communist movement, and the Sino-Soviet schism.

Khrushchev insists that the denigration of Stalin was necessary, timely, and efficacious. This may well be so. But the issue has already been publicly debated at enormous length and one would have wished to hear also his defence against the 'conservative' charge that such 1956 phenomena as the Hungarian rising, the Polish riots, the student unrest in the Soviet Union, the upsurge of nonconformity among Russian artists and intellectuals, and the incipient fragmentation of world communism were directly attributable to the under-considered 'liberal' implications of the policy he called peaceful coexistence.

Certainly there is nothing in these reminiscences to contradict the suspicion that Khrushchev's besetting weakness was an inability to see very far either in space or in time. And it is plain that, once he was firmly established in command, he was no more immune than the next man, de-Stalinization notwithstanding, to the corruptive effect of power. The result was an apparently incorrigible tendency to act arbitrarily and impetuously upon a superficially logical and persuasive appraisal of a situation without truly appreciating its long-range implications. It is, for example, hard to believe that he foresaw the effect on other Communist Parties of his pronouncement that there could be 'different roads to socialism' or, indeed, the lengths to which the Chinese would go in their absolute and implacable opposition to his whole concept of peaceful coexistence.

Khrushchev never, in fact, even began to come to grips with the problems represented by the Chinese Communist Party, and his discussion of Sino-Soviet relations in this book is strikingly ingenuous, petty, and emotional. As early as 1954, he relates, on his return to Moscow from a visit to China, he reported to his comrades: 'Conflict with China is inevitable.' This conclusion was reached 'on the basis of various remarks Mao had made', and Khrushchev then goes on to describe the 'typically oriental atmosphere' in Peking, where 'everyone was unbelievably courteous and ingratiating' and 'it was all too sickeningly sweet' and 'nauseating'. Moreover, Khrushchev continues, 'some of the things Mao said put me on my guard. I was never exactly sure that I understood what he meant.' What he did understand, however, was that the Chinese were uncommonly grasping. When Stalin asked them for a site in China on which to build a pineapple cannery, he was smartly told by Mao Tse-tung to 'give us a credit loan and we will build the cannery ourselves. We will then pay back your loan with the produce from this cannery.' A little later Chou En-lai invited the Soviet Union 'to make us a gift of a university'; and after the Soviet Union had built the road from Ulan Bator to Peking, Khrushchev was understandably taken aback to be told that 'the road from Ulan Bator isn't much use to us. What we really need is a road from Peking through the mountains to Kazakhstan', and then to be pressed to build that too.

So far as we in Britain are concerned there is a certain mild nostalgia in reading about the excitements of the visit of Bulganin and Khrushchev in 1956, but in truth Khrushchev's recollection is disappointingly vague and the impressions he records are in the main trivial and superficial.

More intriguing and revealing to the West as a whole is Khrushchev's account of the Cuba crisis of October, 1962. His apologia for his behaviour in this matter starts with the postulate that the United States was committed to the destruction of the Castro regime by military action. The Soviet Union had an obligation to protect Cuba, and Khrushchev personally conceived the idea of putting missiles into Cuba in order to discharge that duty. The purpose of this move was 'to deter America from starting a war' and, after 'a period of perilous tension', this goal was achieved. The upshot, claims Khrushchev, was 'a triumph of Soviet foreign policy and a personal triumph in my own career as a statesman'. This is essentially the same line as was taken by Kosygin in the first official Russian report on the Caribbean confrontation at the beginning of November, 1962, and though it may have satisfied a Russian audience it is absurdly *simpliste* for other consumers. It is characteristic of Khrushchev that he should express surprise that the Cubans regarded the outcome as 'a moral defeat' for the Soviet Union. Most of the world's qualified onlookers, such as the governments of the main Western powers, most uncommitted governments and a wide range of Communist Party leaderships, shared Castro's view.

The memoirs, then (if that is what they are), are by no means closely analytical; they offer intimate if not always brand-new glimpses of places, personalities and events which, to most of us, by reason of their normal remoteness, are still shrouded in a theatrical unreality; they tell us a fair amount about Khrushchev's own character and personality; and they usefully set one re-examining one's own memories, judgments, and prejudices.

## (*b*) MR. WILSON'S DIARY

AFTER INSTANT GOVERNMENT, instant history: or at any rate instant autobiography. The technique is not very different. Setting the record straight, like governing the country, is largely a matter of the skilful and persuasive use of words. The opening pages of Harold Wilson's personal record are not unlike a political speech or an election manifesto. They determine both the theme and the language in which it is to be expressed. The theme is the transformation brought about by the Labour Government from the appalling legacy of near-bankruptcy in 1964 to the well-based prosperity of 1970. The language is also familiar: it is a record of tough, harsh, relevant, purposeful, specifically socialist measures. Only one or two epithets are missing. Significantly, 'abrasive' has been transferred to Edward Heath, who is also identified as the pioneer of 'instant opposition'.

No doubt remains of Mr. Wilson's consummate skill in choosing and using words. Many readers will have wondered how he would vindicate certain of his past undertakings, but his verbal dexterity never fails. The Nassau agreement on nuclear weapons with the United States Government was to be 're-negotiated', for instance. Very well, Mr. Wilson proposes an Atlantic Nuclear Force, to which Britain and the United States would contribute equal numbers of Polaris submarines. 'This was our answer to the controversial Nassau Agreement.' It passes unmentioned that nothing whatever came of the proposal. But in case the oversight should be remarked, Mr. Wilson later points out that he refrained from asking the American president for the new Poseidon missile as an eventual replacement for Polaris. 'To that extent I was presenting him not with a new Nassau but a Nassau in reverse.' That is all the reader can expect to be told about 're-negotiating Nassau'.

A similar debating skill is to be admired over the equally famous undertaking to repeal the Rent Act passed by the Conservative Government in 1957. Considering that most of that Act is still on the statute-book, it is natural to wonder how the discrepancy is to be explained. The answer is simple: 'We promised a Bill to restore rent control and, in effect, to repeal all the odious provisions of the 1957 Act.' Mr. Wilson has not in fact claimed to have repealed the whole Act, though the casual reader may think he has. Nor is total repeal ever possible of a major Act of Parliament, because however controversial it may be in toto, there are always many clauses in it that are generally acceptable and desirable. It is clearly with this thought in mind that Mr. Wilson has refrained from promising, as many of his followers would like him to do, to repeal the forthcoming Industrial Relations Act. Certainly if he were to become Prime Minister again he would not do so. There is, incidentally, nothing whatever in his memoirs to support the recently canvassed speculation that he has decided not to lead the Labour Party in another general election.

That speculation evidently rests on a misinterpretation of the attitude which Mr. Wilson displays to colleagues and subordinates in writing about them. There is certainly an unusual frankness and even harshness in some of his expressions of opinion. It shows itself not so much in his treatment of senior colleagues like George Brown, whose conduct was often intolerable and who in any case is well able to look after himself in controversy. The same is true of Frank Cousins, who is the subject of a complex and enigmatic criticism:

> I enunciated a 'law' about the coefficient between the publicity attaching to a minister's work and the reality of his achievements. In the past I had known very high coefficients: Frank Cousins I felt had a coefficient less than unity.

In any case Mr. Wilson is unlikely to have either of these colleagues with him again if he forms another government. It is rather his attitude towards the Civil Service that has earned him most opprobrium. Here it is not the individual personalities that matter, for the Civil Service has a collective personality and a very long memory.

Mr. Wilson is no respecter of persons or conventions. His attitude towards the Civil Service is characteristic of his attitude towards the Establishment as a whole, which in turn reflects a refreshingly new conception of social values. Unlike the two previous Labour Prime Ministers, Mr. Wilson made a serious effort to re-mould the accepted conventions of prestige and responsibility in public life. There were innumerable manifestations of this effort: the refusal to confer hereditary peerages and automatic knighthoods; the elevation of new occupations to high honours, such as principals of technical colleges, football managers, and popular entertainers; the insistence on remaining a man of the people, who cleaned his own shoes and had a bottle of sauce on the dinner-table and politely refused to put on a tail-coat to call on the Queen. More significantly, he not only saw clearly the distinction which Bagehot drew between the dignified and the efficient elements in the British constitution; he was determined to give dignity to the efficient, and to make the merely dignified elements efficient as well. To that end he was impatient with some of the formalities of Parliament and he saw through the absurd fiction that ministers alone could be blamed for bureaucratic obstinacy and incompetence.

There was no reason, in his eyes, why civil servants should enjoy a unique combination of power and prestige with immunity from public criticism. The only immunity he dared not attack was their exemption from 'severe restraint' on wage increases. But he has made up for that timidity by the unaccustomed boldness with which he castigated their shortcomings in public. As early as 1966, when his own party gave evidence to the Fulton Commission on the Civil Service, suggesting that sometimes officials misled their ministers and even withheld information from them, Mr. Wilson peremptorily declared that any minister who allowed that to happen would get short shrift from him. In his memoirs he repeatedly blames civil servants for doing exactly that. Officials in the Commonwealth Relations Office misled him about the dispute between India and Pakistan; others were to blame for his belief that sanctions would bring down the Rhodesian government in 'weeks, not months'; the Treasury invented his notorious phrase about 'the pound in your pocket'; and it was 'our man on the spot' who produced a faulty appreciation of the crisis in Anguilla.

Usually Mr. Wilson had no difficulty in dealing with officials who exceeded or failed in their duties. More than once the Foreign Office tried to rewrite the drafts on which he based his efforts to achieve peace in Vietnam. With one of their counter-drafts he wasted no time: 'Politely, but firmly, I indicated to them into which part of their filing system they were free to put it.' Mr. Wilson's alternative draft was not noticeably successful in achieving the object in view, but at least the officials had been put in their place. On one issue, however, he bought himself a boomerang. The episode of the D-Notices in 1967 is still obscure, except to those familiar with the twilight world in which the bitter struggle was fought. But at least there is no doubt that Mr. Wilson mishandled it because, most exceptionally, he says so himself. What made the affair more than usually damaging to his reputation was, of course, that he unwisely chose to do battle on two fronts simultaneously, not only with the official machine but also with the press.

Mr. Wilson's relations with the press are a particularly intriguing and difficult field of study. There is no doubt that he was at times treated extremely badly by the communications media, including television as well as the newspapers. A more recent episode has strongly emphasized the legitimacy of some of his complaints about the BBC, though it occurred after this book was written. Scores of examples may be found in his memoirs, ranging from petulant diatribes about misreporting and misinterpretation to more soberly penetrating judgments, such as that 'the headlines, however sensationalized or selective, fail to measure even the tip of the iceberg in the sea of democratic government, where the heaviest and more lethal pressures are below the surface, sometimes concentrated within the heart of the individual'.

There are many cases in which Mr. Wilson must clearly be given the benefit of the doubt when he accuses the press of misjudgment: his efforts to make peace in Vietnam and the Middle East, and press comments on the expenditure cuts in 1968 and his White Paper on industrial relations in 1969, are all cases in point. Yet he must take some of the blame himself for the fluctuations of his love-hate relationship with the media, and this he declines to do. There is no mention, on the one hand, of the well-calculated wave of propaganda on which he rode to power, nor on the other of his extraordinary outbursts before the television cameras as he opened his speech to the Labour Party conference in 1967.

One of the recurrent weaknesses of his memoirs is in fact the determination to prove himself, on all essential matters, constantly in the right. He does, it is true, give an impression of candour by admitting to occasional errors; but they do not add up to a formidable list. Though doubtful about the way the Department of Economic Affairs functioned in practice, he will not admit that it was a mistake either to set it up or to abolish it. He confidently defends the National Plan of 1965. He has no doubt that it was right to cancel the TSR-2 aircraft, but passes no judgment on the decision to order an American replacement and then cancel that too. The acknowledged errors are comparatively venial. He underestimated the power of speculators against sterling, and the capacity of Whitehall to leak secret information. He should not have yielded to party pressures to dismiss Lord Beeching as Chairman of British Rail; he should have taken the decision to abandon the British presence East of Suez earlier; and he mistimed the introduction of the White Paper, *In Place of Strife*. That is about the sum of it. Most of the other errors for which he was blamed—over arms for South Africa, the sinking of the Torrey Canyon, the appointment of a new General Secretary of the Labour Party, and even the threat to withdraw 'dog licences', among others that have already been mentioned—turn out on examination to have been due to malicious or inadvertent misunderstandings.

The press is held responsible, for the most part, only for the inadvertent misunderstandings; and usually Mr. Wilson's case is soundly based. He entirely clears up, for example, the obscure circumstances in which Peter Shore was present at the crucial meeting of the Privy Council in March, 1968 which led to George Brown's final resignation in protest because he was absent. But the malicious misunderstandings are another matter. For these the Conservative Opposition, either alone or in collusion with the right-wing press, is held chiefly to blame. Mr. Wilson has scarcely a civil word for Mr. Heath from beginning to end. Sir Alec Douglas-Home and Duncan Sandys fare little better. Lesser ministers are treated with a characteristic wit which is always most effective when it is least friendly. Presumed allies of the Conservative leadership, like Ian Smith and Cecil King, are also severely handled. Once or twice Mr. Wilson admits to having been unaware of a secret enemy in his camp: he did not know, for instance, that Lord Cromer, when Governor of the Bank of England, was already a close friend of Mr. Heath; nor that Sir Hugh Beadle, the Chief Justice of Rhodesia, was personally sympathetic with the leaders of UDI. Perhaps the most disturbing feature of his memoirs is that he seems so often to reject entirely the possibility that anyone who disagreed with him could be acting in good faith.

There are exceptions, it is true, but almost all of them are either dead or retired. His admiration for Winston Churchill is unbounded —so much so that he was genuinely embarrassed when President Johnson explicitly compared him with his great predecessor. (To his credit, Mr. Wilson includes one of the unflattering cartoons with which the press hailed this gaffe.) He has scarcely less admiration for Harold Macmillan, whose style he consciously copies in many ways. President de Gaulle and President Johnson are each the subject of penetrating and brilliantly written chapters. But in neither case was there a current conflict at issue at the time. De Gaulle had already retired when he and Mr. Wilson discussed the ethics of cheating at patience. President Johnson had already decided not to seek re-election when Mr. Wilson visited him for the last time. Although at times they had furious altercations, in which Mr. Wilson was inevitably worsted, they had common ground in a mutual fascination with each other's techniques of political manipulation. There are almost no other major figures about whom Mr. Wilson writes with similar tolerance and perspicacity—certainly none with whom he is ever likely to do business again as Prime Minister.

This conclusion points to an important generalization about the upshot of Mr. Wilson's six years in office. His political style has served to narrow the area of political consensus. Since it is widely believed that one of the contributions which Britain can make to European unity is skill in running a parliamentary democracy, there could be serious consequences from the change of character which has come over British politics since 1963. It is not merely a matter of mutual antipathy between the leaders of the two major parties, though that is obvious and damaging enough and has compounded the harm done. But the harm goes deeper. The two-party system used to rest on the convention that there were large areas of fundamental agreement which were never challenged. That is why changes of government were comparatively painless and coalitions were easily formed in times of severe crisis. Today changes of government are by no means painless. The refrain that everything which is going wrong today is entirely the fault of 'yesterday's men' can be heard echoing from both sides of the Chamber without a pause throughout each successive parliament. There is no reason to think it will ever be silenced. The idea of a coalition between the present-day Conservative and Labour leaders is also unthinkable, not solely because of personalities but because no crisis can readily be foreseen in which they would not prescribe diametrically opposite remedies.

It would be absurd to accuse Mr. Wilson of having created this situation, but he plainly revels in it. Although Mr. Heath is not yet so explicitly on record, there is no reason to suppose that he regrets the disappearance of consensus any more than Mr. Wilson. It is a momentous change from the days of Baldwin and MacDonald, Churchill and Attlee, or even Macmillan and Gaitskell. There is no longer any excuse for saying that it makes no difference which party wins elections. Mr. Wilson is determined that it should make a difference, even if that means he has to change his own stance, as in the case of legislation on industrial relations and entry into the Common Market. Admittedly he is convinced that he has not changed his stance on either subject, but the public thinks otherwise; and at least it is certain there is no inter-party consensus. That is not necessarily a bad thing, for consensus can go too far. It is arguable that the mutual compatibility of temperament and policy between Baldwin and MacDonald facilitated the defeatist style of economic and foreign policy in the 1930s. The determination of Churchill and Macmillan not to antagonize the trade unions similarly contributed to the inflationary wave of the 1950s. But most people would judge that Mr. Wilson and Mr. Heath have gone too far in the other direction. What is worse, the process looks irreversible. And what is even more regrettable about Mr. Wilson's memoirs is that they not merely record the process unashamedly but contribute to aggravating it.

His book is therefore to be seen as a political event in its own right, not simply as a record of events. Historians who use it, as they will have to do, will feel obliged to discount a more than usual degree of special pleading. Some of it they will recognize as written with tongue in cheek. They may also be disappointed by the lack of conspicuously new revelations. Among the few titbits, some are tantalizingly incomplete, like *hors d'œuvre* without a meal to follow. Mr. Wilson decides, for example, to appoint Lord Mountbatten as Governor of Rhodesia; he flies to Balmoral to seek the Queen's approval, thus incidentally setting off rumours of an imminent election; and there the story simply ends. When the death of the Speaker in 1965 obliges him to reduce his majority to one by finding a Labour MP to replace him, Mr. Wilson ingeniously finds both a Conservative and a Liberal MP willing to fill the post of deputy chairman of Ways and Means. In the event, the post goes to the Liberal; and Mr. Wilson leaves the name of the Conservative unrevealed to this day. The same discretion, even more understandably, prevents him from identifying the members of his Cabinet who dissented from his own views in successive crises; but more than once he goes to the brink of revealing all, only to step back at the last moment. Only the views of George Brown are regularly revealed and they are generally creditable—in favour of devaluation in 1966, for instance, and of legislation on industrial relations in 1967; but with *In My Way* already published, these are scarcely new revelations.

The total impression is of a prolix and not very well organized diary. Episodes jostle each other on and off the page just as the papers relating to them must have done across the Prime Minister's desk, or the personalities involved in them succeeded each other in and out of the Cabinet room. Scarcely any thread of continuity seems to connect them: such as there is has to be sought through the index, not always with success. There is a certain resemblance to an archaeological site in an early stage of excavation: here and there a fairly complete mosaic, elsewhere some clearly significant but imperfectly identifiable fragments, and everywhere piles of expendable rubble. But students of antiquity find themselves readily at home in such a situation, and there is no doubt that they will derive a vast amount of enjoyment from sorting out Mr. Wilson's monumental fragments of autobiography. They can also look forward to fresh discoveries to come, in the excavation of which Mr. Wilson too can be counted on to play a leading part.

# 2

# A CHALICE FOR YOUTH

## E. M. FORSTER'S UNPUBLISHED NOVEL

IN FEBRUARY, 1915, Forster visited D. H. Lawrence at Greatham, and while he was there Lawrence wrote his impressions of his guest in a letter to a friend: 'He is very nice. I wonder if the grip has gone out of him. I get a feeling of acute misery from him—not that he does anything—but you know the acute, exquisite pain of cramp.' We may take that intuitive diagnosis as essentially accurate: what Forster was suffering from was homosexual cramp, the spiritual and imaginative restraints of a suppressed and guilty sexuality. At the time that he visited the Lawrences he had accepted his sexual nature, and had even written a novel about it, but he had no thought of publishing the book or of revealing his condition to the world; and so, when Lawrence and Frieda began to analyse his problems he responded first with reticence and finally with anger. His cramp might have been painful, but it was none the less necessary: it made his literary and social existence possible.

For Lawrence, Forster's cramp was a pain that could be cured: 'Why can't he take a woman', Lawrence wondered, 'and fight clear to his own basic, primal being?' But post-Freudians know better than that, not only about the persistency of sexual drives, but also about the creative consequences of psychic wounds. The impulse that suppresses and distorts the sexual life may liberate the imagination, though at a price which only the artist can reckon. Forster may have disliked and resented his condition—it seems clear that he did—but it was as central to his art as to his sexual being; to say that he was homosexual is to define not only his private nature, but the nature of his imagination.

With the private nature the critic has no proper business, and it is

---

E. M. FORSTER: *Maurice*. 240 pp. Edward Arnold. £2.

J. R. ACKERLEY: *E. M. Forster*. 28 pp. Ian McKelvie, 65 Lakenheath, London, N14. Paperback, 75p.

easy to respect and continue Forster's life-long reticence. But the homosexuality of his imagination is a critical matter, for it explains both the qualities and the limitations of his work. It informs the essential properties of his novels, the voyeuristic distancing of the narration, the ironic tone, the self-deprecating humour, and it imposes the most serious limitations—the blind spots and imaginative failures.

Most obviously, Forster could not imagine any aspect of the range of experience between men and women—heterosexual attraction, heterosexual relations, marriage were mysterious to him. No wonder he resented having to write 'marriage novels'—the subject was quite beyond his range. If we consider the crucial marriages in his books—Lucy Honeychurch and George Emerson, Lilia and Gino, Margaret Schlegel and Mr. Wilcox, Rickie and Agnes—they seem equally unreal and unrealized; and the one irregular union that he attempted—the one-night affair of Helen and Leonard Bast—is even worse, a case of conception as an Edwardian schoolboy might have imagined it, out of a few facts and a large ignorance.

No doubt this is why one feels in so many of Forster's novels a kind of transference at work, as though one were reading a different sort of story, but translated into socially acceptable terms. *The Longest Journey*, Forster's most personal novel, and the one he himself liked best, is a case in point. It is a 'marriage novel', but not in any ordinary sense; rather, it seems a kind of homosexual nightmare, in which the condition of marriage is imagined—cold, loveless, and degrading. The central relation is not that between husband and wife, Rickie and Agnes, at all, but that between Rickie and Stephen Wonham. Forster confessed in an interview that he had 'had trouble with the junction of Rickie and Stephen. How to make them intimate . . .'—and the difficulty is surely that he was writing a crypto-homosexual story, in which his protagonist is 'saved' by his intimacy with a young man of humble station (Forster himself favoured young men of the lower classes). Forster made the relationship acceptable by basing it on kinship, and by marrying Rickie to Agnes (his abnormality is transferred to his crippled foot), but the curious dissonance remains, that all the heat of the novel is concentrated on the man-man scenes, and the man-woman scenes have a chill repugnancy. Agnes, we are told, had a child, but the statement is incredible: how could a child possibly have been conceived in such a union?

In other novels there are other signs. In *A Room with a View*, for instance, no physical scene between the lovers is treated as vividly as the all-male bathing scene, so reminiscent of the pederastic bathing of Victorian homosexual writing and photography. In it, male nakedness liberates George and Mr. Beebe from their conventionality, and the women, when they appear, are a confining and depressing end to the affair. Over the whole episode a vague spiritual-mythological presence hovers which is evoked in the purplish prose that Forster characteristically employed on such occasions: 'It had been a call to the blood and to the relaxed will, a passing benediction whose influence did not pass, a holiness, a spell, a momentary chalice for youth.' As an account of the effect of pond-bathing this seems rather fruity; but it works better if we take it as a veiled description of sexual feeling—physical and urgent, beneficial but temporary, an event out of the ordinary range of society's possibilities.

Pan is not quite present in that scene, though one can sense him elsewhere in the novels when feeling is released; he is Forster's presiding deity, the spirit of liberation from convention, the god of boys and bumpkins. He appears most overtly in the short stories, but he is also present in Stephen Wonham, and in most of Forster's passionate Italians. Pan may be identified with the force of Nature in Forster, but one must qualify that remark somewhat; for Forster was never really interested in Nature as such, and what Pan really represents is an idea of natural human behaviour—a complete life without conventional restraints, a life that acknowledges 'bestiality'. Which is to say that Forster's Pan is the deity of a homosexual world, or a world in which homosexuality is natural. He is necessary to the stories and novels simply because, in Forster's Sawston-and-Cambridge world, homosexual love could not be a force in itself; it was only by supernatural intervention that direct emotion could find expression.

Looking back over the novels and stories, one must conclude that Forster was incapable of recording deep currents of feeling—sexual feeling most obviously, but other deep feeling as well. The occasions when feeling should flow—sexual love, birth, death—are treated distantly, with a cold casualness; we remember 'Gerald died that afternoon', in *The Longest Journey*, but forget from the same novel 'while he was out his brother died', and 'by the time they arrived Robert had been drowned'—three throw-away deaths of loved persons.

Ordinary emotional states were beyond Forster, and perhaps the moments of melodrama so often remarked in the novels are there because they offered him his only means of indicating strong feeling;

but how gross it always seems—the stabbed man in the piazza, the baby hurled from the carriage, death under a train: extreme stimuli for the feelings they express. And when the emotion is explicitly sexual, the failure is complete. *Howards End* is the weak novel it is because it has heterosexual relationships at its centre—an engagement, a marriage, and a fornication move the plot—and Forster could not handle any of them convincingly. And so the events that should be fully treated are either shuffled off-stage, or are brought on so wrapped in rhetoric as to be quite meaningless (all that embarrassing stuff about 'rainbow bridges', for instance). *Where Angels Fear to Tread* is a better novel than *Howards End* partly because it does not attempt sexuality, or only indirectly: what it is really about is the difficulties a homosexual has in understanding the behaviour of heterosexuals, and Forster knew a good deal about that.

The exception to these strictures is, of course, *A Passage to India*, which is more and more clearly Forster's one achievement. Perhaps Forster learnt about love in India, or perhaps race did what sexual difference didn't do; at any rate, the relation between Fielding and Aziz is the one deeply moving intimacy in the novels, far more intimate than any marriage Forster attempted, or any love affair. It is the principal evidence that he did have a developed heart, for all his donnish reticence.

'How much time does love take?' Forster asks in *Aspects of the Novel*, and he concludes that two hours a day is a handsome allowance. And indeed in Forster's world that is more than enough; setting aside Aziz, one can scarcely find a character in the novels who spends as much time loving as he does in being ridiculous or nasty. This is in part a circumstance of the curious Forsterian tribe that inhabits his world, a tribe that seems designed to make loving, and especially sexual loving, unnecessary, or even impossible. Typically it has at its centre a fatherless family: a widowed mother, some daughters, and one—always just one—rather inadequate son. There are some variations (no daughters in *The Longest Journey*, Mrs. Wilcox for the mother-figure in *Howards End*), but the tribal pattern is strikingly uniform through the novels up to *Passage to India*. The tribe represents restraints: convention, propriety, suburbanism, and the sexual restraints of widowhood and virginity. To escape the tribe is to free the imagination, to move from suburbs to country, from the rule of the C of E God to the rule of Pan, from control to freedom, from no-sex to sex. It is also, in the most personal books, to escape from the world of women to a world of men; woman is the Mother, but man is the Comrade, the brother Rickie wanted but did not have.

In each of Forster's tribes there is a Forster-like character, a boy or young man, ascetic and detached, imperfectly involved in life, and slightly ridiculous. These characters differ a good deal in particulars, and in the roles they play in the actions, but they are always in evidence—in Forster every mother has a son to devour, and every son has a slightly chewed look. Seen together—Freddie and Rickie, Tibby and Philip—they seem a common type without a common function. What they provided for Forster was a steady point of reference, a self in the novel, who can view the emotional lives of others with some ironic detachment, but, because he is a character, can also in turn be viewed ironically. If society disapproves of limp-wristed young men, then Forster will put one in each of his novels, and ridicule him. These are Forster's selves, but seen through the world's eyes, and denied and disinherited by their creator.

Though Forster was homosexual, he lived in a world which believed in marriage and in marriage-novels, and his desire to remain in that world was stronger than his desire to tell the truth about himself. Obviously his work was affected by this disharmony, and certainly his gifts were distorted by it, but it would be too simple to say that the repression of his sexual nature crippled his imagination, or was necessarily a factor in his 'drying-up' as a novelist. One could more readily argue that in fact a *creative* tension existed between the impulse and the work, and that the effort to transform homosexuality into socially acceptable forms was an ordering force, which determined both his characteristic vision and his characteristic tone. He saw the world as emptied of absolutes, lonely, and threatening (the truest expression of this vision is in the concert scene in *Howards End*, when Helen hears 'Panic and Emptiness!' in Beethoven's Fifth Symphony); but he expressed this bleak vision with a self-deprecating irony that refuses to be altogether serious, and never reached toward tragedy. If one says that tragedy and homosexuality do not sit well together, but irony and homosexuality do, this is not to be taken as a judgment of a sexual state, but as an observation of social attitudes. Forster was a sensitive judge of such attitudes, and he wrote, one might say defensively, to preserve his place in the society which would ostracize him if it knew. But cunning defensiveness suited his talent, and he made out of self-deprecation, transference, and evasion a personal and functioning style.

One had always heard rumours that there was one exception: that there was an unpublished novel which eschewed evasion, and was too frank to be published. Now at last we have that novel, and some of the circumstances of its composition. It was written in 1913–14, and in a 'Terminal Note' Forster explains the initial impulse. He had been visiting Edward Carpenter, the Edwardian guru of sandals, the simple life, and 'homogenic love', and while he was there Carpenter's friend, George Merrill, had touched Forster fondly on the backside:

> The sensation was unusual and I still remember it, as I remember the position of a long vanished tooth. It was as much psychological as physical. It seemed to go straight through the small of my back into my ideas, without involving my thoughts.

He returned to his mother, who was taking a cure at Harrogate, and began to write *Maurice*.

The novel came to him easily—no doubt because he did not have to translate his feelings into other terms—and he seems to have written with a sense of private liberation. But having written, he recovered his instinctive cautiousness, and did not try to publish it (not that publication would have been easy in a decade that suppressed *The Rainbow*). He showed it to friends from time to time, and he went on tinkering with it (most recently in 1960), but he was unwilling to endure the disturbance to his quiet life that publication would cause, and he left the manuscript at his death with the laconic Forsterian comment: 'Publishable—but worth it?'

*Maurice* is an example of a common twentieth-century kind of novel, the novel of growth and self-discovery; it belongs to the same category as *A Portrait of the Artist*, *Of Human Bondage*, and *The Longest Journey*. But it differs from those novels in what Maurice discovers—that he is homosexual, and that homosexual love is possible. In his personal circumstances Maurice is Tibby and Rickie and Philip all over again, the Weak Young Man with a widowed mother, sisters, a house in the Surrey suburbs, and a Cambridge education; and though Forster made some effort to make him un-Forsterian by giving him healthy good looks and a rather dull mind, this scarcely matters—he is in essentials true to type.

There is, however, one significant deviation from the tribal pattern; Maurice comes to a happy ending, in fulfilled love with a gamekeeper. Forster mistrusted and disliked happy endings; most novels, he thought, went off at the end as the author huddled resolutions together, and his own instinct was for dissonances. But in this case, he wrote,

> a happy ending was imperative. I shouldn't have bothered to write otherwise. I was determined that in fiction anyway two men should fall in love and remain in it for the ever and ever that fiction allows. . . .

He was writing, this time, for the sake of homosexual love, and was willing to violate his own sensibility to assert that such love was possible. The ending of the novel is clumsy and improbable, and is altogether without the defences of irony that protect the other novels; but it is done that way by intention, to put a human principle above an aesthetic one. This is a very Forsterian thing to do, but it complicates the act of critical judgment, as it complicated the act of creation.

The crucial question about *Maurice* is, what happens when that creative tension between the homosexual imagination and society's restraints which informs Forster's other novels is abandoned for truth-telling? What happens when Forster tries to put 'the private lusts and aches' of his sexuality into fiction? How, in short, does he write without cramp? The answer, alas, is that he has written a novel of such uncharacteristic badness as not to be comparable to any other of his works, a novel almost as good, perhaps, as *The Well of Loneliness*, but certainly no better. He has sacrificed all the qualities that make his work interesting—the ironic tone, the distance, the humour, the touches of shrewd wisdom, the style—and he has gained no commensurate values. The sentimentality that is always close to the surface in Forster (his liberalism was never much more than sentimental humanism) here oozes forth everywhere; indeed both the sentimentality and the prose style are so reminiscent of Edward Carpenter at his worst that one can only regret that trip to Milthorpe, and the pat on the bottom that started it all.

Most serious of all the novel's faults is what can only be described as the incompleteness of the imaginative act. *Maurice* is composed of many short chapters, more of them, and shorter, than in any other Forster novel. This is more than a statistic; it suggests what is indeed the case, that episodes are not fully realized, that the imagination has been imperfectly made verbal. Forster wrote the book rapidly because he was writing from experience, and no doubt for the same reason he did not succeed in turning experience into literary reality. If one examines, for example, the three pages that see Maurice through his public school, one finds a tissue of thin and general statements that might have been written by an Edwardian headmaster: 'Thoughts: he had a dirty little collection. Acts: he desisted from these after the novelty was over, finding that they brought him more fatigue than pleasure'—so much for the adolescent sex life of our protagonist. One is surely not being prurient in suggesting that a novel about the Growth of a Homosexual ought to treat sex more frankly than that.

The heart of the matter is there, in the treatment of sex. Forster may have thought he wrote the book because he had come to terms with his own nature, but the book shows that this is not quite the case; *Maurice* is about homosexuality, but the attitudes it expresses are far from liberated. The language is the language of society—*morbidity*, *perversion* versus *normality*—and the attitude is substantially guilty and regretful. Maurice accepts his condition, but he disapproves of it, and so, one gathers, does Forster, for at the end he turns from the real, social world, and sends his lovers off into a sentimental world of romance, like two Scholar Gypsies; there is to be no assimilation, no contact with society, but rather a sentimentalized form of ostracism.

Nor does Forster give to homosexual love any greater reality than he was able to evoke in his accounts of marriage. One had thought that he was vague and rhetorical with Lucy and George because he did not and could not know anything about their relationship, but he is no better with Maurice and Alec—there is the same poverty of feeling here, the same lack of emotional complexity, the same cramped heart. The language is meticulously decent, but the treatment is as emotionally thin as pornography is. And this, too, must be a consequence of Forster's ambivalence and sense of sordidness; he could not imagine sex that was neither furtive nor repulsive. Love for him may have been a Beloved Republic, but it was never an innocent act.

*Maurice* is interesting as an Edwardian view of homosexuality, but it does not transcend that historical limit, and so, as a friend told Forster when he had read the manuscript, it can only have a period interest—plus, one might add, that morbid interest one has in the unsuccessful work of a good writer. It adds nothing to his achievement as a novelist, and little to his reckoning as a man. If he had published it when he wrote it, it would have been a courageous act, as Carpenter's was when he published *Homogenic Love* and *The Inter-*

*mediate Sex*; but now it appears as evidence of his fearful caution—the sort of thing that Sawston would have understood.

Forster would probably not mind; he had a modest opinion of his place in the record, and did not worry about it, and in any case he would rather have had the kind of immortality that he ascribes to Carpenter, the sort that rests, not on words and deeds, but on the constancy and intensity of affections. (J. R. Ackerley's affectionate portrait, based on an acquaintance of forty-five years, suggests that this was indeed the case.) But the critic can make no estimate of that achievement, and must be content to judge the book. And for that judgment, the words of Mrs. Failing, upon reading Rickie's story, are perhaps the best:

'It is bad', said Mrs Failing. 'But. But. But.' Then she escaped, having told the truth, and yet leaving a pleasurable impression behind her.

# 3
# STATE OF THE DISUNION

It used to be that only the poor were miserable in America, but now everyone is, or thinks he is, and so we have a great many books telling us why and what to do about it. *The New Left* is an anthology of speeches and articles by radical writers, some well known, like Huey Newton and Herbert Marcuse, but most of them unknown outside the movement. *The Greening of America* is a best-seller by a Yale Law School professor, who argues that the new generation of students have developed a life-style which will spread to their elders and save the nation. *The Age of Aquarius* is a reporter's reflections on the national disease, developed after interviews with many famous men, and presented chiefly through the words of these celebrities.

These three books therefore purport to represent three different viewpoints—roughly those of the radicals, the young, and the intellectual establishment. But while they differ, certainly over means, about what must be done, they offer much the same explanation of what has gone wrong, and this explanation is the new conventional wisdom of political sociology. It runs this way. The old left was wrong. In America, at least, the masses are not the victims of the economic greed of the privileged few. Instead everyone—rich and poor alike—is the victim of technology run wild, of an economic and political system out of control, a system that serves only its own systematic needs, destroys human personality, and corrupts what is called the quality of life. There are no human villains of this story, or, rather, the only villains are the well-intentioned liberals whose creature the system is. These liberals, who have run the country since 1932, suppose that bureaucracy, production, and rationalism will make the country great and the people happy, but their programmes have led only to misery at home and a criminal war abroad.

---

Massimo Teodori (Editor): *The New Left*. 500 pp. Cape. £3.75.

Charles A. Reich: *The Greening of America*. 294 pp. Allen Lane The Penguin Press. £2.50.

William Braden: *The Age of Aquarius: Technology and the Cultural Revolution*. 306 pp. Eyre and Spottiswoode. £2.60.

What can be done to break the grip of the system? The authors of *The New Left*, with varying degrees of confidence, hope for a radicalization of the masses, spreading out from increasingly powerful student and Black Power movements. The blueprint (as drafted, for example, by Marcuse, William Domhoff and the radical *Guardian*) shows these groups awakening the anger, first of the minorities cut out of the general prosperity, and then of the prosperous workers and middle class as well. But this blueprint seems shop-worn already. Since 1968—the cut-off date of the collection—radical movements seem to have declined in power, and the grip of false consciousness on the masses seems more secure than ever.

The student radical groups are now split by internal politics. They seem powerful when the non-radical students are active and enraged, as they were last spring over the invasion of Cambodia and the shootings at Kent State, and impotent when the students generally are apathetic, as they have been this year in spite of the invasion of Laos and the trial of Lt. Calley. The campuses are quieter now than they have been in years; the radicals say this is the calm before the next storm, the cynics say that Nixon calmed the universities at a stroke when he introduced the lottery that lets most students know, at nineteen, that they will probably never be drafted. In any case the efforts of, for example, the Students for a Democratic Society to make common cause with blue-collars and hard-hats have come to nothing, and the students at large now seem more occupied by the failing job market for graduates than by the inhumanity of life behind the lathe.

The Black Power movement may be revived, but it seems diminished now, particularly in its impact within the Black community. The police have been efficient—some say murderously efficient—in their efforts of harassment, but for whatever reason the movement has failed to produce leaders of wide appeal or to sustain the excitement of impending revolution. A few months ago the head of the Black Panther Party, Huey Newton, in an extraordinary state-of-the-movement message, said that the Panthers must now, for a time at least, work within the system, and the recent collapse of widely publicized prosecutions of Panthers in New York and New Haven probably reflects this change in the Black militants' advertised image as much as the triumph of due process over prosecutorial hysteria. The era of race riots is not over, of course, and the Black man's relative position in the economy is getting worse, not better. The Black militants have engaged the sympathy and, what is more important, the respect of those White groups that used to admire only Black pacifism. But there remains no reason to think that the worker who fights to keep the Black man out of his union will one day join him on the barricades.

The students and the Panthers are not the only radical movements, but those who claimed larger constituencies have done even less well. The violence-prone Weathermen, for example, have gone farther underground than ever, after the fatal explosion in their Greenwich Village armoury. It is true that some, at least, of the causes once thought radical have now general support, but this is because the majority has co-opted radical issues, not because it has itself become radical. Congress did turn down the SST, America's Concorde, but out of sensible economy, not rejection of technology as such. The war in Vietnam is finally recognized as an obscenity, by almost everyone except the President, but the most impressive participants in the latest march in Washington were the veterans protesting against the war in the name of traditional virtues they came to vindicate and not to challenge. The dilemma of the American left—that the working classes form the base of opposition to social change—remains to mock whatever strategies Marxism can produce for post-industrial societies.

Middle America found Professor Reich's theories much more appealing. The argument of *The Greening of America* is well known: the Corporate State has been sustained by two types of consciousness, the selfish consciousness of small-town America that encourages each man to improve himself and his family at the expense of others, and the liberal consciousness of the technocrat who reads the *New York Times*, has his clothes made in England, and supposes that social problems can be cured by rational planning imposed by a managerial elite. But the Corporate State will destroy itself by producing a contagious new consciousness—Consciousness III—which already shows itself in those Yale undergraduates among whom Professor Reich lives and works, and which must soon become an epidemic. This consciousness expresses itself in experimentation with clothing, sex, music, and drugs; its fundamental principles are spontaneity, freedom, love, and the peace and tolerance that these other virtues must inevitably bring. It is therefore unnecessary to work to improve America, it is only necessary for each man to do his own thing, as Consciousness III spreads from Yale to the suburbs to the factories.

It made everyone happy, this charming confection of Galbraith and the Brothers Grimm, especially middle-class parents glad to be proud of their bizarre children once again, and happy to strike a blow for social justice by switching from gin to pot. It made everyone happy except those who were in fact worried about America, because they knew that if everyone cultivates his own garden no one will cultivate anything else. So the sober critics, asked to criticize the arguments that the public found so persuasive, were appalled, and warned against a general hedonistic cop-out. But the most perceptive reviews were written by members of Professor Reich's new generation itself; in the *New York Times*, as well as in undergraduate papers, they reminded the nation that Professor Reich was only a middle-aged tourist in their country. He had seen the gay clothes and the love beads, but not the desperation, cruelty, and individual tragedy that are just as regular features of the drug culture; he had watched Yale men at play and seen films of the Woodstock festival, but he had not been to Altamont, where the Rolling Stones played to hatred and death, or talked to those who have been to his Eden and are now stumbling back, sick, cut out of a shrinking job market, and cursing the communes as symptoms of the national disease rather than deliverance from it.

Professor Reich has, in fact, missed the nerve of what the students have done. They have indeed given their elders a new style of dress, new slang, and new entertainments, just as their fathers gave the crew haircut to Madison Avenue and then to the red-necks. But some of them served their country better by showing genuine outrage at the social injustice they seemed to see more clearly and earlier than their parents. These were not necessarily or even largely the students who dropped acid and treated themselves as ambassadors from a transcendental way of life. They were the students who are now, for example, young doctors and lawyers trying to make these professions more responsive to the rights of those they are supposed to serve, and ready to experiment with new and highly rational institutional designs to do it.

*The Age of Aquarius* is a title drawn from astrology. In 1948 the sun entered Aquarius, the constellation of peace, where it will stay for 2,000 years. Can man find the harmony this promises? William Braden is a journalist whose beat is the history of ideas, and he can provide scoops like this:

In this country the thalidomide responsible for our atrophied public sector is the atomistic ontology which, as we have seen, is in part at least a by-product of the Newtonian physics that influenced Locke—a fact that adds weight to Waddington's analysis. The best hope for a cure is that unity thing that Molly and her friends have going for them now—or, more elegantly, the Aristotelian concept of an organic society.

Mr. Braden is not sure that we can make the unity thing—Aquarius is possible, but so is Armageddon. He is not even clear about what the goal is, but the key seems to be this: post-industrial society must abandon the idea of atomic individuals asserting rights against each other, in favour of the Eastern ideal, of men who lose themselves in group identity—an ideal represented in America now only within immigrant ethnic groups. We must, apparently, give up our Lockes for bagels.

Mr. Braden reports a leisurely conversation with Bruno Bettelheim about the danger that the student left is a force for fascism, but he does not explore the livelier possibility that his unity thing is fascism itself. He does not explain, for example, how his ideal would be used to test the claims of Black cotton pickers who want to break the natural harmony of the Deep South. Perhaps the stars will bring it about that men can subordinate themselves to the group without subordinating themselves to other men, but that will not take place without a radical diminution in the degree to which men's ambitions and abilities differ, and in the meantime a great many men will prefer Armageddon.

So these three books present ideas that on a second look seem silly: that the American working class is likely to support a revolution, that the students in bell-bottoms have developed a contagious new consciousness, and that an organic society can be achieved without totalitarianism. But why should anyone hold ideas like these? We must look again, more carefully, at the view all three books share: the common diagnosis of how America has gone wrong.

The growth-minded technocrats, who ran the country both before and after the Second World War, assumed that any increase in the gross national product was in the interest of all the people; economic growth provides jobs, and it provides wealth that can be used to make even the jobless better off. The critics now make two distinct charges against that assumption: first, the ideal of production neglects the 'hidden costs' of growth—the damage to the environment, for example, and the damage to personality of the level of competition required to sustain it. These are costs for everyone, though they are not reflected in the price of the products produced, or taken into account by those who decide to produce them. Second, the ideal of production ignores the fact that while economic growth might produce overall economic benefits, the benefit might be distributed unfairly, and, indeed, might make some people worse off than they were before. Unskilled labourers, for example, might be worse off absolutely, if growth eliminates the only jobs they can hold, or relatively, if the middle class can now afford colour television, and advertising makes the unskilled worker want it too.

These are distinct charges, and if we want to undo the mistakes of our infatuation with growth we must pursue them both. We must be more sensitive to the external costs of technological improvement, and to the non-economic needs of people in general. We must also bring up to date competing theories about individual rights—that is, about the circumstances in which individuals or groups are entitled to press claims in spite of the fact that what they want is not in the general interest. There might now be good reason for rejecting, for example, the eighteenth century's catalogue of property rights, and urging general recognition of rights that protect personality, like rights of privacy, instead.

Contemporary critiques of technology, like the three books under review, have become obsessed with the first of these projects and have neglected the second. They cling to the assumption that what is good for one man or group is good for everyone, or for everyone who counts, and the changes they propose in the technocrat's ideology, though in some ways radical, are in that sense limited. The economists of the 1950s attempted to maximize happiness on one set of postulates about what people really want; the new social philosophers want to change these postulates, but not the underlying assumption that all men really want the same thing. This is, of course, an appealing assumption, because it unites the two political issues of what should be done and of how to do it. If some change is in everyone's interest, then the change will be made if we can only somehow teach the public the truth.

The idea is an old one, but it is harder to maintain in the face of the terrible controversies that divide America. The new philosophers have hit on a device for reconciling the fact of conflict with their theories of common interest: the conflicts arise through the work of a common enemy whose victims we all are; this enemy is technology or the corporate state or the system or some other Frankenstein's monster of an abstraction, created by men but now setting man against man for its own implacable and non-human ends. Once that nonsense is accepted, then deliverance from the monster becomes the common cause of all its victims, and we imagine, according to our tastes, the radicalization of the two-car families, or the spread of a new consciousness, or the return to the medieval organic state.

But the concept of a non-personal abstract enemy is a great confusion. It is true that the market economy has hidden costs, for example to environment and personality. It is also true that the costs can and have been publicized, and that technology exists to reduce a great many of them if the public, once informed, is willing to incur the sustained and substantial expense, in conventional comforts and opportunities, that would be required. But the political record shows that so far, at least, it is a myth to suppose that middle America really wants clean cities at the cost of private urban transportation, or communal interracial living at the cost of large lawns, or social justice at the cost of doubled taxes. It is simply a lie that we are all victims of impersonal forces; we are victims only in the sense that we still prefer most of what the system gives us to what we would have if we gave it up. Perhaps the hocus-pocus about consciousness will persuade the public to persuade Congress to give up the SST, or to reduce the influence of military contractors, or to provide for local rather than national planning. But these slight improvements in democracy will count for little so long as the majority continues to be told that, in the end, it must have what it wants.

America must resume the debate about what the minorities—the Blacks, and the poor, and the political minorities—are entitled to have in spite of what the majority wants, and it must resume the debate over techniques for enforcing these rights. This is language that the new philosophers deplore; it suggests the liberal, with his law, administration, planning and linear thought. The radicals say that America has tried the path of liberalism and rights against the state, and that this path has led to its present disasters. That is the biggest lie of all. In spite of its Constitution, in spite of the haphazard work of Warren's Supreme Court, America has not for a long time had political leadership committed to that part of liberal theory. The closest it has come, in recent years, is the extraordinary candidacy of Robert Kennedy, who was killed. The country's leaders have otherwise been in the grip of the economist's dream of optimality, of political decisions which in some way make everyone better off. The technocrats of the 1950s pursued this dream, and made a god of gross national product; the new philosophers, who despise the technocrats, are trapped by it as well.

# 4

# MOON AND MEGALITHS

'I AM FORCED to the conclusion that nothing of any great moment has been established by the astronomical *nouveau vague* [sic] flowing over Stonehenge.' Thus wrote Jacquetta Hawkes in 1967, commenting upon certain theories of Stonehenge which had been proposed, in *Antiquity*, *Nature*, and elsewhere, by G. S. Hawkins and Fred Hoyle. She had begun with the observation that every age has the Stonehenge it deserves—or desires. Having found that cries of delight were provoked from a general audience when she contrasted the wildly jagged stones seen by the Romantics with the smooth regularity perceived by the eye of the classicist, she interpreted the Hawkins-Hoyle stir merely as a sign of our scientific times. Needless to say, she was out of sympathy if not with the times, at least with astronomers who could not even reach 'close agreement . . . on the inevitability of their interpretations'.

Putting aside the rather charming supposition that astronomers live in a harmonious world of objective and inevitable truth, it must be pointed out that Professors Hawkins and Hoyle were, directly or by implication, setting themselves up not as astronomers but as archaeologists. They were applying simple astronomical techniques, but only to offer certain interpretations—largely incompatible interpretations—of the use, if not necessarily the principal use, of the Stonehenge remains.

In fact neither showed himself to be historically very well informed. Much of the time Professor Hoyle managed to dodge the issue by purporting to answer not the archaeologist's problem but the simpler problem of how *we* should design a Stonehenge-type monument. How should we use it to predict eclipses, for instance? Within the outer bank at Stonehenge is a circle of fifty-six holes, dug and

---

A. THOM: *Megalithic Lunar Observatories*. 127 pp. Clarendon Press: Oxford University Press. £3.

ALEXANDER MARSHACK: *Notation dans les gravures du paléolithique supérieur: Nouvelles méthodes d'analyse*. Translated by Mme. J.-M. Le Tensorer and others. 123 pp. Bordeaux: Delmas. 75 fr. (paperback 60 fr.).

refilled soon afterwards, and now named after John Aubrey, who drew attention to them in the seventeenth century. In articles, and in *Stonehenge Decoded*, a book first published in 1965, and now available in paperback (Fontana, 40p), Professor Hawkins had proposed a most implausible theory of the Aubrey holes. They were seen simply as an aid for use in a moderately complicated counting procedure for eclipse prediction, which depended for its validity on the fact that there are certain natural periodicities of eclipse recurrence.

The method proposed was unfortunately of very dubious astronomical value. In spite of its supposed 'remarkable accuracy', at one point Professor Hawkins casually applied one of his rules to our own century, deriving lunar eclipses for 1926 and 1908, both at best imaginary. The trouble with eclipses is that there are infinitely many eclipse cycles (based on a combination of the *saros* and J. N. Stockwell's twenty-nine-year cycle), although most of them are of very little value. At all events, an appropriate eclipse rule could be found to fit almost any large number of holes. Miss Hawkes's fears were understandable: the Aubrey holes had begun to look like one of those hateful digital computers. But then, as every child knows, we might say the same of our fingers without supposing that they have no other use. Have archaeologists not always tended to take labels too seriously? The Beaker People must be turning in their barrows at the thought that posterity remembers them thus.

Eclipses, especially of the Sun, but also of the Moon, are difficult to predict without a tolerably extensive knowledge of astronomical theory, unless it is somehow appreciated that after certain periods of time the eclipse cycle tends to recur. And 'tends' is the right word. Both Professors Hoyle and Hawkins decided that the Aubrey holes told their user that there was a *strong likelihood* of an eclipse at certain times. Now neolithic man might conceivably have formulated general rules concerning eclipses on the basis of eclipses he had actually observed, but he would have been hard pressed to make generalizations from essentially undetected 'danger periods'. How, then, did he proceed? Neither author explained the problem from this end. Professor Hoyle suggested that the circle of Aubrey holes was a representation of the ecliptic (the apparent circular path of the Sun as it moves once a year round the sky). He suggested that there would have been a marker for the position of the Sun on the ecliptic, and others for three highly conceptualized points connected with the Moon.

We know something of the intellectual struggle of the Greeks when they arrived at similar notions more than a thousand years later, but this is itself no argument one way or the other. Even so it is a piece of history worth bearing in mind when we consider Professor Hoyle's claim to see significance in the fact that he was led to an understanding of his own technique from a study of Stonehenge. This, he said, would have been 'strange indeed if Stonehenge had no astronomical connotation'. But the problem was to decide on a historically plausible connotation. The well-documented Babylonian methods of 600 B.C. had seemed to him 'no more than obscure numerology'. He was also constrained to add at the end of a paper describing his own solution: 'a most remarkable point still remains. The method could not work.' No wonder that professional archaeologists were sceptical.

Despite all this, it was really Professor Hawkins's show, a fact of which we are reminded by quotations from the *Daily Express*, the *Daily Mirror*, and *The Observer*, on the covers of the re-issued *Stonehenge Decoded*. The real secret of Stonehenge, as every news editor knows, is that the whole world loves a Druid. (The Druids of course had nothing to do with the building of Stonehenge.) Professor Hawkins produced his book out of a handful of articles, slender, but of some originality. In them he had shown restraint, but the book, hastily assembled with the collaboration of one 'neither astronomer nor archaeologist', threw sobriety to the winds. Setting aside the melodramatic and autobiographical style, and even overlooking its central astro-archaeological theses, the book was filled with misunderstandings, half-truths, and irrelevancies. Its artless but condescending tone was well adapted to a popular audience, but surely its author cannot have remained so untouched by the purely archaeological criticisms made at the time as to think that a re-issue is a substitute for a new edition. The tragedy is that he has something worth saying, and that by refusing to refine it he is failing to communicate with those whose judgment is worth having.

It has long been recognized that the 'avenue' at Stonehenge is directed towards midsummer sunrise, and seventy years ago Sir Norman Lockyer even tried to calculate from this the date of construction. (His method was at best probabilistic, since we do not know whether sunrise was taken as the first glint of the Sun, or the appearance of the full Sun, or some intermediate state.) More than a century ago Edward Duke had noted other stones aligning with the sunrise at the time of the solstice. Greatly moved by a dawn visit to the monument in 1961 Professor Hawkins and his assistants calculated the directions of 120 'significant' lines drawn between the positions of pairs of stones as marked on relatively small-scale charts. A quite irrelevant fact, of which archaeologists were so suspicious, and of which he was inordinately proud, was that the directions were calculated with the help of a computer.

It was found that some directions occurred more commonly than others, and that these coincided with the computed directions of sunrise and sunset at the times of winter and summer solstice, and also with certain extreme directions of the rising and setting Moon. Which calculation was done first is a matter on which the book and the original article do not agree. Between writing the two, he heard that C. A. Newham had found an alignment with sunrise at the equinoxes. Returning to his charts he found more significant alignments which he had previously overlooked, and in the book was able to add eight equinoctial directions to his earlier lists.

Although the archaeologists were irritated by the overall crudity of the book, when their annoyance had subsided they began to nibble away at its astronomical core. They pointed out that Professor Hawkins had mixed different building periods in his alignment points; that the plans he was using were not reliable, and that many of the stones had been disturbed; that the horizon selected was a crucial factor in deciding the direction of a rising or setting object in the sky, and yet that the bank around the monument might well have been high enough to provide the horizon in the west. It was even suggested that some of the points through which Professor Hawkins drew his lines were not stone-holes at all, but had a natural origin, which implied that many of the supposed alignments were fortuitous. But no one can really be said to have demolished the general thesis that Stonehenge incorporated *some* astronomical alignments.

It is extremely unlikely that this will ever be rigorously disproved: and that we can say as much is almost entirely due to the labours of Alexander Thom, until ten years ago Professor of Engineering Science at Oxford. Professor Thom has always studiously avoided Stonehenge, with all its uncertainties, but over the years has collected together an immense amount of information on more than 600 megalithic sites throughout the British Isles, having personally visited more than three-quarters that number, and having surveyed more than half. In this way he has made possible a statistical analysis of his findings, which are remarkable not only in themselves but for the relative absence of irrelevant historical speculation.

*Megalithic Sites in Britain* appeared in 1967, in the wake of *Stonehenge Decoded*, and at first attracted unfavourable comment, largely by association. There is little doubt that most of Professor Thom's book will stand the test of time. In it he shows that the men responsible for the circles built nearly 4,000 years ago were capable of working within very narrow limits. Professor Thom underscores the urgency of accurate surveys. He shows that the Avebury site, for instance, was set out with an accuracy approaching one part in 1,000; and yet even scales of yards and metres on some modern plans might differ by more than one part in 100. Thanks to the accuracy with which the rings of megaliths were set out, Professor Thom was able to show that they were designed on at least six non-circular geometrical plans—as ellipses, for instance, or flattened 'circles', with component circular arcs drawn from different centres.

These centres were themselves at the vertices of right-angled triangles of at least four or five different sorts, but always having sides made up of simple multiples of a fundamental unit—what Professor Thom called the 'megalithic yard' (2.72 modern feet). This is not to suggest that the theorem of Pythagoras was known, for it was evidently believed, for example, that a triangle with sides 41, 71, and 82 was right angled, which it is not. Here for comparison it is worth remembering the Old Babylonian 'Pythagorean triangle' tablet, Plimpton 322, which is of roughly comparable date, or a little older.

Professor Thom showed how the architects of the megaliths were obsessed with lengths of integral numbers of megalithic yards, even to the point of distorting the circles—with due attention to a neat geometrical construction—to give an integral periphery. He showed conclusively that multiples of the unit (2½ and 10 yards) and submultiples (down to 1/40, in the cup and ring markings) had been used.

If Professor Thom's conclusions as to neolithic metrology and geometry were astonishing, what he discovered of the astronomy of the time was even more so. He showed for site after site a preoccupation with the Sun at the solstices. He proved that a calendar had been in use in which the year was divided into eight, sixteen, or even thirty-two parts. But he also left no doubt in the mind of an impartial reader that some of the alignments were lunar, while some pointed to the rising or setting of one or other bright star. Dates are deducible from the directions of the latter, dates which tend to be within a couple of centuries of the nineteenth century B.C. The lunar orientations were touched on in *Megalithic Sites*, but only briefly, and *Megalithic Lunar Observatories* now supplements the earlier volume. The author's results are, if anything, more interesting than before.

To appreciate the achievement of those who observed from the megaliths, while keeping their achievement in proper perspective, we should at least keep half an eye on the probable evolution of their methods. Once it was noticed that the Sun rises and sets over a different point of the horizon on successive days, that at midsummer it reaches its greatest displacement along the horizon in one direction (north), and that in midwinter it reaches the other extreme, it would have been natural to fix the two turning points with permanent direction markers. These might have been a pair of stones, or an avenue, or a stake or stone taken in conjunction with some distant natural object, such as a mountain top, for a foresight. (This last method, found in many of Professor Thom's examples, is obviously potentially very accurate, a minute of arc being easily achieved. One foresight, Mount Leinster in Ireland, is ninety-one miles from Parc-y-Meirw. It is not absolutely clear, incidentally, that Thom is right to ignore refraction in azimuth when sighting over a coastline.) It seems likely that some calendrical or religious motive—or both—might explain the wide acceptance of this first type of observation.

Perhaps comparable lunar observations were made almost simultaneously, but it is unlikely that the nature of the Moon's fluctuating habits of rising and setting were fully appreciated at all quickly. Although in any month the Moon's rising and setting points fluctuate between certain limits, as do the Sun's over a year, yet the limits themselves now vary as between successive months. The full cycle of the second fluctuation takes more than eighteen years. And then again, there is another very slight oscillation of the limits, due to an effect which the sixteenth-century Danish astronomer Tycho Brahe is generally supposed to have been the first to discover.

Professor Thom shows that several megalithic observatories (a name which is certainly not out of order) give conclusive evidence that the first two effects were allowed for, and very strong evidence that some alignments can only be explained in terms of the effect discovered by Tycho. Since there is a temptation to see in this some sort of priority of discovery, it is worth adding that Tycho described the effect, and separated it from cognate effects, in the conceptual terms of the geometry of the sphere. The megalith builders, with a tenacity, perseverance, and minuteness of which Professor Thom's own work is reminiscent, at first merely staked out lines pointing to extreme positions of the Moon as it crossed the horizon. The two sorts of activity were not at this stage really comparable.

But this is not to say that genius was wanting in the ancient world, for the precise positions of the theoretical extremes were not in all strictness immediately observable. Professor Thom holds that in Caithness certain fan-like arrangements of stones are devices for calculating the true, but generally unobservable, lunation extremes. The problem is a highly complex one, and his views are not likely to go unchallenged. He offers two modern solutions, and finds that one may be fitted to the archaeological remains; but he can hardly be said to have explained by what route the originators of the Caithness rows arrived at the supposed solution. This detracts from the completeness of his argument, but certainly does not refute it. There were, as he shows beyond all doubt, giants in the earth in those days.

Professor Thom is usually almost too cautious in his claims, but on one or two occasions he allows himself to speculate freely. He clearly knows at first hand the hazards of sailing in western Scottish tidal waters; but is it legitimate to assume, as he does, that the tides must have been *correlated* with the Moon's motion 4,000 years ago? Not improbable, perhaps; but would this explain the motive for building so many observatories? If so, what price the thesis of Mediterranean influence? And, if so, was there any appreciation of the far subtler correlation between *eclipses* and the different periodicities which may in principle be guessed at rather than deduced from the lunar observatories? It is extremely difficult to know where to stop. It is all too easy to accept without a second thought even such a sentence as 'The object then was to predict the dates of the maxima of the perturbation cycle.' The megalith builders marked out the maxima, certainly, but the claim that they dated them, that is, that they recorded long time intervals, is one which demands at least an argument about plausibility. And then, as argued before, is not the ascription to these people of the very concept of a 'danger period' for eclipses lacking in plausibility?

Professor Thom's brilliant work leaves us with many unanswered questions. At a simpler level, are there road or barrow alignments to be found? (There is a suspiciously straight footpath running from a tumulus in North Tidworth in the direction of the avenue at Stonehenge.) Why so many observatories? Is Silbury Hill—giving it a structure on top, perhaps—an articificial astronomical sight? (Just think of all that recent digging when a theodolite and a step-ladder might have revealed all. How natural that there should be nothing *inside* it!) Was the intellectual coherence evidenced by neolithic design mirrored by a deep social conformity? Was there perhaps an academic rivalry between different groups, or did some sort of central neolithic National Trust supervise their activity? Where did astronomy fit into the religious life of the community? And, above all, where did it all start?

As Professor W. Hartner has explained, an early awareness of the movements of the constellations is apparent in an Elamite seal impression of the fourth millennium B.C.; but this is far from being the earliest artifact of prehistoric astronomy. In his large quarto volume, beautifully illustrated with photographs, and—like Professor Thom's books—with excellent line drawings, Mr. Alexander Marshack presents material evidence for systematically recorded lunar observation extending in an unbroken line from Aurignacian and Perigordian cultures to the end of the Magdalenian, that is, the upper (i.e. later) palaeolithic period, from about 36,000 to 10,000 B.C. This all strongly suggests a source for the calendars of the later agricultural peoples.

For ten years Mr. Marshack has been studying engraved bone and stone artifacts, on which are sequences of marks which have been seen by others as evidence for a decimal system of counting, as hunting tallies, or as a ritual, ceremonial, or sexual symbolism. Although he is apparently aware of thousands of examples, very many of which support his claims, his book deals with only six, all from the Musée des Antiquités Nationales, Saint-Germain-en-Laye. His commentary (originally written in English but first published in this French version) admirably explains, and in detail, his methods of microscopic analysis of the marks (suggesting, for instance, that they were put on a given object at different times). He also presents his own notation for summarizing the intentions of the engraver.

The reasons for thinking the marks to be a lunar notation are strong. The length of a month is approximately twenty-nine-and-a-half days, but the precise time of a new Moon (or of a full Moon, for that matter) is not easy to distinguish, and a casual observer unaware of the precise period will often introduce extra days of lunar invisibility. Reckoning to or from the first time he sees the new crescent, to or from the last crescent visible, and making a mark for each day, he will score perhaps between twenty-seven and thirty-one marks in a 'month'. The artifacts discussed do indeed have markings in multiples of this sort, while the marks seem also to be grouped fairly naturally into quarter months. Although this summary might seem intolerably vague, the book itself should go far to convince the sceptic. It should be added that the markings occasionally have the appearance of the appropriate lunar phase.

There is obviously much to be learnt from Mr. Marshack's meticulous approach. When he finally publishes his evidence for the ubiquity of the markings, and for their association with animal and anthropomorphic drawing and symbolism, it should be possible to add substantially to our knowledge of the cosmic and spiritual attitudes of palaeolithic hunting communities. And rather than scatter his pearls in divers obscure articles, may we not hope that he will write a sequel for the same publisher?

Our knowledge of prehistoric life, and pre-eminently of its astronomical aspect, has come a long way during the past decade, and for this we should be grateful to the enlightened few who have suppressed a human tendency to read one's own sermons in stones, and unhistorical truth in everything. The time has come for professional archaeologists to throw off the feeling that they are being ever persecuted by occultist pyramid-measurers.

# 5

# FICTION OF 1971

## (*a*) V. S. NAIPAUL

### *In a Free State*

RACIAL QUESTIONS have been central to almost all V. S. Naipaul's fictions, and over the years he has become thoroughly expert at capturing the subtle divisions, the minute, insidious tensions and humiliations that race, once it *is* a question, can engender. It has always been possible, however, while admiring Mr. Naipaul's delicate and cutting gifts, to argue that the racial situations he has explored have been fairly marginal to what most people would think of as the Racial Situation. Brilliant as he is at rendering the pomposities and solitudes of the Caribbean Indian, whether at 'home' or in a shabby London exile, the very nature of his material has not allowed him to surrender a deep sense of its absurdity. To have such big ideas and such small prospects! Some such feeling has usually been at the bottom of even his most compassionate portrayals.

This has not struck one as a limitation, except where Mr. Naipaul himself has clearly been trying to push beyond it into something larger, into some more general meditation on the whole problem of place and placelessness, the rooted and the eternally uprooted. He has not seemed to possess an imagery wide-ranging and resonant enough to support such grand ambitions. Nor has he appeared to be a writer of sufficient sexuality, of sufficient aliveness to the violent ingredients of racial feeling. He has seemed too fastidious, too ironical, too poised an artist ever to start playing with apocalypse. One was not surprised to hear that his books were not thought much of in America.

---

(*a*) V. S. NAIPAUL: *In a Free State*. 256 pp. André Deutsch. £1.75.
(*b*) WILLIAM GOLDING: *The Scorpion God*. 178 pp. Faber and Faber. £1.75.
(*c*) WALKER PERCY: *Love in the Ruins*. 403 pp. Eyre and Spottiswoode. £2.95.
(*d*) MARY MCCARTHY: *Birds of America*. 318 pp. Weidenfeld and Nicolson. £1.75.
(*e*) JORGE LUIS BORGES: *El Informe de Brodie*. 151 pp. Buenos Aires: Emecé.

*In a Free State* suggests, does more than suggest, that such expectations have been glib and hasty. Throughout the book, irony and pathos are assimilated to a version of placelessness which is the opposite of narrow or eccentric. In this new book, the placelessness is global. In other words, Mr. Naipaul's essential perception is that no one belongs to the place he belongs to, that we are all both owned and disowned by our origins, that, imprisoned as we are by where we come from, we are yet perpetually drifting, 'in a free state', and in fear:

> Perhaps that had been the only pure time, at the beginning, when the ancient artist, knowing no other land, had learned to look at his own and had seen it as complete. But it was hard, travelling back to Cairo, looking with my stranger's eye at the fields and the people who worked in them, the dusty towns, the agitated peasant crowds at railway stations, it was hard to believe that there had been such innocence. Perhaps that vision of the land, in which the Nile was only water, a blue-green chevron, had always been a fabrication, a cause for yearning, something for the tomb.

The book is full of transients, of tourists, exiles, colonialists, emissaries; it has three major settings, Africa, America and England, and in each of these states the state of most of those we meet is itinerant, yearning, sick for a home that isn't home.

The most striking aspect of the novel (if one can reasonably call it a novel; it is really three stories—one very long—encased between two documentary diary entries) is that Mr. Naipaul himself has managed to become more wide-rangingly itinerant; there is no sense of strain or fabrication in his attempt, in the long title-story, to penetrate the English colonialist consciousness, and in the tale set in Washington he actually turns to his advantage a dim, undetailed grasp of American locales: an Indian accompanies his master to the Promised Land, cuts loose from him and is lost—as we see him, baffled and terrified, groping around in this utterly alien, indifferent city, we can also hear and see, as a kind of permanent, irremediable backcloth to his kind of isolation, the conflagrations of racial violence. Seeing America through his eyes, we see it as an element, of menace and destructiveness, rather than as a location. And this works; it is a beautifully made, very troubling little tale.

In the title-story Mr. Naipaul also evokes, as a distant but encroaching murmur, the violence of the continent, but in Africa he is far more assured and painstaking in his local detail, and it is on this story that the book's main burden rests. (The third story—about the relationship between two Indian West Indian brothers based in London—is somewhat laboriously oblique, and much more predictably Naipaul-ish than the others.) Set in an independent African state, newly free but now torn by an inter-tribal war, 'In a Free State' focuses on the dilemmas and delusions of an English couple who get caught up in the war's climax. Bobby, an old-style paternalistic civil-servant, is a homosexual who has long been used to wooing native boys with a few shillings and a murmured, 'I wish I was your colour'. The book opens—in a startlingly impressive scene —with Bobby making overtures to a young Zulu in the still smartish bar of a once all-white club; the Zulu leads him on and then, at the crucial moment, turns and spits at him. Bobby, pathetically dressed up in a brand new native shirt, leaves the bar; everyone has witnessed his humiliation. And this humiliation is the first of many, spiralling humiliations that await him on the journey he is to take the following day, a journey which stage by stage builds up into a painful allegory of the Colonial Retreat.

Accompanied by Linda, a representatively shallow, hard-bitten, subtly distraught colonial wife (and the relationship between her and Bobby is masterfully complicated), he is bound for the Southern Collectorate, the region still in control of the country's about-to-be-ousted king. In spite of the events of the night before, he sets out in contented mood; he loves Africa, he is neutral, he still cherishes all the old colonial assumptions and mannerisms while being totally, indeed gushingly, ready to adapt to the new order. Why should he be in any danger? What the story dramatizes is the steady erosion of this confidence, the revelation of areas of hatred and brutality that Bobby in his kindly, stupid way had never even guessed at, the gradual stripping-away of empty dignities, impotent authorities and self-indulgent decencies.

As they drive, Bobby and Linda come across one signal after another, and each more explicit than the last, that the game is irrevocably up. Building from minor impertinences, through blatant insults, to explicit violence, the African's self-assertion is paralleled by the disintegration—from indulgent toleration through haughty insecurity to blind bafflement and panic—of the Englishman's whole sense of who, or where he is.

It is brilliantly done; without sacrificing any of his calculatedly suspenseful timing, Mr. Naipaul is yet able to incorporate into the narrative a complex and inclusive discussion of the intricacies of the colonial mentality. And he manages also not to caricature or sensationalize the African; menacing as he appears, his own doom hangs over him. The country is no more *his* than it is Bobby's. Mr. Naipaul proposes a desolate vision, but his real achievement is that he does not allow it to devalue the absurd, ugly and, at times, heroic efforts that are made to mitigate it.

## (*b*) WILLIAM GOLDING

### *The Scorpion God*

WILLIAM GOLDING has just turned sixty, an age when a man has made his life, done the best of his work, shaped and expressed his mind if he is ever going to. In Golding's case the work is modest in quantity (he has written a good deal less than Forster, for example), and has come out of a creative career of less than twenty years; nevertheless, it is all of a piece, a unified and impressive accounting of a unique imagination. When those first novels appeared, the originality of their conception was so great that many readers (and some critics) never got beyond the invention to the imagination; the astonishment with which one discovered the minds of the pre-human, or the ego of a dead man was blinding. And to find such an imagination functioning in the 1950s, in England, was even more extraordinary. Golding seemed to belong to no school, to exist quite outside fashion; one could not even be certain that he had read Joyce.

Now that the shock is past, we can see that Golding is in fact a very conservative novelist, as he is a conservative thinker. This is not to say that he is not original, but only that his originality has not needed more than the traditional novelistic tools to express itself. He does not play with reality, and he does not, like many novelists since Joyce, hold his readers on the arid level of language. He is concerned to tell a story, to engross, and to render experience. But he is also and above all concerned that experience should reveal its meaning, that fiction should tell truths; that is to say, he is a serious moral artist.

Golding has never been much concerned with the immediate present, and certainly seems to have no feeling that the present moment in human history is unique. His classical training, and his amateur interests in Egyptology and archaeology have encouraged him to see man's story as an evolving one, and have fed that quality of his mind that is most individual, and that makes him irreplaceable—his sense of the human *species*. His humanity reaches back beyond history, and finds us there; he is an anthropologist of the imagination. He is primarily interested in the cruxes in the evolution of consciousness, and the childhood of individuals or the childhood of races serves him equally well, providing those points at which a mind opens imaginatively to knowledge, learns to use fire or to impose discipline, learns evil or love or the nature of death. His courage in attempting such subjects is admirable, and when he has failed, he has failed courageously.

*The Scorpion God* is not major Golding, but the book is nevertheless a pure example of Golding's gift and it will help, perhaps, to fix the nature of that gift. It consists of three long stories, of which one, 'Envoy Extraordinary', is something of a make-weight (it was published first fifteen years ago). The title story is from Golding's Egyptological side; set in ancient Egypt (exactly how ancient other Egyptologists will know), it turns on the moment when a man, by a leap of imagination, chooses to become a God. The best text for further elucidation is Golding's essay, 'Egypt from My Inside', in which he describes what he calls 'the heart of my Egypt': 'It is to be at once alive and dead; to suggest mysteries with no solution, to mix the strange, the gruesome and the beautiful; to use all the resources of life to ensure that this leftover from living and its container shall stand outside change and bring the wheel to a full stop.' By treating the unfamiliar with familiarity, explaining nothing, he teases the reader into the strange world of the story. It is as brilliant a tour de force as *The Inheritors*, if on a smaller scale.

The other story, 'Clonk Clonk', is somewhat less satisfying. It is one of Golding's 'childhood of the species' stories, set apparently in Africa (there are rhinos and chimpanzees), at a date that the last paragraph suggests was at least a hundred thousand years ago. In this stage men, appropriately, are childish and polymorphously perverse; women, however, are women—knowing, material, and wisely deceitful. As a fable of the relations between the sexes the story is clumsy; as a fable of a growth of consciousness it scarcely works. One must judge it one of the honourable failures.

'Envoy Extraordinary' will be familiar to Golding's admirers from its first appearance in the collection titled *Sometime, Never* and, in dramatic form, in *The Brass Butterfly*. It is unique among Golding's writings in that it is witty and amusing, and quite lacking in the solemnity that rather weighs down his other work. Though classical in setting, it plays with anachronisms in a cheerful, unserious way—though the story has its Golding-esque point about civilization and its discontents.

Golding has said that he wrote *The Inheritors* to refute Wells's *Outline of History*, and one can see that between the two writers there is a certain filial relation, though strained, as such relations often are. They share the fascination with past and future, the extraordinary capacity to move imaginatively to remote points in time, the fabulizing impulse, the need to moralize. There are even similarities in style. And surely now, when Wells's reputation as a great writer is beginning to take form, it will be understood as high praise of Golding if one says that he is our Wells, as good in his own individual way as Wells was in his.

## (*c*) WALKER PERCY

### *Love in the Ruins*

THIS NEW NOVEL from Walker Percy will neither bolster nor weaken his reputation—just keep it running straight and level. It's a biggish book of smallish import, turning out to be more interesting for its unintentional revelations than for the illumination it offers about present tendencies in the United States. The story is set about a decade in the future, with politics polarized towards two extremes; the Knotheads are a supercharged version of present-day Republicans, and the Leftpapas are the latter-day Democrats—although just how Left they are is not made clear, and is only the first of all the crucial things that are not made clear.

The country is falling apart. The one man who might be able to fix it is Dr. Thomas More (a descendant of the saint) who has invented a gadget (the lapsometer—and guess what the lapse is from) for diagnosing psychic conditions and curing them with a dose of ionization. Dr. More likes women, and has three of them shacked up with him in a derelict motel where they await the apocalypse, which may, or may not, occur on July 4, the Devil (no kidding) having pinched the first batch of production models of the gadget and distributed them to the populace of Paradise, More's home town. A lot more could be said about the book's details and events, but the thing to hold on to is Mr. Percy's central notion of psychic upset: it is grace that we have fallen from, and it is to grace that we must be restored.

If we refer the book's themes back to Now (and we are plainly meant to do this) we find that everything would be much nearer to being all right if only everybody would cool it—get the mind back in tune with the body, and be whole. This is a charming notion, but unfortunately has little to do with the problem, which is to give an account of the main reasons why things went so wrong that people ceased to cool it in the first place. In Mr. Percy's future—and therefore in his present—psychic disturbance is anterior to its causes. His future is consequently not only extrapolated and exaggerated, but inverted. In a book that tries to be a diagnosis, the very intelligent Mr. Percy has come up with another set of symptoms. It makes you wonder, not to say shake in your shoes, that a man of Mr. Percy's equipment and qualifications can seriously propose that Western Man (his own words and capitals, and it should be said that the notion that the American somehow typifies 'Western Man' is itself symptomatic) is ungovernable *in the abstract*. The book teems with entertaining eccentrics but has few real characters; the reason being, one fears, that its theme is above all that. What we are offered is not men but Man, and it appears that Man has got to change his head. More, who is a Catholic and knows all about Original Sin, apparently has the qualifications to help him try.

Closely allied to this thesis is the remarkable way in which the book fails to present a credible projection of the actualities of the current American crisis. The politics of its future are not recognizable as American politics at all. One of the things that mark the American present is that the two major parties are, as near enough as makes no difference, united in failing to see that it is American foreign policy which exacerbates domestic upheavals. In Mr. Percy's future the two parties are meant to be polarized—and yet a Vietnam-style war (this time in Ecuador) continues to rage. Which party is for, which against? We are not told. Presumably the Leftpapas are against, but be that as it may, in what else does their Leftness consist? Equally puzzling is the total absence of any pressures from the intellectual community, which does not seem to even exist. Is there no draft then?

The whole picture has a dream-like incoherence, and in this resembles Kurt Vonnegut (the late Vonnegut, not the Vonnegut of the un-flashy but carefully thought-out *Player Piano*) more than the SF writers of the 1950s who supplied—supplied through middlemen, the spoof writers of the 1960s—the incidental themes and gimmicks which make the book so variously and tiresomely recognizable. For the picture of the consumer-society running to decay the canvas was primed by SF writers like Pohl and Kornbluth. The *affektlos* inability of everybody concerned to judge the import of what is going on was an invention of Terry Southern and has already been raced into the ground by himself and his epigones. Put it together and it adds up to a complete abnegation of thought—the book is riding on the depleted crest of a wave that is already washed up. To see how tired the book is, set it beside the best utopian novel of the 1950s, Bernard Wolfe's *Limbo '90*. Wolfe could not write half as well as Mr. Percy, but he isolated his central problems and thought them through.

Nevertheless there are, in *Love in the Ruins*, the incidental pleasures we expect from the author of *The Movie-Goer* (although the hangover of movie-goer themes is not one of them). Mr. Percy's descriptive powers have the clinical precision of the creative writing class, but there is no denying their quality of evocation. When he writes about the way a swarm of gnats 'hangs over the water motionless and furious, like a molecule' you are honour-bound to tip your lid. Moments like that save this worthy but weary novel from total factitiousness. Mr. Percy is plainly worried about his country, but one of the reasons the rest of us are even more worried is the *way* he worries: he just doesn't seem to see that it is not the business of politics to produce a new man.

## (*d*) MARY McCARTHY

### *Birds of America*

If, like Miss McCarthy, you live on the Left Bank in Paris, the ghosts of the Enlightenment are your daily companions—statues, street-names, even restaurants, proclaim that Voltaire, Diderot and the spirit of the *philosophes* are still the honoured mentors of French civilization. Moreover, what latter-day Candide, in search of Eldorado, would cross the Atlantic in the hope of finding the ethical beauty of natural, harmonious society? It is in Voltairean mood, wryly nostalgic for the New World innocents and yet critically conscious of Europe's failure to live up to the ideals of *Liberté*,

*Egalité* and *Fraternité*, that the expatriate Miss McCarthy charts the tragi-comic enlightenment of her nineteen-year-old hero, Peter Levi, as he leaves his American nest.

Peter is a philosophy minor, son of a Jewish Italian refugee who teaches history at Wellesley, and an ex-concert-playing harpsichordist, now with her third husband. It embarrasses him to explain that he likes 'the net effect of serial monogamy'—chiefly because, besides not having to be jealous of his various half-siblings, he knows that his mother adores him. Once, in answer to his fifteen-year-old Oedipal prayers, he had her to himself for a blissful summer in Rocky Port, New England. She and Mother Nature jointly embrace the America fast disappearing, even in Rocky Port—the innocent tradition he loves:

> reading aloud to children in the evening, Fourth of July sparklers and fireworks, Easter-egg hunts, Christmas stockings with an orange in the toe, popcorn and cranberry chains on the Christmas tree, ducking for apples at Hallowe'en, shadow pictures on the walls, lemonade, fresh cider, picnics, treasure hunts, anagrams, checkers, eggs, golden-rod, home-made cakes, muffins, popovers and corn breads, fortune-telling, sweet peas, butterfly nets, narcissus bulbs in pebbles, Trillium, Spring Beauty, arbutus, lady's-slippers, cat's cradles, swings, bicycles, wooden ice-cream-freezers, fishing with angleworms, rowing, ice-skating, blue-berrying, hymn-singing.

And, for Peter, bird-watching. So that when, four years later, the Great Horned Owl and the three cormorants have left Rocky Point along with plain yoghourt and salt codfish, Peter cheerfully accompanies his mother to a night in the local gaol in defence of the freedoms America has lost and in defiance of the new vulgarity.

Arriving in Paris armed only with his beloved (but rapidly embarrassing) old motor-bike Rosinante and staunch intentions to live up to the highest Kantian ethical standards, Peter begins his sobering self-education. He learns, even on the journey, that in the Great Diaspora of his people an American is mortifyingly recognizable—worse than being a Jew, he decides, since there is no 'dignified history of martyrdom', nothing to be proud of. Indeed, almost the worst—and funniest—of his Parisian days is Thanksgiving, at which, in the lavish apartment of a Nato General, he not only tackles his fellow expatriates on Vietnam but falls in love with the demure, killjoy, vegetarian Roberta.

To his dismay he discovers that being an egalitarian is a good deal more problematical than being a Civil Rights worker and that his mother's 'classical style' is incompatible with democracy. For instance, revolted by his upbringing at the fifthy state of cheap hotel lavoratories, Peter wages a solitary, hopeless, and, he realizes, furtive hygiene campaign. Questioning his pharisaism, his need to avoid appearing critical of the prevailing mores, his awareness of being *different*, he parodies the worst scruples of the penitent—and those who remember *Memories of a Catholic Girlhood* will appreciate the panache of Miss McCarthy's painfully funny authenticity.

At least, he feels, the spectacle of a student demonstration, with an 'airy ballet' of gendarmes swinging capes, is uplifting compared to the savagery back home (it is 1964, still). Until the capes are revealed as lead weapons, the police arrest his new friend in error, his treasured *Fatshedera* plant is trampled in the gutter, and the US consul is cynically overcome with merriment at Peter's concern. The non-personality of the animal world he observes with a bird-watching group on Sundays seems a possible solution to society's ills—identity, to Peter unattainable, might then belong naturally to occupation, as in the Middle Ages. But this, like all his other *idées géniales*, merely indicates to Peter's advisor Mr. Small that he is too inward-looking, not making full use of the challenge of self-realization, the richly rewarding decision-making device of his junior year abroad—maybe he's even in need of psychiatric treatment.

His image of the virtuous Roberta shattered too, Peter spends Christmas in Rome. And here, in his paternal homeland, things look better. For one thing, the world's problems do not clamour for solutions; even poverty seems an acceptable natural state. Best of all, he can contemplate Art. But Mr. Small, the unavoidable Pangloss of modern student life, has also come to Rome. Not, he proudly claims, for the Sistine Chapel, but, armed with tape-recorder and drop-out disguise, to prepare a mammoth depth study of the tourist experience. He's delighted with his field trip among the Beats: 'Some of them are extraordinarily attractive, as human beings. Last night, I smoked grass with a diversified group . . .', he explains, and Peter spots the phraseology of his bird-watching books as Mr. Small outlines the flyways, migrations and common urges of these deviant minorities. It saddens him, once again, to find that it is the ludicrous Pangloss who believes in Man—he himself prefers 'most art to most people'.

Particularly he prefers anything—except a tormented conscience—to the final gesture into which Paris forces him on his return. Appalled by his venal philanthropy now that he is once more among the temples of 'icy reason', he shelters a filthy incontinent, stinking *clocharde* in his room overnight. And, to crown the horror of hearing that Johnson has bombed Hanoi, Nature itself turns on him savagely; even the sage of Königsberg can offer no consolation.

The didacticism of Miss McCarthy's theme in no way blunts her wit; indeed, the challenge of the *philosophes* and the attempt to make her Candide a convincingly likable as well as serious fall-guy hero seem to have stimulated her into some of the funniest scenes she has ever written. Like all such *contes moraux* in which a symbolic figure makes a tragi-comic pilgrimage, however, *Birds of America* will seem to many of her admirers too episodic, too obviously a vehicle in which the protagonist merely suffers various rituals, in which arguments are aired but emotions never involved. It is also, of course, a splendid excuse for Miss McCarthy to describe Paris, Rome, and their inhabitants—all of which she does with relish, great skill and more justice, perhaps, than the caricature-sketches of her fellow Americans.

It may be in keeping with the novel's ironical tone to have given the chapters such coyly literary titles as 'Round Table, with the Damsel Parcenet' or 'Epistle from Mother Carey's Chicken' (though the aptness of 'Greek Fire' is lost by misprinting it, in the text, as 'green'); but Miss McCarthy would have done well to avoid the self-consciousness of 'a sociologist hight Mr. Small'. Only the scrupulous attention that Miss McCarthy expects in her readers, however, pin-points such objections. This is an enormously enjoyable, intelligent, civilized novel.

## (*e*) JORGE LUIS BORGES

### *El Informe de Brodie*

*El Informe de Brodie* is the first book of new stories that Borges has published since *El Aleph* nearly twenty years ago. He makes no excuse in the preface for his abstinence from fiction, unless there is one to be derived from his teasing acknowledgment of the young Kipling as a model for the old Borges. In his later stories, says Borges, Kipling was an artificer of labyrinths and anxiety comparable with Kafka or Henry James; earlier he had produced some 'laconic masterpieces' in a more direct manner. Borges claims to have been travelling in the other direction, declaring that in *El Informe de Brodie*: 'He intentado, no sé con qué fortuna, la redacción de cuentos directos. No me atrevo a afirmar que son sencillos. . . .'.

Thankfully, the stories in *El Informe de Brodie* do not quite live up to this dreadful promise; they may be, for the most part, simpler than the best of Borges but they are not transparent, and the agnosticism towards the ultimate nature of his own creations to which Borges holds looks very much like a preliminary move in his game of withholding from readers what he wants them to think out for themselves. (But how treacherous of his publishers to have evacuated Borges's preface of its irony and printed wild remarks on the cover about 'an unforeseen shift in his aesthetic', as if anyone could possibly welcome that.)

The majority of the eleven stories in *El Informe de Brodie* carry, as their author's letter-heading, a reference to their own source. They are explicitly 'narrated', since the act of narration figures as a first episode in the story as printed: the stories have been told to the narrator before being told by him. Borges counts on this gentle alienation effect to dispossess the narrator of his story, as well as to emphasize to what extent it is fictitious. *El Informe de Brodie* is punctuated by reminders that with each successive telling a story mutates, as it is embroidered or censored by the teller, concerned with making good use of his temporary ownership of it. The story itself may have begun as a private experience but with its first transmission it was surrendered to the public world, and although the revisions made to it by the mouths through which it passes may be trivial they are the one loophole that Borges leaves for the inclusion in a literary work of those fashionable elements of style and originality.

The pre-eminence of an episode over its protagonists is made very clear in *El Informe de Brodie* and is even, now and again, grasped by the protagonists themselves, aware of being upstaged by what is happening to them. In 'El Encuentro' two men who quarrel at a game of poker take up knives and fight to the death with a dexterity belied by their ignorance of knifemanship. Essentially, it is not they who are fighting but the weapons, museum pieces once wielded by legendary Argentinian buffs of the *duelo a cuchillo*. This is not Borges being fantastic but strictly literary, the precedence of knife over man being a recognition that anecdotes will, if recorded, survive their actors. Borges is richly entitled to his claim that he writes fiction as a 'realist' even if it is hard to keep in mind, while reading him, what a scrupulous form of realism he practises.

Similar re-enactments of historical or cultural episodes crop up so regularly in *El Informe de Brodie* that they give this set of stories a coherence lacking in any of Borges's earlier collections. The topos of the duel is especially prominent, although it may be transposed into a context where nothing more belligerent can pass between the adversaries than a demonstration of conflicting attitudes. The most involved and, in the psychoanalyst's sense of the word, 'over-determined' story of all is called 'Guayaquil', the name of the town in Ecuador where there was a historic confrontation between Simón Bolívar and San Martín in 1822.

The confrontation in Borges's story is between two academic historians variously and consistently differentiated. They are rivals for the privilege of deciphering a newly discovered letter by Bolívar which may or may not disclose what passed between him and San Martín when they met. The narrator's opponent is a Jewish refugee from Europe who stands for the mastery of persons over events and whose features are, to the narrator's mind, *trop meublé*. The narrator himself is a native South American and heroically bookish. The meeting passes without discernible crisis but by the end it has been settled, tacitly, that it is the other historian who will go to read the letter: there has been a replay of San Martín's renunciation of ambition at Guayaquil, down to the crucial detail that neither renunciation has yet been explained.

It is, however, the shrinking Borges-figure who has supplied this account of the scholars' duel, not the man of action, handicapped, as a fictional character, by his involvement with the excessive furniture of the phenomenal world. 'Guayaquil' is itself a replica of Bolívar's letter and the testament of the man who won, inviting sedentary decipherment by yet a third generation: the reader. This story embodies, in a blindingly ingenious scheme, the victory of Borges's 'realism' over the deceits of what is commonly known as 'realism' by looser literary theorists.

In the preface to *El Informe de Brodie*, Borges gives his support, not for the first time, to an inspirational theory of literary composition and dissents from the fanciful rationalism of Poe, who believed that the writer could calculate backwards from the effect he wanted to produce to the linguistic signs for producing it. There is, one need hardly say, no sign whatsoever of any inspiration in Borges's new stories, but there is, in a story like 'Guayaquil', reassuring proof of this intellectual man's continuing faith in contrivance and in the need always to leave room between what is unique—life—and the generic means of recalling it—language.

# 6

# OBSERVATIONS ON POWER

ELIAS CANETTI claims that Kafka is the only Chinese poet produced by the West. Yes, even that face could be, with little variation, a Chinese face. Arthur Waley shared this opinion, not from a study of the face but from the prose (that other, secret face made public); he knew Kafka as well as he knew Po Chü-I. It is not only the economy, the suggestive subtlety of words, but above all Kafka's interest in small things, his projection of personal situations into the humanly insignificant, animals even. He migrates into the minute, the mole in its burrow, Gregor Samsa waving his insect legs in bed. This is more than symbolic transformation of feeling into form, it is kinship, an oriental migration of souls.

*Der andere Prozess*, Canetti's short study of Kafka's letters to Felice Bauer, is perhaps the most revealing essay on Kafka ever published. Like every book worth reading it tells us as much about the author as his subject. At last Kafka is matched in thought and prose. But more: there is for Canetti a propriety in the subject, and we learn from his book why good writing is simply enthusiasm made manifest in characteristic form. The list of Canetti's publications is brief, he selects his subjects with care, and here is the justification, a theme from the past which reminds us of what Lessing said long ago (about the historical dramatist): that he doesn't choose a subject because it has happened, but because it has happened in such a way that he could hardly have invented it better for his immediate purpose. This time it is Canetti who migrates into the spirit of Kafka, that spirit breathing under the transparent membrane of prose; his own feeling finds form there.

From the beginning, Canetti's work has been an image (in the fiction) and description (in the philosophy) of the individual's relationship to power. It is an obsession which itself generates power. In

---

ELIAS CANETTI: *Der andere Prozess: Kafkas Briefe an Felice*. 128 pp. DM 5.80. *Alle vergeudete Verehrung: Aufzeichnungen 1949–1960*. 139 pp. DM 7.80. Munich: Hanser.

*Alle vergeudete Verehrung*, Canetti's latest book, a selection from his notebooks of the period 1949–1960, the Old Testament is described as a history of divine power; of all writers, he says in his study of the letters to Felice, Kafka is the greatest expert on power. But is there any writer whose creations seem as powerless as Kafka's? They endure, accept, humiliate themselves. How then can he be the greatest expert on power? It is just this abasement which reveals Kafka's preoccupation with power. 'My writing was all about you', he said to his father—or was it God the father or the Father-Judge in the unending trial which is the human situation, the Last Judgment which is never final but a court in standing session, a continuing process, the trial of facing daily and eternally the tests of contact with experience? The environment is power and has to be coped with. Kafka's answer is to advance by retreating. Canetti might have had him in mind when he speaks in these published notes of one who can only find his way home by straying on devious paths; each time he has to find a *different* way there.

There is no contradiction between power and the humiliating situations, in soul and body, of Kafka's characters. Impatience is the principal human sin, says Kafka; it is because of impatience that we were expelled from Paradise, it is because of impatience that we do not return there. Canetti is convinced that Kafka's migrations into the minute are gestures of constructive defence. Patience is stubborn resistance to distractions. Kafka would like to work in a remote cellar far from the light, undisturbed, sealed off. The distractions of normal life are too much for him; he does not live, he only creates life. Power is the family, his fiancée, the formal ceremony of betrothal in Berlin where the captive writer is incomprehensibly paraded in public, arrested without knowing he has done anything wrong. And then six weeks later at the Ascana Hotel, the 'court of judgment' where his engagement to Felice is broken off. He goes away to carry out the verdict of society in the only way he knows, in writing, which is always for him a conjuration of spirits. K. dies 'like a dog . . . as if the shame would outlive him'. But Kafka lives on, like a dog. He often calls himself a dog. He likes the term, he finds it appropriate. Self-abasement is the best defence, the individual conceals himself and power passes by, looking for responsive targets. Saint or lunatic? Canetti remarks in *Alle vergeudete Verehrung* that the gesture of the true idiot moves him more than that of the Almighty. We are approaching the two ends of Heinrich von Kleist's circular world, the two ends which join in the identical grace of God, and the inanimate object reacting only to natural laws.

Both in theoretic and in fictional work Canetti comes back again and again to paranoia as the most revealing attitude to Power. Power exists only in relation to the individual, the individual is his relationship to power. The paranoiac becomes his own God in the world he has made. There is only one point of view, central and absolute and confined in a box of delusion. Each of the four main characters in Canetti's novel *Die Blendung* (1935) represents this kind of obsessive defence. One way to resist power is to capture it all and become its source and justification. Three of the characters choose this path and become lunatic rulers in their realms. Another way is to withdraw, really withdraw beyond the periphery of life to the anonymous and the inanimate. This is what happens to the fourth character, Peter Kien, in Canetti's novel. Kien is a dedicated scholar, a sinologist with a huge private library 'in the sky'—in his head *and* on the top floor of a block of flats, with windows only in the roof. The library is his life. When he is attacked, when his private world of scholarship is threatened, he withdraws, he petrifies himself, he becomes his name. That label of individuality becomes static. Stone or shell, the protection is there. Another defence is voluntary blindness; Kien shuts his eyes and excludes the distracting world and its power; blindness becomes a weapon against time and space. He is in the remote cellar far from the light.

But Peter Kien is not Franz Kafka. The insect survives in the cellar, it is his comfortable home, he re-turns the metamorphosis by making insect-life seem more real than daylight existence. The insignificant is tough and endurable. Kien does not become insignificant, only isolated, stifled in a box where he finds death, not creation. He, too, is a lunatic ruler in his realm of fantasy, a ruler who goes under, suppressed by superior force. The insect escapes to live again. Life begins with the smallest cell, hardly worth noticing.

The shape of Canetti's work is form given to observations on power. During his student days in Vienna between 1924 and 1929, he resolved, suddenly one day as if struck by illumination, to dedicate his life to the study of crowd phenomena. The conscious association with power came later, but of course the theme was already there: he was at school in Frankfurt at the time of the inflation and saw mass demonstrations, the mob in the streets. But the greatest external influence came on July 15, 1927, the day the Palace of Justice in Vienna went up in flames. Significantly, this was the year the first idea for his novel *Die Blendung* came to him. That book too is red with fire and violence. It characterizes not only individuals sealed in paranoiac shells, it characterizes an age of anger and misunderstanding. It must be one of the indestructible novels. It is fantasy made precise, but so is our society. It is comic and horrifying—human. And human too, for a reason beyond imaginative craftsmanship: its theme is the central issue of all life, the confrontation between individual organization and external force. This is the nature of Canetti's illumination.

The pressures on any separate organization are immense. Every form is a moving equation of energies, transformed and transforming through pressure. The human individual is, like every other form, a separate organization, precariously balanced. He can dissolve into the crowd, the ocean around him, uniformity. The survival of the individual depends on his response to the field of force through which he moves, picking his way to avoid collision like a shopper in the street. Napoleon tells us that most of the time he had no definite plans but only projects: 'Instead of obstinately seeking to control circumstances, I obeyed them, and they forced me to change my mind all the time.' These 'circumstances' are external force, unexpected reinforcements on the other side, a change in the weather, casualties, toothache. Vision, in poet and soldier, is the ability to react with spontaneous accuracy to external forces. The individual cannot survive as an institution or monument but only as a changing shape, flexible in the order which is never finally ordered, as he himself is never final and complete.

Peter Kien turned to stone is the man who believes he can live in his own rigidly ordered private world, immune to force. But nothing is immune to force. If you do not negotiate with force you have to crush or be crushed. There is nothing creative here. The kind of false and common order in which nothing is to change, nothing is to be out of place, nothing may ever be different, is described by Canetti in *Alle vergeudete Verehrung* as a self-made desert. Nowhere in nature is there an order which is fixed and unchangeable, but humanity insists on its suicidal monuments, in private and in public. This is why Canetti's fiction is the image of an actual world where objects sheathed in misunderstanding meet in angry collision. Where there is no adaptable negotiation there can only be collision. Living form is energy in cooperative delineation. The box of delusion is mute, based on arid misconception, always in opposition, since it knows no cooperative gesture. More frustratingly, it is in opposition to the fundamental nature of life. The effect is anger, in individuals, in nations. Canetti grew up in a Europe of conflicting monomanias, but who can say that his immediate environment was the sole arena of public and private idiocy? He speaks for the human condition.

When Canetti wrote *Masse und Macht* (1960), the first volume in a planned study of crowd psychology and the aspects and gestures of power, he related the individual's postures of self-preservation to the grander public acts of the ruler. Paranoiac and ruler seem identical to him in their inner structure, and there is certainly evidence from recent history that he is right. The attitude of the one is interpreted as delusion set against the whole of mankind; in the other it is called heroic conviction (depending on your point of view). Canetti began to write this book towards the end of 1948 after years of concentration and study, a time dominated by a veritable 'rage for learning'.

Earlier, in Austria until the pressure of a paranoiac ruler drove him to Paris in 1938 and in the following year to London, where he still lives, speculation on crowds and power yielded place periodically to the other diversions of a creative writer. His migration and the outbreak of war changed all that. The fixed institution had shown its true nature, which is an offence against law; it had become licentious. The extremes of rigid form and absolute licence are equally inimical to life. Here again are two ends of a circular world which join, but in violence not creative grace. Licence too is madness, a prejudice in favour of chaos; it doesn't negotiate, it doesn't shape and realize itself in creative interplay with external force. It insists and collides. Only law can give us freedom, says Goethe. This law is a developing pattern of fact conditioned by energy. Impatience is an offence against this pattern, impatience which led to man's expulsion from Paradise and prevents his return there. Canetti's patient dedication to study is an attempt to see the law. Understanding comes from knowledge.

Canetti is a scientist by training. His doctorate at Vienna was gained for a dissertation in chemistry. Musil was an engineer, Gottfried Benn a doctor, Hermann Broch trained in philosophy, psychology and mathematics. When Thomas Mann displays his enormous erudition in the dialogues of *Der Zauberberg* and *Doktor Faustus*, or makes Professor Kuckuck entertain young Felix Krull in the dining-car to Lisbon with an elaborately detailed account of the growth of all life, he is not trying to blind us with science. On the contrary, he is using it to open our eyes. The detail is sacred, the fact which connects. It is natural, in every sense, for Musil to begin his story of Viennese life in *Der Mann ohne Eigenschaften* with a scientific report on the weather over the Atlantic. Everything matters. The poet Arvers on his death-bed in Rilke's *Die Aufzeichnungen des Malte Laurids Brigge* comes back momentarily from his final coma to correct a nurse about the spelling of a word. Then he dies. 'He was a poet', says Rilke, 'and he hated the approximate'.

This fantastic world is precise in every detail, and every detail is a vestige of energy. There is nothing vague about life except our contemplation of it. Canetti's passion for learning is an effort to make this contemplation exact. There is no other basis for fruitful response. While everything in the environment changes, it changes from specific form to specific form.

It is curious that back in the 1930s the protagonist of *Die Blendung* was a fanatical scholar who proved inadequate for life. But there is nothing of Kien's self-made desert about Canetti's scholarship. In that novel he described a man in a box, a man who could not make connexions. The most difficult thing in the world is to see what is there, without prejudice or expectation, to have only variable projects not plans. Canetti is open, flexible, everything which the stiff structures clashing so violently in *Die Blendung* are not.

The detail must be known, but the profounder knowledge is that everything changes as form succeeds form, and there can be no finality. It is characteristic of Canetti's natural gift for development that he instinctively resisted the dangers inherent in passive study. Perhaps he had his own Peter Kien in mind. Knowledge is necessary for informed judgment, but satisfaction comes only from the spontaneous gesture which springs from a creative combination of conscious *and* unconscious. This is where energy stretches out to energy, transforming and being transformed. So in 1942 he slackened the grip of his studies by devoting one or two hours each day to writing notes on whatever came into his head, freely and with no thought of revision or publication. He had done this irregularly before, but what had once been peripheral now became a necessary expression of personality.

The first selection from these notes was published in 1965 as *Aufzeichnungen 1942–1948*. The second is *Alle vergeudete Verehrung*, which takes us up to 1960. In a sense, these books are by-products of

*Masse und Macht*: they accompany the preparation and composition of that work. The three books taken together give us the portrait of a man in relentless pursuit of truth, but it is the notebooks which speak of the soul, where pursuit is unending. They too move from specific form to specific form. Canetti follows his own dictum that the writer must speak as if it is the last sentence allowed to him.

Rilke remarked that fame is the sum of misunderstandings that gather round a name. We in England can congratulate ourselves that we do not misunderstand Canetti: we hardly know him. It becomes wearisome to mention his name and wait for the flash of recognition which so seldom comes. *Die Blendung* was brought out in English (translated by C. V. Wedgwood), by Cape in 1946 as *Auto-da-Fé*, and it is available in Penguin Modern Classics. Gollancz published *Masse und Macht* in 1962 as *Crowds and Power*. That is all we have in English, apart from a brief essay on his friend, the sculptor Fritz Wotruba, published in Vienna (Verlag Brüder Rosenbaum) in 1955. The Japanese will shortly do better: Canetti's complete works are about to be translated into their language. In Germany his reputation has grown considerably since *Die Blendung* was re-issued in 1963 by Hanser, who have also published all his books since then. He has suddenly become what he always was—an individual and important literary figure.

# 7

# ROMANTIC REVISIONS

## (*a*) THE PHYSICAL KEATS

THESE BOOKS mark the 150th anniversary of the death of Keats; and they suffer a little from commemorating him as a classic. He thought he would be among the English poets after his death, and Miss Hewlett quotes Arnold's verdict: 'He is—he is with Shakespeare.' This at once raises the problem of the Arnoldian prejudices of Keats critics today. Though praising Keats for fascinating verbal felicity, Arnold felt his poetry lacked sustaining thought; it was made out of sensations—he disapprovingly points to the letters to Fanny Brawne and the incident, recorded by Haydon, in which Keats poured cayenne pepper on his tongue to give claret a finer savour—rather than ideas. Romantic poets didn't know enough. To a Victorian, cramped in the posture of Rodin's thinker, burdened by seriousness and the dignified depression of George Eliot in Trinity gardens with F. W. H. Myers, the Romantics were too young and too untroubled to be of help; the lovely lyrical wail of Shelley, Byron's play with his own discretions, the gusto with which Keats preyed on experience, had all proved unavailing.

The verbal luxury of these poets was for Arnold a sign of their infantile quality; the Victorian poet, desperately reflective, a troubled adult rather than a visionary child, needed to write with greater plainness, with stern seriousness. Arnold could only salvage part of

---

(*a*) *Keats at Wentworth Place: Poems written December, 1818 to September, 1820.* Introduction by Dorothy Hewlett. 66 pp. London Borough of Camden. 40p.

TIMOTHY HILTON: *Keats and His World.* 144 pp. Thames and Hudson. £1.75. *The Odes of Keats and their earliest known Manuscripts.* Edited by Robert Gittings. 79 pp. Heinemann. £3.50. *The Poems of John Keats.* Edited by Miriam Allott. 772 pp. Longman. £3.

(*b*) JAMES DYKES CAMPBELL: *Samuel Taylor Coleridge.* 319 pp. Lime Tree Bower Press. £3.50. *The Collected Works of Samuel Taylor Coleridge.* Volume 2: *The Watchman.* Edited by Lewis Patton. 477 pp. £5.25. Volume 3: *Lectures 1795: On Politics and Religion.* Edited by Lewis Patton and Peter Mann. 512 pp. £6.30. Routledge and Kegan Paul.

FRIDA KNIGHT: *University Rebel.* 320 pp. Gollancz. £3.

Keats by arguing that despite his sensuous excesses—Mr. Hilton records an 'immortal' dinner party at Haydon's at which Lamb became mad with drink; Keats on one evening led a discussion of 'the derivation of the word *C——t*'—he had the makings of a philosophic poet, and only death prevented him from becoming one. And indeed, the early deaths of the Romantics do seem peculiarly apt, since they are poets of adolescent confidence and energy; the only one who survived, Wordsworth, became a Victorian, and stiffened into the apologist of Duty.

Thus Arnold divides the early, luscious Keats from the later, flinty one. The early Keats, still under the baleful influence of Leigh Hunt, is warm and pulpy, specializing in slippery contacts of lips, warm pressures of hands, wine, women, and snuff; the later Keats, the Keats of Mr. Gittings's annus mirabilis, doesn't luxuriate in experiences but questions them—

> Do I wake or sleep?

—and aims not for colour and sensuous effusion but for the severe and marmoreal:

> Then saw I a wan face
> Not pin'd with human sorrows,
> but bright blanch'd
> By an immortal sickness which kills not . . .

He is on the verge, in the Arnoldian view, of becoming a Victorian poet, concerned to console and instruct men; and indeed Miss Hewlett says that the odes are '*great utterances* where every rift is loaded with ore', a phrase which suggest Arnold's touchstones. Yet the ore Keats spoke of in advising Shelley was surely not nuggets of golden reflection on human kind, as Miss Hewlett seems to assume; he meant sensuous decoration. He felt Shelley's verse to be too rapid and abstract and intellectual, and advised him to weight it down with colour and feeling, like his own. Shelley's poetry is haunted by the 'awful shadow of some unknown power'; in Keats there are no shadows, nothing invisible and remote, all is palpable, full and rich. Shelley's autumn poem looks forward to a future awakening; Keats's is content to savour the ripeness of the present.

Miss Hewlett's misreading derives from an Arnoldian desire to make Keats respectable, as does her argument that *The Cap and Bells* is a product of disease and frustration and not worthy of inclusion in her selection of poems written at Brown's house. The judgment is a curious one, for, rather than being a reversion to the earlier fairy manner at a time when he ought to have been devoting himself to philosophic verse, *The Cap and Bells* is a perfect complement to *Hyperion*. In the epic fragment Keats chastens his earlier lush style, while in the satire he sneers at it, parodying Hunt and making his own earlier delicate fancies seem grotesque (the broth made from the thighs of moths, for instance). The poems are complementary failures, because both strain beyond the trusting animal spirits of the early lyrical Keats; to exclude one and overpraise the other is to rewrite his development in the Arnoldian way.

In the introduction to his fine comparative edition of the odes and their earliest manuscripts, Mr. Gittings gives a similar Arnoldian account of the later Keats, seeing the odes and the epic as a developing argument, a working out of solutions to life. Keats's 'self-created philosophy of Soul-Making' (compared by Mr. Gittings with the theodicy of Bishop Butler) is glossed from his letters. This seems a doubtful procedure: the letters offer hints, metaphysical guesses, intimations, rather than a developed system of thought; once again it is an Arnoldian fallacy to assume that a poet needs to be armed with a criticism of life—for the Romantics, glimpses, guesses, odd visionary spots of time were enough. If the late poems are a sequence—which, reading them chronologically in Mrs. Allott's splendid edition, one doubts, for the questioning ones are interspersed with frolicsome pieces and fairy poems—they are one emotionally rather than intellectually. Their unity is that of a certain mood, and their development is in the increase of emotional temperature rather than in the growth of insights into explanations. Can that most non-committal, satisfied, steady of poems, *To Autumn*, really be called, as it is by Mr. Gittings, the final poetic realization of Keats's personal philosophy? Mellow and swollen with its own richness, it can't be interrogated.

Keats is not a reflective poet: as John Jones put it in his recent study, whereas Wordsworth wanted to make sense of life, Keats only wanted to make the most of it. This is why he is a pictorial poet—and Mr. Hilton's book usefully follows the suggestions of Ian Jack's *Keats and the Mirror of Art* by reproducing some of the Poussins and Claudes on which Keats drew. The Nature of Wordsworth opens into immortality, that of Shelley is fraught with intellectual beauty, with the luminous powers and presences released in the Turneresque atmosphere of Act IV of *Prometheus Unbound*; but Keats doesn't wish to pierce through Nature to something beyond: it is the plump appetizing reality of things which attracts him, and his poetry celebrates this reality by making pictures of things. Pictures make things palpable, prove them upon the pulses. The music of Shelley is, in comparison, abstract and ethereal:

> Light of life, thy lips enkindle . . .

Keats delights in synaesthesia, the rich confusion of senses: 'snow-light cadences melting to silence'. His predatory instinct leads him to fuse dissimilar kinds of pleasure, and a controversial case of this occurs in the 'Ode on Melancholy':

> When the melancholy fit shall fall . . .
> Then glut thy sorrow on a morning rose,
> Or on the rainbow of the salt sand-wave,
> Or on the wealth of globed peonies;
> Or if thy mistress some rich anger shows,
> Emprison her soft hand, and let her rave,
> And feed deep, deep upon her peerless eyes.

Bridges commented: 'Among the objects on which a sensitive mind is recommended to indulge its melancholy fit, the anger of his mistress is enumerated with roses, peonies and rainbows, as a beautiful phenomenon plainly without respect to its cause, meaning or effect.' Likewise the sonnet printed by Mrs. Allott as No. 44 melts together Sappho, a sleeping infant's breath, a woodland rivulet, and a poet's death. The appetite for the beautiful is undiscriminating: Keats is like Browning's bishop, equating

> A fancy from a flower-bell, someone's death,
> A chorus-ending from Euripides

—or Mallock's caricature of Pater in *The New Republic*, Mr. Rose, who finds equally pleasant 'a beautiful face, a ruined temple, a death-bed, or a line of poetry'. Mr. Gittings, with an Arnoldian anxiety to cover up these avid Huntian cravings in Keats, proposes an alternative reading: 'Mistress' has a capital in the earliest surviving draft, so Mr. Gittings argues that it refers to personified Melancholy, not to the girl-friend with whom the Cockney Johnny Keats—Arnold's 'merely sensuous man'—is grappling. The reading is more decorous, but less true.

Arnold said Keats was with Shakespeare; Mr. Gittings writes of his successes of 1819 that 'his nature, striving for a Shakespearean universality, seemed miraculously to have achieved this aim'. The letter in which Keats differentiates the egotistical sublime of Milton and Wordsworth, in which the mind and will impose themselves on everything in the poem, from the negative capability of Shakespeare, who darts into sympathy with his subjects, has given critics licence for a misleading identification of Keats with Shakespeare. Yet negative capability is a distinction of dramatic invention, and Keats, like the other Romantics, is the least dramatic of poets; his sensual, caressing way of lingering over a subject is the obverse of that dramatic and novelistic imagination which keeps its distance, recognizing the separateness and individuality of its subjects. Keats, like Lawrence, dotes on his subjects, hangs on them—

> As if increase of appetite had grown
> By what it fed on.

This is not the same as Shakespeare's impartial relishing of Iago or Imogen; it is more the greedy, devouring enthusiasm Hazlitt called 'gusto'. Hazlitt complains that Claude saw landscapes without feeling them, that he lacked Keats's power of synaesthesia: he does not 'interpret one sense by another. . . . His eye . . . did not strongly sympathize with his other faculties'. Gusto is 'the power or passion defining any object'—the colouring of Titian (whose 'Bacchus and Ariadne' Mr. Hilton shows Keats recalling in *Sleep and Poetry*) has it, but the flesh-colouring of Vandyke, bland and null, hasn't: 'The eye does not acquire a taste or appetite for what it sees.'

For Keats, as much as Dickens, to whom Christmas dinner was more important symbolically than the Nativity, and whose last written words were 'and fell to with an appetite', is the poet of eating, of voracious appetite. Leigh Hunt had complained that the poetic spirits of the English were too sour and saturnine, and recommended cream as a poetic subject; and in writing of Keats he continually uses images of feeding to suggest his sensuous gobbling up of things: his is 'the young poetical appetite, obtaining its food by the very desire of it'. The sensations are at first ethereal and palpitating: the tender pressures and ardent listlessness of *Endymion*, the 'breathless honey feel of bliss'; these mature into the mellow scenes of the Autumn ode: the slow luxurious tricklings of the cyder-press, 'the last oozings hours by hours', the satisfied sense of plump fruitful things, gourds or hazel-shells, swollen with the weight and obesity of their ripeness.

*Hyperion* fails because it renounces the pleasures of sense—'savour of poisonous brass and metal sick'—for something more austere. Keats's development is not from a Spenserian chamber of maiden thought to Shakespearean bitter-sweet fruit, but from appetite dreaming of fanciful food to appetite gorging itself on a feast of real things; not from sensation to vision but from sensation to more intense sensation.

An Arnoldian guilty conscience about poetry having to be a criticism of life has made critics reluctant to admit that Keats's is poetry of enjoyment, of what Hunt called 'the sheer license of animal spirits'. Keats's verse is, as he said of Barry Cornwall's, 'composed of Amiability'. Too often he is seen as moving, like Shakespeare in Dowden's version, from idyllic seclusion into tragic struggle and thence on to the heights of poetic serenity; the truth is that he changed hardly at all, but simply became more confident. The last odes are implicit in the very earliest poems of 1814 and 1815 printed by Mrs. Allott:

> Fill for me a brimming bowl
> And let me in it drown my soul . . .
> I want as deep a draught
> As the e'er from Lethe's wave was quaffed

—or—

> Byron! how sweetly sad thy melody!
> Attuning still thy soul to tenderness

—or—

> Hast thou a goblet for dark sparkling wine,
> That goblet right heavy, and massy, and gold?

Keats is a bard of passion and of mirth.

He is also a poet of relaxation—even of indolence and sleep; it is his dozing quality which Tennyson found so congenial, and drew on for his Lady of Shalott and Lotos-Eaters. He doesn't aspire to epic because of its strenuousness, its celebration of action, as Arnold did; he is dreamy and passive, and for him the long poem is a 'place to wander in'. As one could go for walks in the landscapes of Hobbema or Claude, so one can travel in poems—'Much have I travelled in the realms of gold', he writes in the poem on Chapman's Homer, and in another on Homer he is

> one who sits ashore and longs perchance
> To visit dolphin-coral in deep seas.

He writes of *The Floure and the Leafe*, 'this pleasant tale is like a little copse'; *The Story of Rimini* provides a bower for the spirit of the lover of poetry, just as the thing of beauty in *Endymion* keeps a bower quiet for us. In Mrs. Allott's poem No. 29 to Cowden Clarke, verse is a stream on which the poet drifts, like the Lady of Shalott,

> scarce knowing my intent,
> Still scooping up the water with my fingers.

All this is most un-Arnoldian—he would have thought it lazy and self-indulgent, like the mill-owner Thornton in Mrs. Gaskell's *North and South* who argues that 'we are of a different race from the Greeks, to whom beauty was everything, and to whom . . . a life of leisure and serene enjoyment . . . entered in through their outward senses. . . . I belong to Teutonic blood . . . we do not look upon life as a time of enjoyment, but as a time for action and exertion.' Milton, the poet of action and exertion, was death to Keats; in Mrs. Allott's poem No. 67 he is overcome by hot flushes at the sight of a lock of Milton's hair, and feels he lacks the vaulting power of the epic poet, just as in the early poems on the Elgin Marbles he regrets that he lacks the eagle's wings of Haydon and can't soar into Grecian grandeur. Instead, characteristically, ' 'tis a gentle luxury to weep'.

Keats's feeling for a poem as a bower, a place of rest, links with his pictorialism. For pictures too open up imaginary spaces. If a Romantic poem is a bower, a Romantic picture is a magic casement opening on to strange distances, like those in the Claudes which appealed to Keats—Mrs. Allott shows him remembering the 'Landscape with the Father of Psyche' in the poem to Reynolds. Earlier paintings contain and mark off a certain limited area; but those of the Romantics are windows into the remote and mysterious, the foam of magic seas, or the ringing plains of windy Troy. Romantic art doesn't so much hold the mirror up to nature as open a window on to something beyond nature. Thus Burne-Jones denied that a picture was a photograph: it was 'a beautiful romantic dream of something that never was, never will be—in a light better than any light that ever shone—in a land no one can define or remember, only desire'. Mr. Hilton, like a good Arnoldian, quotes Keats's early comment that poetry

> should be a friend
> To soothe the cares, and lift the thoughts of man

to prove that he was an Arnoldian after all. Keats is unjustly charged, he says, with 'self-indulgent escapism and revery'. Yet reverie and escape aren't necessarily things to be ashamed of, as Mr. Hilton assumes; they are at the centre of Keats's art, and an illustration on the very same page shows us why—it is of the operating theatre of Old St. Thomas's Hospital with a box of sawdust under the table to catch the dripping blood. It is this from which Keats retreated into his poetic copses.

For he is, as John Bayley pointed out in his Chatterton Lecture in 1962, the first poet to be troubled by the disparity between art and life. Hence his attractiveness to the Pre-Raphaelites (on whom Mr. Hilton published a book last year). *The Eve of St. Agnes* is a Pre-Raphaelite poem, for it was inspired by engravings of the frescoes from the Campo Santo, Pisa, which provided a justification for the primitive Nazarene art of the Brotherhood; and they often painted scenes from it—Holman Hunt in 1848, Arthur Hughes's triptych in the Tate in 1856—while Millais spent a night shivering in the Jacobean bedroom of a deserted country house in order to capture the winter moonlight silvering the breast of Madeleine as she undresses. Rossetti described *La Belle Dame Sans Merci* as 'the germ from which all the poetry of my group has sprung'. Yet Tennyson and the Pre-Raphaelites are as untrue to Keats, in their way, as Arnold: their dim golden dreams weaken him; they have none of his avidity. Nothing is palpable enough, it is all too soulful; refinement has taken over from lip-licking delight, and their sadder, withdrawn mood is very unlike the sensuous excess and luxury of Keats. Their misinterpretation of him is in fact similar to Arnold's: they make this most physical of poets seem spiritual; and the critics of this century have pressed the misunderstanding even farther, to make him seem theological.

## (*b*) THE RADICAL COLERIDGE

SAMUEL TAYLOR COLERIDGE was in or around Bristol much of 1795 and 1796, in his twenty-third and twenty-fourth years. He married, became a father, delivered two series of lectures (an enterprise which he shared with Southey, nearly two years his junior), and between March and mid-May 1796 he edited ten numbers of a political and literary journal, *The Watchman*.

Some six or seven years after this he had substantially shifted his positions, rejecting his Hartleian necessitarianism, and repudiating his passionate (if ambiguous) alliance with the democrats. Some parts of *The Friend*, in 1809, appear as an argument with his own tousle-headed, impassioned, Bristol youth. The argument was continued in *Biographia Literaria* (1817) with such tergiversation that he succeeded in convincing himself: the friends of his *Watchman* days (he alleged) 'will bear witness for me how opposite even then my principles were to those of Jacobinism or even of democracy'. Although no such friends thrust themselves forward to give his convenient testimony, the matter of Coleridge's youth was already becoming enwrapped in a familiar Coleridgean obscurity. Despite James Dykes Campbell's sober attempt to assemble a factual account (first published in 1894 and now reprinted) and the numerous recoveries of recent scholars, some part of that obscurity has remained to the present day.

All but its last vestiges are now removed in two well-edited volumes of the *Collected Works* (under the general editorship of Kathleen Coburn), in which Peter Mann and Lewis Patton present the political and theological lectures of 1795 and *The Watchman.* Barbara Rooke's edition of *The Friend* has already appeared in this series (reviewed in the *TLS* on January 8, 1970) and we await only David Erdman's edition of *Essays on His Times* (culled largely from the *Morning Post* and *Morning Chronicle*) to have a definitive view of Coleridge's evolution from 1795 into the early 1800s.

William Blake apart, no English writer of the past 200 years can have been served by such an eminent congregation of North American and British scholarship. Apart from the *Collected Works* (and leaving aside many notable biographical and critical contributions), we now have the superlative edition of *The Notebooks* (by Kathleen Coburn), the more reticent edition of the *Collected Letters* (by Earl Leslie Griggs), and Carl Woodring's learned *Politics in the Poetry of Coleridge.* Coleridge, who completed so little work to his own final satisfaction in his own lifetime, and who, in any case, succeeded so rarely in giving to his ideas consistent and systematic organization, now appears laid open to view as a veritable literary Herculaneum, excavated by half a hundred highly skilled posthumous literary amanuenses. These two new volumes of the *Collected Works* both belong to the best tradition of this scholarship.

Coleridge is the very acme of the editor's author. As John Livingston Lowes first showed in *The Road to Xanadu*, scarcely a line came from Coleridge's pen which was not derivative of some literary experience. Week after week, year in, year out, this literary input continued; and week after week it returned, well or ill assimilated, in letters, notebooks, poems, articles, lectures. One of the fascinations of Coleridge is not in his originality or force of intellect (which is too often overrated by scholars who have a professional bias to confuse width of reference with creative originality) but in the energetic catholicity of his interests. Whatever happened, *as a literary experience*, in the 1790s or early 1800s, turns up in some form in his writings: every controversy, every philosophical hang-up, every new literary mode, chance-hap millenarial prophets like Richard Brothers, anti-Jacobin professionals like John Reeves, squalid diplomatic deals with the King of Naples, voyages of discovery—whatever was written about somehow caught his eye, was ingested, and then thrown out again, usually in some oblique, unpredictable context.

Everything is there. And hence the temptation to scholars to use his texts, not in their own right, but as a clothes-line to hang everything upon. And there are, indeed, long passages of the 'Lectures on Revealed Religion' when Coleridge himself is doing little else than stringing up other men's washing. Bursting upon the Bristol scene as an impassioned reformer in February, 1795 (his lecture 'On the Present War', published in *Conciones ad Populum*, can—in the pamphlet literature of 1793 to the Peace of Amiens—be compared, in its tone of absolute moral rage, only with a few passages of Gilbert Wakefield, William Blake, or William Frend), he and Southey gathered around themselves an audience which, in all probability, was laced with young ultra-Godwinians, necessitarians and deists. With a characteristic mixture of courage, egoism, and perversity, Coleridge immediately set out, in his theological lectures, to challenge the prejudices of the 'infidels' among his supporters, by grounding his own idiosyncratic reformism upon Christian precept and revelation.

But—characteristically again—he could rarely get around to preparing each lecture until the day before. His borrowings from the Bristol Library are known, and, with the help of these records and of his own wide reading, Dr. Mann's annotations show us Coleridge, like a young and harassed WEA lecturer, grabbing an armful of books at noon on the eve of a lecture, retiring to his lodgings, working through the night, and emerging with a (generally unfinished) manuscript at the eleventh hour before delivery. No wonder a friendly commentator noted that 'Mr. C— would . . . do well to appear with cleaner stockings in public, and if his hair were combed out . . . it would not depreciate him in the esteem of his friends'. The wonder is that in this brief period of intense concentration he put together, not notes for a lecture, but a tolerable draft of its greater part.

This was done, however, at the cost of great intellectual indigestion. Whole paragraphs and even pages were copied, sometimes word for word, sometimes with significant revision, from the pile of half-gutted books at his elbow: from Hartley and Priestley, from Maclaurin on Newton, from Lowman on the *Civil Government of the Hebrews*, from Cudworth's *True Intellectual System of the Universe*, Balguy's *Divine Benevolence Asserted*, and Michaelis's *Introduction to the New Testament*. In several cases Dr. Mann notes that evidently only the first volume of a multi-volume work has been consulted.

There were six theological lectures, and much of the first four are taken up with a hotch-potch of derivative philosophy and Christian apologetics. Their interest (apart from serving as a guide to Coleridge's reading) lies in the manner in which Coleridge organized and deployed fragments of other men's thoughts, and in occasional prefatory or transitional passages which are wholly his own. Also of interest is the way in which Coleridge prepared the ground for a confrontation with Godwinian philosophy. On all these points Dr. Mann is a percipient guide.

Carefully prepared as it was, the confrontation between Coleridge and Godwinism never came about. Often announced (in his letters, in his notebooks, in *The Watchman*) as the philosophic tourney of the decade, Coleridge always retired after a preliminary flamboyant canter around the field. Dr. Mann insists at several points that the theological lectures dispose finally of the notion that Coleridge, in 1795, was an ardent disciple of Godwin. And he indicates very clearly those passages where Coleridge was beating the bounds between them—in particular, those many, echoing passages where Coleridge insists that benevolence must be nurtured, in the first place, by the 'home-born' feelings.

But to move from this to the suggestion that the issue is raised, in these lectures or in *The Watchman*, to the level of mature philosophical argument is to read back into 1795–96 fifteen years of subsequent evolution. It is also to carry the work of an editorial amanuensis too far. Coleridge was in fact inhibited from offering this confrontation for two reasons, one temporary, the other to prove permanent. The first is that both Godwin and the Coleridge of 1795–96 derived their view of man's nature from common Hartleian (and sometimes Priestleyan) roots. So long as Coleridge moved within the premises of Hartleian necessitarianism, he was a prisoner to premises from which Godwin derived conclusions which he repudiated.

The second, more permanent, inhibition was a habit of impatience when arguing with deism or atheism: at a certain point, Coleridge would simply throw up his arms and pass over to rhetoric, often of a vulgar and bigoted kind. Atheism, for Coleridge, *must* indicate a capitulation to mere sensuality: the matter is not argued, it is asserted as a commonplace. An atheist was 'an intellectual Deformity'. The theological lectures begin with a dream-sequence in which Sensuality and the Monster Blasphemy are discovered together in a 'Vast and dusky Cave'. The sensuality of the atheist was so axiomatic that (in the third lecture) Coleridge denies to him the possibility of aesthetic experience:

> to a Sensualist and to the Atheist that alone can be beautiful which promises a gratification to the appetite—for of wisdom and benevolence the Atheist denies the very existence. The Wine is beautiful to him when it sparkles in the Cup—and the Woman when she moves lasciviously in the Dance but the Rose that bends on its stalk, the Clouds that imbibe the setting sun—these are not beautiful.

In *Religious Musings* Coleridge had thrown in the line: 'Ye petrify the inbrothell'd Atheist's heart', and Thelwall quite properly took him to task for 'one of those illiberal & unfounded calumnies with which *Christian* meekness never yet disdained to supply the want of argument'. But neither then nor later did Coleridge learn to supply this want, when he came to a similar point in his argument. By denying dignity and sensibility to his opponent, he denied dignity and rigour to his own argument, and descended time and again to mere exclamation and apologetics.

At times he descended to something worse. When he exclaimed, after a vivid caricature of some notions in *Political Justice*, 'Your principles are villainous ones! I would not entrust my wife or sister to you—Think you, I would entrust my country?', he was descending to the very level of anti-libertarian and anti-intellectual lampoon which was the stock-in-trade of John Reeves and of the *Anti-Jacobin*: a kind of smear with which Mary Wollstonecraft was only too familiar. It was a kind of vulgarity with which Godwin, for all his cold-bloodedness, was never contaminated.

Fifteen years later Coleridge made an apology of a sort to Godwin: 'When I had read [your works] religious bigotry, the but half-understanding your principles, and the *not* half-understanding my own, combined to render me a warm & boisterous Anti-Godwinist.' So far, in a private letter, to Godwin. But in other private and public places he referred with increasing smugness to the fact that he, Samuel Taylor Coleridge, had never, for one moment, fallen into the ways of the Infidels. In March, 1798, he was writing to his brother, the Rev. George Coleridge: 'I wish to be a good man & a Christian—but I am no Whig, no Reformist, no Republican.' In 1809 in *The Friend*: 'I may safely defy my worst enemy to shew, in any of my few writings, the least bias to Irreligion, Immorality, or Jacobinism.' And in that fine piece of fiction, chapter ten of *Biographia Literaria* (1817), he purported to explain the failure of *The Watchman*: 'I made enemies of all my Jacobin and democratic patrons . . . disgusted by their infidelity and their adoption of French morals with French psilosophy [*sic*].' This is smug and smear together: his 'democratic patrons' were all immoral and all infidels; STC alone survived in purity.

The last two lectures on revealed religion (V and VI) are of greater originality and greater interest. The ghosts of these two cannot be exorcised by disclaimers in *The Friend* and *Biographia*. Bias to irreligion they may not show; but bias against the Established Church is to be found in plenty, and the later Coleridge—soliciting the Bishop of Llandaff's subscription for *The Friend*, and (in *Biographia*) celebrating Britain's good fortune in its Church establishment—must have been glad that they never got farther than manuscript. As a radical Dissenter, young Coleridge wished to show the infidels among his auditors that they were taking up arms, not against the true Christian revelation, but against its manifold corruptions in the worldly churches: 'They may not determine against Christianity from arguments applicable to its' Corruptions only.' The rhetoric of Lecture V is one with which William Blake also was familiar:

> He who sees any real difference between the Church of Rome and the Church of England possesses optics which I do not possess—the mark of antichrist is on both of them. Have not both an intimate alliance with the powers of this World, which Jesus positively forbids? Are they not both decked with gold and precious stones? Is there not written on both their Foreheads Mystery? Do they not both SELL the Gospel—Nay, nay, they

neither sell, nor is it the Gospel—they forcibly exchange Blasphemy for the first fruits, and snatching the scanty Bread from the poor Man's Mouth they cram their lying Legends down his Throat!

This—with more imagery of the Whore and 'Mother of Abomination'—is written hastily; one supposes after an all-night session, hair tousled, linen unkempt; and a paragraph or two later the manuscript breaks off. But this is Coleridge *talking* sedition, in a way in which his colleagues of those years were to remember, but in a way in which it was neither prudent nor (in the prosecuting climate of 1795–96) possible to go into print. The customary teasing paradoxes and involuted ambiguities of the printed page are not present. He speaks, *tout court*, of 'the idolatrous doctrine of the Trinity, and the more pernicious dogma of Redemption'.

This is the Coleridge who loathed black vestments, and who preferred to preach, in Dissenting meeting-houses, in a blue coat with brass buttons; who could refer in his (late 1795) lecture, 'The Plot Discovered', to 'whole flights of Priests and Bishops, black men, and black men with white arms, like magpies and crows that pick out the eyes of sheep'; and who was not above writing slyly to a fellow Dissenter, during his tour to solicit subscribers for *The Watchman*, that his occasional sermons were helping forward his editorial business: 'The *Sacred* may eventually help off the *profane*—and my *Sermons* spread a sort of sanctity over my *Sedition*.'

'I know he cannot preach very often', John Thelwall hazarded early in 1798, 'without travelling from the pulpit to the Tower.' And the final lecture (VI) explains this judgment too. For Coleridge, still under his pantisocratic impulse, sketched out—with references to Moses Lowman's version of Hebraic agrarian law (previously set out in Lecture II)—a critique of the institutions of property (and, in particular, of commercial imperialism and industrialization) in the light of a visionary communistic republic. His critique of society is based, not upon abstract Painite demands for equality of political right, but upon a wider claim for socio-economic equality.

This had already been set forward in *Conciones ad Populum*; arguing with the comfortable middle-class radical, with his faith in political machinery, Coleridge had declared:

It is a mockery of our fellow creatures' wrongs to call them equal in rights, when by the bitter compulsion of their wants we make them inferior to us in all that can soften the heart, or dignify the understanding.

The same point is central to Lecture VI:

The poor Infant born in an English or Irish Hovel breathes indeed the air and partakes the Light of Heaven: but of its other bounties he is disinherited. The powers of intellect are given him in vain—To make him work like a brute beast he is kept as ignorant as a brute beast.

Every level of society is polluted: 'Selfishness is planted in every bosom, and prepares us for the Slavery which it introduces.' At the point where the lecture appears to be moving towards a communistic peroration, it breaks off.

Whatever is made of this fragment, it certainly qualifies in a devastating way the extraordinary, and pat, opening to Essay VI of *The Friend*: 'From my earliest manhood it was an axiom in Politics with me, that in every country where property prevailed, property must be the grand basis of the government.' But we must leave further reflection upon these interesting recoveries to the reader's judgment, prompted by Dr. Mann's excellent editorial advice.

The rest of these two volumes of the *Collected Works—The Watchman*, *Conciones*, *The Plot Discovered*, &c—are Coleridge's more direct political journalism of these two years. The writings have always been available, if inaccessible; and are adequately presented by Professor Patton, with some useful appendixes of contemporary documents.

He is especially helpful in presenting *The Watchman* in perspective. The legend has grown that, owing to Coleridge's unworldliness and his erratic alternations of indolence and energy, *The Watchman* was a shoddy production, always late for the printer, increasingly chucked together from cannibalizations from the general press. Professor Patton shows, on the contrary, that (despite some innocence in business experience) Coleridge ran, for ten numbers, a competent and regular politico-literary miscellany. His borrowings from other journals were no more than eighteenth-century convention allowed. Moreover, the extracts from parliamentary debates and national newspapers, far from being chucked in haphazard to make up copy, were an important part of the initial intention of the periodical (to keep provincial reformers alert to important political developments in England and France) and—in their selection, abridgement, and editing—cost Coleridge as much effort as did the original contributions.

To reinforce this judgment, certain other comments may be added.

The idea for *The Watchman* took fire at a unique moment in the 1790s, during the temporary solidarity brought about among all brands of disputing reformer (Foxites and plebeian democrats, Dissenters and 'infidels') by the campaign against the Two Acts. The Midlands and the West Country had been active in this great agitation, and the audience for a periodical seemed to lie ready to hand. The cause was self-evident, and dictated the title. 'Watchman' echoed through many passages of Isaiah and Ezekiel which were beloved by Dissent, and which set Coleridge happily in a prophetic role:

> I have set watchmen upon thy walls, O Jerusalem, which shall never hold their peace day nor night; ye that make mention of the Lord, keep not silence. . . .

Yet three months later, when *The Watchman* eventually appeared, the solidarities of December, 1795 had dispersed, and reformers and opponents of the French War were already withdrawing indoors. The chilly dusk of persecution was upon them, and the night of oppressive orthodoxy, which stretched from 1798 to the last years of the wars, lay ahead. Few radical journals survived 1796. Thelwall's *Tribune* concluded in April, 1796. In Sheffield, James Montgomery, the editor of the *Iris*, was in prison. In Norwich a miscellany appealing to a similar provincial audience, *The Cabinet*, had closed at the end of 1795. The attempt of leading members of the London Corresponding Society to run a *Moral and Political Magazine* in 1796 ended, despite the claims upon the loyalty of the society's membership, in disaster—a disaster which, in the view of Francis Place, struck a crippling blow at the society's finances. There need be no wonder that Coleridge got no farther than the tenth number. When additional difficulties are considered (the demands of his young household, the fact that his London bookseller refused to send any money for numbers sold), it is surprising that he got as far as he did.

The available audience was probably only large enough to support the two journals towards which Coleridge guided his readers in his valedictory essay: the discreet *Monthly Magazine* (in which Dissenting reviewers took in Dissenting washing) and Benjamin Flower's pugnacious *Cambridge Intelligencer*, which had far better coverage of the news and commentary of interest to reformers than Coleridge could command. But, small as it was, this audience was of real importance. It is the failure of the editors to locate this audience which constitutes the only substantial criticism of their work. Indeed, so far from removing the last vestiges of obscurity about Coleridge's political position in 1795–96, they have actually added new misunderstandings of their own.

It will never be possible to write down the names and addresses of Coleridge's supporters in these years. No subscribers' lists have survived for *The Watchman*, as they have, by good fortune, for *The Friend*. However, even without such aids, Coleridge's intellectual reference-group need not be in doubt. Generations of literary critics have established the convention that Godwinism was coterminous with intellectual ultra-radicalism; and that any intellectual who signalled a major disagreement with Godwin must thereby have been moving away from the 'left'. Godwin occupies so important a place in mainstream intellectual history (the history represented by hardback publications and monthly or quarterly reviews) that this misunderstanding is easily made. But the attentive reader of the *Morning Chronicle*, the *Iris*, the *Cambridge Intelligencer*, the pamphlets and correspondence of the time will get a very different view. For many provincial reformers, Godwinism was neither here nor there: it was an exalted argument carried on in London. Alternative radical vocabularies lay to hand in the Lockean celebration of the Glorious Revolution; in plain Painism; or in the radical traditions of Christian Dissent. Godwin, by disclaiming political societies and activism, and by ducking the whole question of France, had nothing to offer to middle-class sympathizers with the Norwich or Sheffield 'patriotic' societies. Indeed, the typical young Godwinian, like Wordsworth's friend Montagu, was too busy discussing universal benevolence to get into the rough-and-tumble of political argument: petitions against the Two Acts, public lectures, *The Watchman*, agitation against the war.

He was also too canny. Godwin was victimized by scandal and lampoon, but he was never brought to trial, to be transported or imprisoned, as were Thomas Fysshe Palmer, William Winterbottom, or Gilbert Wakefield. A number of these radical Christians had a quality of commitment which the authorities sensed as more dangerous than the most advanced philosophical radicalism. In 1795 there was a small, but significant, new wave of this commitment among the young, who had their heroes (in Gerald, or Palmer, or William

Frend), who lamented the hounding of Priestley out of the country, and who began to throw up spokesmen of their own.

Coleridge was exactly such a spokesman: his position was difficult, but it was by no means unique, nor was he as isolated as he later came to pretend. This can be seen in page after page of *University Rebel*, Frida Knight's very lively new life of William Frend. In matters of scholarship Mrs. Knight belongs to a different league from Dr. Mann and Professor Patton: her style occasionally is novelettish; she has received no grants from the Bollingen or other foundations. She is an 'amateur' historian (that is, unpaid), who has already written a sound study of Thomas Walker, the Manchester reformer.

Her book is a triumph. Year after year the North Atlantic ocean is darkened by the wings of migrating scholars—the English flying over to scrutinize (English) manuscripts secreted in the Huntington Library, the Berg Collection, the Pierpont Morgan or the Pforzheimer; the American scholars crowding out the British Museum or moaning at the lack of scholastic technology at Dove Cottage. Meanwhile Frida Knight has got on a bicycle (or perhaps a telephone) and tracked down two important collections of William Frend's letters, in the hospitable keeping of two descendants, as well as important related material in lesser collections, including the Ely Diocesan Records. Her work is a very salutary reminder that, despite wars and salvage drives, much important material from the 1790s onwards survives in private attics; and that the real finds in scholarship lie off the main migration routes, and fall only to those with persistence and tact.

From these materials she has written a most readable book. It flags in the second half: partly because her subject flags, but partly because she is interested in the drama of William Frend, the intrepid radical drummed out of Cambridge after a ludicrous mock-trial in the Vice-Chancellor's court in 1793, and she fails to show the same interest in Frend's unitarian thought. She has the same quality as she gives to one of her own characters—'a refreshing tendency to disregard points of doctrine in favour of general truths'—but since Frend himself was much concerned with doctrine, this is sometimes a disqualification. At such points she dives off into her store of letters, and produces a few pages of personalia: but personalia so vivid that we might be sitting at Frend's elbow.

Frend, as she shows, overplayed the drama of his 'trial', and failed to make of it the principled occasion which it might have been. He had neither the experience nor the temperament to carry such public notoriety. But he emerged quite uncompromised; exalted in the eyes of those students who, like Coleridge, had supported him; and as he matured (in banishment from the University) his naive integrity and his unheated intransigence carried him as far as the London Corresponding Society, for which he spoke and for whose prisoners he collected money.

Earlier, when Frend's scruples about the Trinity had led him to resign his curacy, he had exchanged the clerical black for a blue coat with brass buttons: such a coat as Coleridge preached sedition in during 1795. If we wish to plot Coleridge's position in the intellectual firmament in 1795 it is far more important to take bearings on Frend than on Godwin. It is also important to take more accurate bearings than Dr. Mann and Professor Patton do upon the popular reform movement. On this point, the 'amateur' has a better sense of the times than the professional scholars.

Coleridge had been drawn into the great agitation against the Two Acts and he had no doubt jostled against the elbows of hundreds of new allies, reformers of all degrees. The Prospectus of *The Watchman* explicitly declared that

> it's chief objects are to co-operate (1) with the WHIG CLUB in procuring a repeal [of the Two Acts] and (2) with the PATRIOTIC SOCIETIES, for obtaining a Right of Suffrage general and frequent.

Professor Patton has something to tell us about the Whig Club, but, although he is normally so voluble, he refuses the second fence altogether. In the editors' joint introduction to the *Lectures* the failure to look steadily at the same point enlarges the area of misunderstanding. Coleridge's attitude to Godwinism, it is suggested, 'affected his attitude to the whole radical movement that had come into existence in the 1790s'; and:

> He was much distressed by the thought that Godwin's disciples, or radicals infected with Godwinian ideas, could be capturing the leadership of the people. Holcroft, for example . . . played a leading role in the activities of the London Corresponding Society.

'It was the power of such men and their influence on the masses that claimed Coleridge's fearful attention. . . .' Holcroft played no role in the LCS and probably was never a member. He had supported the more genteel Society for Constitutional Information which (like the

Friends of the People) had ceased to have any national presence by 1795. Godwin had *never* supported the popular 'patriotic societies', by which all England understood, in 1795, those numerous provincial centres of democratic 'mischief' of which the LCS was the metropolitan mother. Indeed, he chose the moment of agitation against the Two Acts to single out the LCS and the popular tribune, John Thelwall, for specific attack. 'Ordinarily', propound the editors, Coleridge 'would have shared Godwin's fear of associations', but he was overborne by enthusiasm at the time of the Acts to join with their members in common agitation. They have no warrant for this proposition; nor can one easily see how they are able to decide what an eccentric and unstable twenty-three-year-old would 'ordinarily' do in time of national emergency.

What one *knows*, from the record, is less than this. We know that Coleridge, in 1795, chose—like John Thelwall in London—the open method of proselytizing public lectures: one clause in the Two Acts was specifically aimed at such lecturing, and Coleridge once suggested that government had been aiming not only at Thelwall but also at himself. We know that Coleridge was a star orator in the Bristol agitation against the Acts. We know that the prospectus to *The Watchman* specifically announced cooperation with the patriotic societies. And in *The Watchman* itself several telling contributions (sent in by the Rev. John Edwards, another Frend-like Christian, and Priestley's successor at the Birmingham Meeting) gave a sympathetic blow-by-blow account of the persecution, under the Acts, of Binns and Gale Jones, the 'missionaries' of the LCS. And we know that in 1796 Coleridge began a warm correspondence with the people's tribune, John Thelwall.

Taken together, these facts suggest that the curve of Coleridge's commitment, in 1795–96, took him very close indeed to the popular societies—or towards their more intellectual component. If he was moving away from Godwin, with his aloof elitism and his canny avoidance of persecution, he might, in these years, have been moving *towards* political activism, like his mentor, William Frend. Indeed, to publish *The Watchman*, and to travel the provinces for subscribers, is evidence of exactly such a stance.

By neglecting the alternatives to Godwinism, the editors discourage such a reading; and they leave us with a Coleridge who is a total individualist, in a unique posture, swatting hostile ideologies like wasps on every side. They support their reading with negatives:

'No evidence has been found that (patriotic) societies in 1795 were at all active in Bristol.' Perhaps not: historians have been less helpful on such points than they might have been. But there was a lusty Bristol Constitutional Society in 1794, small in numbers but confident: 'It is our firm opinion', they wrote to the LCS, 'could we but arouse them, that patriots would become nearly the majority of our city.' There is no reason to suppose that the society had ceased in 1795; it showed signs of activity as late as 1797. Certainly, the tone of Coleridge's letter to George Dyer in February, 1795, does not suggest that his lectures were delivered in an unformed political context:

I have endeavoured to disseminate Truth by three political Lectures.... But the opposition of the Aristocrats is so furious and determined, that I begin to fear, that the Good I do is not proportionate to the Evil I occasion—Mobs and Mayors, Blockheads and Brickbats, Placards and Press gangs have leagued in horrible Conspiracy against me—The Democrats are as sturdy in the support of me—but their number is comparatively small....

'Uncouth and unbrained Automata' had scarcely been restrained 'from attacking the house in which the "damn'd Jacobine was jawing away"'.

It is more than probable that the Bristol of 1795–96 had, like Manchester, Nottingham, or Norwich, some more or less formal organization of reformers: perhaps overlapping circles—polite reading-groups and discussion clubs, some of whose more ardent members also supported a more popular reform society. Very possibly these 'democrats' would have supported Southey and Coleridge in their lectures, gathered signatures against the Acts, and bought *The Watchman*. But the editors are determined to leave Coleridge floating weightless in political outer space, subject to no atmosphere or force save the repulsion of Godwin and the remote gravitational pull of Burke.

In support of their reading they bring to bear several passages from Coleridge's own letters which should not have been employed without more careful critical scrutiny. Writing to Charles Lloyd's father, late in 1796, he referred to 'politicians and politics—a set of men and a kind of study which I deem highly unfavourable to all Christian graces'. But this sentence, alongside much other pious humbug, comes from a letter in which the author was attempting to calm the anxieties of a conventionally-minded father, whose disturbed son Coleridge had recently taken under his roof and patronage. It is no more useful as evidence than a phrase from one of those numerous calming letters which young lecturers in English or Sociology are no doubt at this moment indicting to parents in a similar predicament:

> While appreciating that it is sanctioned in youth culture, I myself have for long discouraged my students from the use of cannabis and other narcotics. Julia's idealism does her credit, but I am sure she will soon outgrow the practical revolutionism of misguided sects. . . .

If critics properly demand a discipline of reading (these words in this order), historians must with equal propriety demand their own discipline (these words in this context). And with no one is this discipline more necessary than with Coleridge, who combined a sensitive and often exciting ambivalence of attitude with a chameleon-like capacity to modify the colour of his opinions according to his correspondent. It is greatly disheartening to find Dr. Mann concluding his acute and learned preface to the *Lectures* with the uncritical use of whole passages of the notorious letter which Coleridge wrote in October, 1803, when he had just heard of Emmet's death, to Sir George Beaumont. The event recalled to him, with acute shock, his own agitational youth:

> Fortunately for me, the Government, I suppose, knew that both Southey & I were utterly unconnected with any party or club or society. . . . I disclaimed all these Societies, these Imperia in Imperio, these Ascarides in the Bowels of the State. . . . All such Societies, under whatever name, I abhorred as wicked Conspiracies.

This, and so much more—an incoherent, contradictory, torrent of self-exculpation—is evidence only about Coleridge's state of mind in October, 1803. Not a sentence in that letter has any worth whatsoever as historical evidence, unless confirmed by other sources. As autobiography it is wholly corrupt. One is not, of course, labouring the petty point whether Coleridge was a card-holding member of a Bristol Constitutional Society or not. If there was such a society, it was probably so loosely organized that it did not have cards; and if it had, Coleridge probably forgot or on some scruple or other refused to join it. The point is the trajectory of Coleridge's allegiances in these years. And this (we have suggested) the editors have at this point obscured. It came very close to that of William Frend and of Gilbert Wakefield; and such a trajectory, if it had not been arrested by the retirement of Stowey, would almost certainly have led him to prison.

It was not only Hazlitt who remembered him as an ardent seditionist, until as late as 1797. When Coleridge denied his Jacobin sympathies in *The Friend*, Southey remarked: 'If he was not a Jacobine, in the common acceptation of the name, I wonder who the Devil was.' The editors dismiss this comment as 'spleen'; but there are others, which they overlook, which still have to be explained away. Professor Pollin has recently brought to light Thelwall's annotated copy of *Biographia*: where Coleridge wrote 'how opposite even then my principles were to those of jacobinism or even of democracy', Thelwall exclaimed: 'Mr. C. was indeed far from Democracy, because he was far beyond it, I well remember—for he was a down right zealous leveller.' There is ample testimony of the way in which Coleridge's verbal sedition shocked the primmer relatives of Thomas Poole at Stowey. Fifty years later an old clergyman in the Quantocks was still found to be clucking over the 'sad democratic nonsense' talked by Coleridge in those days:

> 'It was a time of great political excitement, and, you see, we didn't change our opinions, but they did', said the vicar with a twinkle in his eye. . . .

One would not wish to deprive the vicar of his small octogenarian triumph: but perhaps he had misunderstood Coleridge's meaning? If so, then someone rather closer to Coleridge had fallen into the same misunderstanding. In April, 1799, the unhappy Sara (with Samuel in Germany) was under the necessity of applying to Poole for aid to pay the household bills:

> My principal reason for troubling you now is, to beg you will send me ten guineas, for I expected Coleridge would have thought of it, but he has not. . . .

The letter had two irritable postscripts. First: 'The Lyrical Ballads are not liked at all by any.' And the second: 'It is very unpleasant to me to be often asked if Coleridge has changed his political sentiments, for I know not properly how to reply. Pray furnish me.' No doubt the admirable Poole furnished the ten guineas, and 170 years of scholarship have done something to assuage the first postscript. But, in the matter of the second, Sara is still awaiting a definitive answer.

The editors do not finally 'furnish' Sara. Their command of intellectual history is impressive, and Dr. Mann, in his editorial introduction, clarifies much. He insists properly upon the unitary development of Coleridge's thought, even where that unity is the exfoliation of successive interrelated ambiguities. From these first lectures onwards there can be traced consistencies of preoccupation. As Dr. Mann writes:

> The fundamental emphases in his religious and political thinking that the lectures reveal suggest that his early work could be more accurately and justly seen as an intellectual *reaction* against the philosophy of the revolution, sharing the moral and social concern of the revolution, certainly, but resisting some of its most important controlling ideas about the individual, society, and religion as they appeared, at least, in the work of Godwin and Paine.

This is just; and, provided that one bears in mind that the 'philosophy of the revolution' is identified with Godwin/Paine, the point is proved. But if this proviso—a proviso which might be applied with equal validity to that other revolutionary, William Blake—is forgotten, one could be led on to false conclusions. Dr. Mann writes that Coleridge's 'later intellectual progress can be seen not simply as an apostasizing rejection of his ideas of 1795, but as a more profound exploration and development of them'. Yes; but an exploration and development in only *one* of several possible directions; and in a direction which involved a distinct apostasy towards other alternatives and, indeed, towards some of that 'moral and social concern' which had illuminated his youth.

For in the glowing paradoxes of his notebooks, lectures and letters of these years, one has glimpses of abundant alternative possibilities of development: Coleridge the millenarian, Coleridge the communitarian Christian, Coleridge the revolutionary (rather than Burkean) critic of utilitarianism. Coleridge astonishes one, between 1794 and 1798, because of his capacity to contain within himself so many oscillating, contradictory philosophical impulses, each one momentarily realized, in a flash of illumination. If we speak of 'exploration and development' we must also speak of limitation and rejection. And the question of apostasy remains important, not because one wishes to nag at his biographers but because only this sense of covert self-betrayal explains the vehemence, the guilt-ridden and tortuous incoherence, of some of his later writings when he approached this sensitive area.

The contradiction in which Coleridge was immersed in 1795–96 was not only philosophical: it was also social. He was a utopian revolutionary who, nevertheless, was profoundly nervous of 'the mob' and who could see hope only in converting his own class or, at most, the educated and moralized artisan. However far these writings go in extremes of *opinion*, they show consistency at this point. In *The Watchman* (VI) he was writing of 'that greatest of evils, a revolution begotten by an unprincipled and extravagant government on a miserable, ignorant, and wicked people'. (Twenty years later he had forgotten about paternity, and wrote of revolutions as if they were malodorous virgin births.) In his antiwar lecture of 1795 (in *Conciones ad Populum*) his abuse of the putative father, William Pitt, went beyond all measure:

Heaven has bestowed on that man a portion of its ubiquity, and given him an actual presence in the Sacraments of Hell, wherever administered, in all the bread of bitterness, in all the cups of blood.

But in the same lecture he warned that the avowal of political truth should be made only among those 'whose minds are susceptible of reasoning: and never to the multitude, who ignorant and needy must necessarily act from the impulse of inflamed Passions'. 'General Illumination should precede Revolution', and the 'small but glorious band . . . of thinking and disinterested Patriots' should 'plead *for* the Oppressed, not *to* them'.

The self-isolation of a utopian intellectual revolutionary has rarely been more explicitly defined. But the powerful pressures in experience which led Coleridge to this position are not always borne in mind. The crowd did not, in 1795, offer itself in England as any kind of organized democratic force. It was the mob of the Gordon Riots: the Church-and-King mob which, only four years before, had burnt down Priestley's laboratory; the price-fixing crowd which historically, had often turned against Dissenting and Quaker corn merchants, and which throughout 1795 was clamouring against the middle-men: the Church-and-King bullies who attacked the meetings of patriotic societies (whose membership, if plebeian, was selected from a self-educated, self-respecting elite), and which was scarcely restrained from beating at Coleridge's own lecture-room doors. And if he turned to France, the mob also seemed to be an engine of destruction, pulling down impartially aristocratic privilege and the utopian hopes of the middle-class republican. As he wrote in *Conciones*,

The Annals of the French Revolution have recorded in Letters of Blood, that the Knowledge of the Few cannot counteract the Ignorance of the Many; that the Light of Philosophy, when it is confined to a small Minority, points out the Possessors as the Victims, rather than the Illuminators, of the Multitude.

The communistic revolution of his 'theological' lectures must be preceded by a moral revolution within each individual:

> Let us exert over our own hearts a virtuous despotism, and lead our own Passions in triumph, and then we shall want neither Monarch nor General. If we would have no Nero without, we must place a Caesar within us, and that Caesar must be Religion.

From this position, a bridge might easily be thrown forward, across which he might pass, evacuating his youthful utopianism and occupying the territory of Burke and of the Established Church. But these recovered lectures establish firmly the seditious levelling of the lands he left behind. In Thelwall's copy of *Biographia* at the line, 'I retired to a cottage at Stowey', there is this marginal annotation:

> Where I visited him & found him a decided Leveller—abusing the democrats for their hypocritical moderatism, in pretending to be willing to give the people equality or privileges & rank, while, at the same time, they would refuse them all that the others could be valuable for—equality of property —or rather abolition of all property.

Still, in 1797, Coleridge's criticism of the revolution was from the 'left'. But the watchman had left his post, and the night was coming on, not only without but also within. The watchman's uniform, the blue coat with brass buttons, was, no doubt, packed away in one of Sara's trunks. It was not to be the last time that the leftist intellectual critic was to find, in the impotence of his own self-isolation, an excuse for a reconciliation with the status quo. The undulating Quantocks were more inviting than Botany Bay; the great elms around the church tower at Stowey were an image of greater security than the banks of the Susquehanna. In July, 1797, he was visited by John Thelwall, and they settled down to talk in a quiet dell among the hills. 'Citizen John', said Coleridge, 'this is a fine place to talk treason in.' 'Nay! Citizen Samuel', Thelwall replied, 'it is rather a place to make a man forget that there is any necessity for treason.'

# 8

# 'GIVE ME YOUR PANTS'

A VERY SERIOUS JOURNALIST once inquired of Buster Keaton whether the hapless little men who were so often the heroes of his films were a conscious anticipation of the human situation in the 1930s, when the individual found himself menaced by increasingly authoritarian regimes. Keaton thought for a while, and then replied: 'In those days we used to think of one gag, and then we used to think of another gag.' Chaplin has written in his memoirs of how he would go to the studio in the morning empty of ideas:

> With a bare notion I would order sets, and during the building of them the art director would come to me for details, and I would bluff and give him particulars about where I wanted doors and archways. In this desperate way I started many a comedy.

Perhaps the most hilarious moment in the often depressing lives of the people who make us laugh comes when they find themselves taken up by intellectuals and analysed by academics. The look on their faces as they read of what some superior mind imagines them to have done may resemble the slightly shifty air of the rising low comedian when royalty comes to his dressing room. Should he have hidden the bottle of stout and covered *The Stage* with *The Times*?

The film farces of Will Hay are now receiving serious attention. 'The Goon Show' and the sketches of Tony Hancock have become classics. The process accelerates. The smart magazines of the year after next may be filled with reassessments of those 'Carry On' comedies that are still culturally on the wrong side of the tracks. Fortunately, these canonizations are usually confirmed after the creators are dead or their work is over. But the exaltation of any art form that has genuinely popular origins always carries with it the dangers of destroying the spontaneity that brought that form to birth. Folksong is no longer of the folk when experts begin to collect it. Craftwork degenerates as soon as tourist boards exploit it for the souvenir

GEORGES FEYDEAU: *Four Farces*. Translated by Norman R. Shapiro. 346 pp. University of Chicago Press. £5.40.

trade. In the same way, the vigour of certain popular and commercial forms of entertainment may unwittingly be gelded by admirers for whom they were never intended.

We approach, therefore, with some anxiety Norman R. Shapiro's introduction to his translation of four farces by Feydeau. What is the Associate Professor of Romance Language and Literatures at Wesleyan University doing here?

BOIS-D'ENGHIEN. Give me your pants.
BOUZIN. Please, Monsieur Bois-d'Enghien! Please!
BOIS-D'ENGHIEN. Come on, be quick about it! Your pants or I shoot!
BOUZIN. Of course, Monsieur Bois-d'Enghien . . . anything you say! (*Petrified, he begins to remove his pants.*) My God, this is terrible! Running around without my pants, and in a strange house!

But Professor Shapiro gives us only moments of uneasiness:

Feydeau is, uncontestably, the Bach of his genre; and his compositions—the word is not out of place—have a kind of awesome grandeur about them in spite of their levity and seeming triviality. They are like great Bergsonian machines, in which characters seem reducible to the status of inanimate things, mere parts of the mechanism; and situations, growing in size, or gathering momentum, or reversing their elements into monstrous quid pro quos, become almost tangible in their terrible concreteness.

If Feydeau were alive, he might have survived such analysis through his engaging and often cruel self-mockery. He began by writing drawing-room monologues, and showed his quality at twenty with *Un Monsieur qui n'aime pas les monologues*, in which the reciter delivers a lengthy example of the very genre he is attacking—the kind of brilliant inversion that was to be a feature of the later plays. After an apprenticeship in short pieces, Feydeau's first great success came at twenty-four with *Tailleur Pour Dames*. He was then faced with the not uncommon anti-climax of a dozen or so partial successes and a comment in *Figaro* that 'he would work to better advantage if he took the trouble to develop his ludicrous entanglements and link them together by some kind of logic'.

It was now that Feydeau showed his particular qualities. He retired from the theatre for two years and studied the works of Labiche, Meilhac and Hennequin. He emerged with the sure technique of the later plays, and after a period of collaboration with Desvallières he never again faltered. Here, perhaps, was one of the few examples of a playwright who listened to his critics, returned to his masters, and came back to deliver what the critics and the public wanted. Not, however, without a certain cynicism:

When I am arranging all that madness that unleashes the spectators' glee, I am not amused by it. I keep the cool, calm poise of the chemist measuring out his medicine. I put into my pill a gram of imbroglio, a gram of licentiousness, a gram of observation. As well as I can, I grind them all into a powder, and I can tell, almost without fail, the effect that they will produce. . . . When the work is done, what a relief! I regain my freedom.

'The persons and actions of a farce are all unnatural and the manners false.' This was Dryden's definition. It is true of the surface; but every farce of quality has beneath the posturings the horrid reality of the comic postcard. Mothers-in-law *are* a menace, men *are* fixated on breasts or buttocks, they *do* at times see women as devouring monsters; and behind Donald McGill's skinny men in swimsuits, or the smallness and baldness of the Robertson Hare stereotype, lie very real fears of inadequacy or impotence.

The actions of a farce are exorcisms of murderous thoughts, lust, deceit, betrayal and secret shames. They are also a release for the pressures imposed on us by our liberal consciences. Where else can progressive and fastidious people roar with laughter at foreigners, at smelly breath or bad complexions, at a man with no roof to his mouth, at the sad lecheries of old and middle age, at deafness or mental subnormality? And where else can the sex war be fought so openly and crudely—between men absurd in underpants, and women who are either avaricious little schemers or fearsome dragons simultaneously rapacious for respectability and bed?

When it comes to bed, French farce is very different from the English variety. In Pinero, at the old Aldwych, or at Brian Rix's Whitehall, the characters were mostly innocent of the sexual misdemeanours they appeared to have committed. The outrage of the vicar or the wife, our symbols of respectability, was comic because it was unjustified. With Feydeau's characters sex really happens. When they are found in a bedroom, penetration, in its legal sense, may actually have occurred. When a lover throws out his mistress, there is a moment of practical reality when he throws after her a dressing gown and slippers. When a comic servant wants his day off, it is quite plainly to relieve his sexual needs. Farce, in France, was not for a family audience. This allowed it to acquire a hardness, a truth to the facts of life, that all our debaggings and glimpses of knickers evade. It was this licence that encouraged Feydeau to take many a well-worn sexual gag just one step further—dangerously close to that point where laughter becomes hysteria; where an adulterer found in a cupboard without his trousers is *almost* feeling what a real man would feel in that predicament.

If we are honest, it may be doubted whether the intellectual ever enjoys farce as much as he pretends. He sits through the laughs as a voyeur, watching the pleasure the actors give the audience without taking part himself. A kind of irritation may afflict him. Reviewing the first performance of *The Importance of Being Earnest*, Shaw wrote: 'Though I laugh as much as anyone at a farcical comedy, I am out of spirits before the end of the second act, and out of temper before the end of the third, my miserable mechanical laughter intensifying these symptoms at every outburst.' It is his need to analyse that makes this outsider a spectator of spectators, the urge to explain the jokes that dries his laughter. He feels at a disadvantage, a little cut off from the rest of the human race; whatever he may say or write, the last laugh is not with him. As A. B. Walkley wrote of Grock: 'Clowns may enjoy a secret, malign pleasure; they proudly confront a universe which delights in them but cannot describe them.'

The actors and writers of farces are busy getting themselves from one gag to the next; the audiences laugh from their bellies; the success of the show is measured by the takings. Why, then, does the intellectual persist in trying to find some significance in a popular entertainment that has nothing to do with him? He risks becoming a comic character himself—the Mad Professor of many an uproarious night. He is like a Freudian digging for symbols in nursery rhymes, an art critic who has never left his mother lecturing on primitive cultures, an avant-garde composer taping tribal music.

Determined to avoid condescension, humbled by untutored achievement, he can only acknowledge some primeval vitality—and hope by absorbing it to rejuvenate energies that may be failing in his own declining culture. It is, perhaps, an increasing sense of the madness of life that leads us now to take the farcical view of it seriously. If the theatre of the absurd remains a minority entertainment, Hollywood has done very well out of treating serious subjects farcically. *Dr. Strangelove* was that old stand-by, the funny foreigner. *M.A.S.H.* and *Catch-22* use techniques that go back to Plautus and Menander. Dryden must turn in his grave to see reason so fallen that farce can become the consolation of reasonable men.

Professor Shapiro has translated the early *Par la Fenêtre*, *Le Mariage de Barillon*—where we find what is perhaps the first use of the immortal line 'My God, what a night!'—*Un Fil à la patte* and the one act *On purge Bébé*. His versions read easily. It is a greater achievement that they seem actable. He rightly warns intending performers of the immense difficulty of playing these pieces, and one's heart sinks at the thought of the flounderings to come on many an amateur stage. But Feydeau, as if his own professionals were not entirely to be trusted, provided copious stage directions. He not only details the precise position of every property and piece of furniture; he gives us a running commentary on the state of mind of every character. Such orders to actors as 'Heaving a sigh of relief' or 'At a loss' or 'Still in high spirits' are now resented in the theatre as intrusions on the director's authority. But the director Jacques Charon is quoted as a warning:

I don't dare to make a change in any of Feydeau's directions. . . . Once I left out a couple of instructions which, I thought, were unimportant. A few scenes later the whole play toppled, the plot came askew. Not only every word of dialogue by Feydeau, but every gesture, is carefully thought out by the author.

These instructions are so precise that we imagine Feydeau miming the parts as he wrote them. How far was he acting his own predicaments?

Professor Shapiro writes well about the edge of madness that Feydeau's characters are always so perilously skirting. Their author knew that borderland. Looking at his portraits in this book, we see in the eyes that withdrawn melancholy that so often seems to shroud the clown. Towards the end of his life, when his comedies took a bitter tang and were increasingly concerned with domestic themes, Feydeau left his wife and family and went to live in a hotel. His wife, Jean-Louis Barrault has slyly suggested, was often the muse for his later work. A critic, reviewing *Le Mariage de Barillon*, commenting on its mad inventiveness, flippantly suggested that the author would end his days in an asylum. He was not far wrong. A lifelong sufferer from what was then called melancholia, Feydeau would nowadays be diagnosed as depressive and filled up with drugs and given shock treatment. We should be grateful that he found his own therapy in making other people laugh.

Dryden's definition wears thin when we come to the later playlets, here represented by *On purge Bébé*, well translated as *Going to Pot*. This little masterpiece exploits every twist and turn of marital discord in a way that far heavier and more serious plays have never excelled. Here, in sixty pages, is a farcical version of that theory of role-playing in relationships that has not only inspired many modern dramatists, but forms the basis of work by psychiatrists like R. D. Laing and Eric Berne. One sees here the other playwright Feydeau might have been if his own pain had not forced him to write comically of the things he could not bear to face seriously.

Professor Shapiro seems admirably fitted to write the book for which his introduction here is an appetizer: the biography of a writer of farces for whom life was a miserable business and the farcical view of it the only hope of sanity. It was a hope that nearly failed poor Feydeau. It may fail us, too. 'The curtain falls on a scene of wild confusion.'

# 9

# STYLES IN HISTORIOGRAPHY

## (*a*) EXOTIC CONSERVATIVE

LEWIS NAMIER was on all counts an outstanding personality, and has earned an outstanding biography. Julia Namier was his wife for thirteen years, and had known him for five years longer. Every biographer, however consciously and deliberately self-effacing, enters into the biography which he writes side by side with its subject. This is an intimate and moving book. Unquestionably, Lady Namier's influence on her husband's last years, though never in the remotest degree self-assertive, was very great, and she gave his life a sheet-anchor which had hitherto been lacking. The whole book is in some sense suffused by this rich experience, and by the meeting of these so different, yet congruent, personalities.

Another element in its composition will quickly become apparent to the reader. Namier throughout his life was prone to searching, and sometimes painful, self-examination. The assured authority of his pronouncements, his arrogance in controversy, covered an inner core of tormenting doubt. In his last years he poured out his soul, and laid bare the experiences of his past life, his frustrations and his predicaments, in a way he had never done before. Namier was always an expansive and exhaustive talker on any topic near his heart. Towards

---

(*a*) JULIA NAMIER: *Lewis Namier*. 347 pp. Oxford University Press. £4.25.

(*b*) E. F. JACOB: *Essays in Later Medieval History*. 223 pp. Manchester University Press. £1.90.

L. F. SALZMAN: *Edward I*. 224 pp. Constable. £1.75.

REGINE PERNOUD: *Héloïse et Abélard*. 295 pp. Paris: Albin Michel. 19.50 fr. *Jeanne devant les Cauchons*. 127 pp. Paris: Éditions du Seuil. 13 fr.

HENRI GUILLEMIN: *Jeanne, dite 'Jeanne d'Arc'*. 251 pp. Paris: Gallimard. 20 fr.

DUC DE LEVIS MIREPOIX: *Saint Louis: roi de France*. 373 pp. Paris: Albin Michel. 27 fr.

F. GRAUS, K. BOSL, F. SEIBT, M. M. POSTAN and A. GIEYSZTOR: *Eastern and Western Europe in the Middle Ages*. Edited by Geoffrey Barraclough. 216 pp. Thames and Hudson. £1.75 (paperback, £1.05).

MAURICE KEEN: *A History of Medieval Europe*. 309 pp. Routledge and Kegan Paul. £1.75. Penguin. Paperback, 40p.

the end he talked, as Lady Namier records, in the hope and intention that she would be his biographer. Characteristically, he wanted to get the facts right. Large sections of the book, for which no other witness exists, are pure autobiography, told in the words of an understanding and deeply sympathetic listener.

Another source, less widely and fruitfully exploited here, might have been provided by the recollections of the very numerous men and women, of varied occupations and interests, with whom he came into contact at different periods of his life. Some, perhaps most, of these are no longer alive; some, including perhaps those with whom he clashed most sharply on controversial issues, may be reluctant to write. Almost the only reminiscences to appear so far in print were in a volume of *Acquaintances* by Arnold Toynbee (1967): these, though not very substantial, add a few agreeable touches. Lady Namier quotes a few letters from an apparently extensive archive, and some tributes from former students and others. But this is, by and large, the story of Namier and of his views and reactions, not a study of the issues in which he became involved.

For most readers, the central theme of Namier's life and of his biography will be the sharp impact of this exotic figure on the traditional English scene, and the eddies and two-way reactions which it set up. From this point of view, the early and obviously autobiographical chapters deserve the generous space allocated to them, though they still leave much that we should like to know. Born in Russian Poland, the homes of his childhood were two successive estates at the eastern extremity of Austrian Galicia, not far from the Russian frontier. His father was a medium-sized landowner, a polonized Jew, no longer a Jew and yet not quite a Pole; by profession a liberal and a reader of John Stuart Mill, in habit a martinet and a compulsive gambler.

When, in 1908, at the age of twenty, after a year at Lausanne University and a year at the London School of Economics, Namier (still under the name of Bernstein) came to Oxford and entered Balliol College, he was already in search—unwittingly—of a new life and a new identity. He was 'socially omnivorous'; as Lady Namier puts it, 'belonging to no group, he was uniquely acceptable throughout Balliol'. Toynbee's account of his arrival shows how he polarized the society into firm friends and sceptics or mockers. It was a foretaste, at a crude and simple level, of many later experiences. The citadel of English prejudice was breached only slowly, and never completely. The story was one of the irresistible force meeting the immovable mass.

Balliol was the starting-point of a career; 'they taught me to think', was Namier's later generous tribute to that unique institution. During the next few years, he was gradually shaking off, on vacation visits, the ties of allegiance that bound him to family and to Central Europe. He changed his name by deed-poll—twice: first to Naymier, then, being dissatisfied with the un-English spelling to Namier; and he acquired British nationality. By 1912, after a flirtation with the seventeenth-century Puritans (whose attraction did not last long), he had succumbed to the lure of the British Empire. Before 1914 he was already preparing for a book on 'The Imperial Problem during the American Revolution'.

Compared with the beginnings, the remainder of Namier's career seems relatively plain sailing, and is well known. A short period of military service in 1914–15 was followed by employment in one of the political intelligence departments, which badly needed his specialized knowledge of Central Europe, and then in the Foreign Office. An interlude of teaching at Oxford; and then three years of business and journalism in Vienna and Prague, with the avowed intention of making enough money to finance further historical research—a period of which he rarely spoke in detail, though he was known to boast mildly of a financial expertise beyond the scope of most academics and intellectuals.

The return to England in 1925 opened the period of his greatest financial stringency, when he had to live on his own resources and on limited grants; but this was also the period of his greatest historical creativity, which produced *The Structure of Politics* and *England in the Age of the American Revolution*, published in 1929 and 1930. It was also at this time, in 1929, that he first became associated with the Jewish Agency in London, as its political secretary. Finally, in 1931, his appointment as Professor of Modern History in Manchester brought him for the first time academic recognition and financial security.

The development of Namier's opinions makes an interesting sociological as well as psychological study. Like nearly all the intelligent young in Central and Eastern Europe, he was drawn to 'socialism', without any very clear definition of the term. The seeds were sown in boyhood by an intelligent tutor, also a polonized Jew, who achieved some distinction in political journalism, and by early hero-worship of Pilsudski, the implications of whose brand of national socialism had not yet been revealed. But the socialism imbibed by the adolescent Namier had a peculiar stamp. As Lady Namier records,

> The general political and economic assumptions were Marxist, but the urgent concern was with agrarian reform—the righting of the dispossessed native Ruthenian peasantry's wrongs.

The cause of the Ruthenian (or Ukrainian) peasant majority of East Galicia, and the attempt to save them from the fate—which befell them—of annexation by Poland, which was the chief preoccupation of Namier's period of service in the Foreign Office and at the Peace Conference, earned him the undying hostility of the Polish nationalists, and helped to complete his breach with his family.

It is significant that the first oppressed people with whom the young Namier identified himself were not the Jews but the Ruthenians. It is more significant—for this bias remained with him for life—that they were peasants, not urban dwellers. Namier's mature political thinking, as he more than once proclaimed, revolved around the holding of land: political struggles were struggles for the possession of land.

But this feeling went deeper still. When Namier entered L.S.E., in 1907, he duly enrolled in the Fabian Society, and met the now famous leading Fabians of the day. But this was not his milieu. As he walked the sordid streets of Central London, he was overpowered by 'perplexing culinary stenches, spiced with coal dust', and saw 'the bleary faces and misshapen bodies of nondescript women'. The miseries of starved and land-hungry peasants he could understand and pity. The misery of urban poverty was a horror that passed his understanding, eluded his sympathy, and excited only revulsion.

The years in Oxford transformed him, in more than legal status, into a loyal British subject. It does not need to be stressed how much he still remained a foreigner, in outward aspect and manner, in his knowledge of Europe, in many of his habits of thought. But, with the zeal and thoroughness of the newcomer, he set out to assimilate and to make his own the fundamental assumptions and attitudes of the society to which he had given his allegiance. With the approach of war, hatred of the Germans, endemic—not without reason—among the Slavs of Central and Eastern Europe, came to reinforce and stimulate his British patriotism. By 1914, in so far as this could be achieved by conviction and deliberate choice, he was a devoted member of the British establishment of that still imperial epoch.

It fitted into this picture that he should have immersed himself in English history, and have taken as his chosen field the great period of the unchallenged pre-eminence in English society and government of the land-holding aristocracy. This choice also influenced the sectors of contemporary English society to which he most naturally and eagerly sought access. Some rather unfair fun has been poked at Namier's addiction to the British landowning classes. He met some of them when he sought access to the hitherto untapped resources of their family archives. Mrs. Dugdale, A. J. Balfour's niece, whom he met during the First World War and with whom he worked at the Foreign Office, became a firm friend, and helped to ease his way into the society of the English countryside. Incidentally, she, earlier than he, became a fervent Zionist.

Though any label attached to so many-sided and complex a figure is liable to mislead, it seems proper to call Namier a conservative historian. In his two major works, he was the chronicler and analyst of a ruling class. He was not one to gloss over its defects or abuses; but he admired its effectiveness; he admired any system which, however oddly and paradoxically, worked, and preserved order and civilization. He took little account of the turbulence bubbling beneath the surface of life in the cities, which was to erupt just at the end of his period. Richard Cobb recalls a student who told Namier that he thought of doing research on the Sans-Culottes, and was met by the question: 'Why are you interested in those bandits?' One catches an echo of the old disgust at the sight of urban squalor. Still, relating to the group which sparked off so mighty an historical conflagration, it was an odd reaction.

It was perhaps the tiredness and disillusionment of old age which led him to a more and more outspokenly elitist view of history. The rudeness of students who harshly attacked a paper he had read at a seminar in Oxford in the 1950s, combined with the rudeness of a British Railways ticket inspector provoked bitter reflections on the 'new vulgarians' and the destruction of urbane living. Some years earlier he had written:

> Nazism, from the very outset so far as the Jews are concerned, starts with the worst characteristic of what is usually described as Bolshevism—disregard of the rights of persons and property, and the joy of humiliating people of higher standing and education than their tormentors.

One shrinks a little from the comment when one reflects that the vast majority of the Jews who went to the gas-chambers—or of the Russians who went to Stalin's camps—were not people of 'standing and education' in Namier's sense.

The famous charge that Namier 'took the mind out of history' is true only in one strictly limited sense. For Namier, common sense and enlightened self-interest were, and should be, the motive forces of history. He had the traditional conservative mistrust of abstract ideals; the invocation of abstractions like 'democracy', 'socialism', or 'self-determination' seemed to him empty and dangerous. His major excursion into European history—the others were brilliant occasional essays on limited topics—was a slim volume on the revolutions of 1848, which started life as a British Academy lecture in 1944. Though much expanded from the lecture, it remained in essence an incomplete fragment, without summing-up and without conclusions. Tribute was paid to peasant discontent and to the forces of nationalism. But only scorn was reserved for the ideologues in Paris or Frankfurt, who dreamt of toppling thrones and reviving the principles of the French Revolution. The very title, *The Revolution of the Intellectuals*, indicated the character of the fiasco. The moral, implicit here, more explicitly expressed elsewhere, was clear: the pursuit of political ideals spelt the end, not the beginning, of political wisdom.

It is nevertheless tempting to believe that Namier's youthful idealism, driven underground in the pursuit of his historical studies, surfaced again in his mature years in his devotion to Jewry and to the creation of Israel as a national unit in a world of nations. Namier's Zionism was for many years his central and overriding preoccupation. Yet its course was neither smooth nor simple. Namier's first association with the Zionist organization in 1929 was short-lived, and ended in a quarrel which has never been documented on either side; though, when he referred to the Executive as 'an absurd group', he was evidently condemning its methods and perhaps some of its policies, not its aims or ideals. The crisis of Jewry in the 1930s brought him back, and both then and throughout the Jewish agony of the Second World War he identified himself wholly and unreservedly with the Jewish people, and gave himself unsparingly to the cause of Israel.

After the war, he was uneasy at some of the methods by which the Israeli state established itself (twenty years earlier he had indulged the dream of Israel as a British Dominion); and when, in 1947, his closest friend and supporter among the Zionist leaders, Chaim Weizmann, expressed shocked and uncompromising disapproval of his Christian baptism and marriage, the breach was difficult to heal. Eleven years later, Namier and his wife visited Israel for the first and only time. He was profoundly moved by his reception. He was now an aged and ailing man; and any ambiguity in his divided loyalties to Christianity and Jewry melted away in the mood of warmth and reconciliation. It was a deeply-felt leavetaking of a central episode in his career.

Lady Namier fairly enough disclaims any call to assess Namier's work as an historian. But in the world of scholarship in which he chiefly moved the question has to be raised. The devil's advocate may have some searching points to make. Namier's two major works on English history have revised our view, probably for good, of certain aspects of the political scene in a span of the eighteenth century. But what the volumes contain is a series of essays. However bright and penetrating the illumination they provide on chosen topics, they do not add up to a history of England in the period; nor do they place the limited period to which they relate in the perspective of what went before and what came after. The analysis is static. The sense of the unending flow of history is missing. Namier is a great historian—so much cannot be gainsaid. But is he, like Acton, a great historian who has written no history?

Much nonsense has been talked about Namier's 'method'; he has, it is said, 'namierized history'. His originality consisted in the systematic thoroughness with which he investigated the affiliations and backgrounds of a group of individuals. The method justified itself by the illumination it enabled him to provide on a single institution, whose workings were governed by, or reflected in, the attitudes of these individuals. It was not a key to the study of history. It was useful in a limited sphere, and had its limitations and also its dangers. Namier devoted his last years to one enterprise—a vast encyclopedia of Members of Parliament of all periods—whose value has yet to be demonstrated. Bricks are important. But a pile of bricks is not a house. And should the master-builder spend his time in a brick-field? Perhaps nemesis awaits the historian who seeks to expunge ideas from the historical process.

These doubts, which only posterity can resolve, in no way exterminate the melancholy fact that the British scholars kept Namier at arm's length and, throughout his working life, refused him admittance to the inner sanctum of scholarship. When he stood for a fellowship of All Souls in 1912, a majority of the fellows, as Pollard recorded in an unpublished letter, 'shied at his race', and two other historians were elected. Revulsion against the unconventional and un-English, rather than antisemitism in particular, was probably the culprit; a well-integrated British Jew, even in 1912, would not have incurred this discrimination. That was a long time ago. It is less excusable that, in the later 1920s, when he was working on his masterpiece in straitened financial conditions, no Oxford college was willing to open its doors to him. It is almost inconceivable that, after the Second World War, at the height of his powers and his fame, he should have been twice passed over in Oxford for chairs of Modern History and of International Relations. A conscience-stricken university did indeed confer on him more than one honour and distinction. But these were honours commonly awarded to outsiders.

Namier was an angular personality, relentless and sometimes overbearing in argument. Gifted by nature with acute powers of perception, he nevertheless became, when mounted on his hobby-horse of the moment, impervious to the reactions of the listener; and he never learnt that constant reiteration can be counter-productive. Yet all this did not weigh, or should not have weighed, in the balance against the magnitude and quality of his attainments. He towered above his contemporaries. His writings are an imperfect tribute to his intellectual stature. His widow's biography attests his stature as a human being.

## (*b*) RETICENT MEDIEVALISTS

THE RELATIONSHIP between published work on medieval history and the progress of scholarship in the subject is an unusually complex one. Like all such relationships in academic disciplines, it is largely determined, and therefore distorted, by purely commercial considerations; but in addition, medievalists have developed what might almost be described as a tradition of non-publication. Some of the most respected scholars of the past few decades have produced a remarkably small output of books, preferring to concentrate on smaller-scale studies destined for learned journals. In part this is genuinely dictated by the nature of their research; but it must be admitted that there is also an element of timidity in the unwillingness to expose large-scale theses to detailed dissection. Where nervousness of this kind becomes all-pervasive, its effects are thoroughly unfortunate. It helps to push scholars in the direction of becoming an esoteric coterie, interested only in writing for each other; and at the same time it leads to deliberate neglect of the great issues of the past, in favour of minute investigation of its byways. These two perversions, in combination, present the greatest threat to the health of medieval studies today. The line between proper concern for truth and morbid determination to achieve omniscience is narrow, and is being overstepped too often. On the other hand, short essays can be vastly illuminating when they serve to expound a broader vision of history. E. F. Jacob's *Essays in Later Medieval History* is a splendid example of this.

Professor Jacob has always been a master of the essay form (his *Essays in the Conciliar Epoch* is still the best book in English on the subject), and although the pieces brought together in this book were written over a period of nearly thirty years, they have a remarkable consistency of style and approach. The aim is always to light up the period as a whole by studies in depth of individuals (Reynold Pecock, John Stratford, John of Roquetaillade), business transactions (the work of proctors at the papal court, and of founders of institutions) and subsequent historiography (Johan Huizinga and the Conciliar historians). As an envoi there is a delightful essay on the *Book of St. Albans*, that pot-pourri of fifteenth-century snobbery, heraldry, and field sports. Professor Jacob is at his best on the *Book's* disquisition on angling, about which he writes with an authority and enthusiasm born of the highest practical expertise.

In the three essays on clerks, there are profound insights into the exact nature of the changes taking place within the church at a time when, as Professor Jacob puts it,

> There was the problem of how to deal with the forces of the Wycliffite movement, forces encouraged by the naturally satirical and dramatising temper of a rising middle class, individualist and not infrequently anti-clerical, but in no way anti-religious.

Pecock came to grief because his reliance on reason and the vernacular to solve the church's problems outran the mental agility of his superiors; Stratford's career illustrates all too clearly the appalling dilemma facing great prelates, helplessly immersed in secular business, yet deeply troubled over the consequent neglect of their spiritual duties; while it is not perhaps too far-fetched to regard John of Roquetaillade's magical exercises as a kind of retreat into fantasy from the pressing problems of the real world.

Professor Jacob is fully aware of the diversity of response evoked by the situation of the church, and his method of approach is a useful disincentive to remain satisfied with simple generalizations. In his essay on Huizinga and the thesis of 'the waning of the Middle Ages' he gently takes the author to task for excessive concentration on cultural decline, pointing out that many of the changes in the way of life of the later Middle Ages can be explained more convincingly as consequences of particular governmental activities. Again and again Professor Jacob returns to the importance of the positive ferment within the church, and its implications for secular society. As he says, once enough studies have been made of individuals, their thoughts and concerns, 'we shall think of the early Tudor Age as no pallid aftermath of the Middle Ages, but their fruition, in an atmosphere of greater order and security'. If we do come to such a fuller understanding, it will be very largely through the teaching of this most humane and sensitive of historians, and the extraordinary sympathy with his chosen period these essays, like all his other work, convey.

Collections of essays of this kind form a major part of recent publications in the medieval field—R. W. Southern's magisterial contributions are outstanding among them—but a desire to cut through the complexities of detailed research to the heart of the Middle Ages undoubtedly accounts for the large numbers of biographies which are appearing. Straightforward biography is notoriously one of the most difficult forms for a medievalist. His sources are ill-fitted to it, and the gulf dividing modern and medieval thinking on individual personality is almost unbridgeable. Perhaps this is why a good number of recent biographies are the work of authors who are not, in the fullest sense, professional historians, and are attempts at interpretation rather than narrative. Certainly, some of the 'professional' biographies of recent years appear very dry in comparison with the amateurs' more daring work.

One such, L. F. Salzman's *Edward I*, is cast in an extremely old-fashioned mould: eight chapters of a strictly narrative account of Edward's life and reign, in which political and military history predominate heavily; a chapter assessing his character; and an appendix devoted to 'The Legal, Constitutional and Financial Background' of the reign. This last is scarcely adequate evaluation of Edward's importance in English legal history, or of the period of his reign in the development of parliament, over which controversy has been raging. Moreover, the book entirely omits any serious investigation of the internal structure of the court, of Edward's relations with those who served him, or the creation and working of the vast administrative system required to sustain expeditions to Wales, Scotland and France, and a programme of King's Works unprecedented in scope and effectiveness. Analysis of this kind is essential to any understanding of the conditions of the reign, and its absence leaves Dr. Salzman's narrative curiously detached from reality.

In his preface he defines his aim as being to bring out the personality of the King, so as to illustrate its influence on the events of his reign, in contradiction to the antiheroic trend of modern historiography. Certainly he gives interesting glimpses of Edward's incidental characteristics—his love of jousting, his affection for his family, his delight in display, and even a certain sense of humour; but he fails to convey a sense of the sheer formidableness of the man whose bones inspired Bruce with so much more awe than did the living reality of his son. His more serious comments on Edward's character present the reader with no more than the traditional stereotype of a hero-king. 'Edward . . . could respect a good adversary and was above petty spitefulness'—yet he humiliated and executed the utterly defeated Wallace. He 'could upon occasion, evade an inconvenient obligation, [he] was incapable of deliberate treachery'—his conduct during the Barons' War was hardly consistent with so favourable a judgment. It is unfortunate that Dr. Salzman has paid so much more attention to his career as king than to his apprenticeship as the Lord Edward, for his personal policy in the earlier years explains more about the man himself than do his actions when he had to discharge the responsibilities of the crown.

As an account of the events of the reign, the book is clear, though excessively condensed; but much of the interpretation suffers from a failure to take into account modern work on the period. It is strange, for instance, that Dr. Salzman makes no mention of the part played by the great Continental master-mason, Master James of St. George, in the construction of the Welsh border castles, which epitomizes the huge size of the operation. Most of his discussion of parliament and the legal advances of the reign is confused with the general narrative, and is seriously misleading. He accepts, without qualification, Stubbs's outmoded view of the parliament of 1295 as a Model Parliament, and says nothing of the judicial basis of parliamentary authority. In dealing with Edward's statutes he fails to explain their usefulness as revenue measures, and in general he is far too ready to accept record evidence at its face value, rather than inquiring what decrees meant when translated into practical politics.

In sharp contrast to a traditional book of this kind are the much fresher biographical studies by scholars who are less obsessed with the reproduction of original sources and more interested in providing a coherent framework of an explanatory kind. Some extremely good books of this kind have recently appeared in France, one of them being Régine Pernoud's *Héloïse et Abélard*. Mlle. Pernoud is, very clearly, writing the woman's side of the Héloïse and Abelard story. It is not a new approach—Helen Waddell's *Peter Abelard*, although a novel, has already treated the great romance from this point of view, with exceptional sympathy. But Mlle. Pernoud is less in love with Abelard, and her account is the more convincing. For her, his original attraction to Héloïse was a matter of 'l'intellect et les sens'—it contained not a shadow of emotion. In this he was 'un parfait prototype d'universitaire'. The purely donnish element in Abelard's make-up is traced through his early adventures in the Schools, to the affaire itself, and on to his subsequent correspondence with the Abbess of the Paraclete. At each stage it is seen as limiting Abelard's capacity for responding to other people, and understanding the full force of Héloïse's devotion. There is no attempt to play down the reality behind the donnishness—Mlle. Pernoud accepts Abelard for what he was, one of the greatest and most original scholars and thinkers of European history; and her summaries of his philosophical concepts are sensible and comprehending, if somewhat simplistic. But her interest is primarily in his personality, and while her portrait cannot be claimed as definitive, it is a real contribution to our understanding of a most enigmatic figure.

Only on wider issues are her opinions more questionable. Abelard was one of the brightest stars in the intellectual firmament of his time, but he was not the only one: nor was the dialectic of which he was the acknowledged master the only branch of thought making great strides during his time. From Mlle. Pernoud's treatment of the subject it would be easy to derive an unbalanced picture of the age on either score.

Mlle. Pernoud displays another side of her historical erudition in a small book, *Jeanne devant les Cauchons*. In it, she takes the story of the life, trial and death of Joan of Arc as the text for a sermon on historical method. Its moral is the necessity for the historian to surrender himself unreservedly to the original records of the past, and it is worked out through the destruction of successive legends about Joan. The theories of Joan as the stool-pigeon of a court faction, or a royal bastard, or as having escaped the fire by substitution, are comprehensively and ungently demolished. A good number of historians are arraigned, in terms which recall the polemics of J. H. Round, but Mlle. Pernoud's severest strictures are kept for Henri Guillemin's recent book, *Jeanne, dite 'Jeanne d'Arc'*.

Here she draws up a devastating indictment of misunderstanding and misuse of documents, sheer ignorance of available sources, mystagoguery about secret cupboards in the Vatican archives, and above all, a sublime readiness to supplement ascertainable fact with imagined incident. Even if some of her criticisms are exaggerated, the weight of them is sufficient to deprive M. Guillemin's book of any claim to be considered as a serious contribution to knowledge. Mlle. Pernoud calls it anti-history, with some justice.

Yet her own case is overstated. History is not a matter of abstract truth revealed through documents, totally independent of the opinions of the historian; throughout *Jeanne devant les Cauchons* she herself is forced to argue from her judgment of the veracity of the records of Joan's trials and retrials. In doing so, she does not betray her craft, for assessment is essential to the historian's function. Her book is disturbing, rather, for its revelation of the growing gulf between the outlook and standards of the amateur and the professional historian, each driving the other to extremes.

One very important reason for this is the swift decline in knowledge of Latin among educated people in the past few decades. For the professional medievalist Latin is more than an indispensable tool: it is the language in which his period lives, moves, and has its being. There is an inevitable frustration in being forced to communicate only in an alien tongue, with all the loss of nuances it involves. The temptation to take a high line, and aim serious writing on the Middle Ages solely at the diminishing audience of those who have Latin, is almost overwhelming. But refusal to meet the challenge of the decline of the classics is a counsel of despair.

Fortunately, it is not a universal reaction. The editors of that admirable series 'Nelson's Medieval Texts', now taken over by the

Oxford University Press, respond to the problem by printing texts and translations in parallel, with a well-judged minimum of critical apparatus. So far as possible, the provision of both text and translation should be extended to quotations in secondary works; one may even hope that this will stimulate interest in the original language. Where this is not possible careful translations alone have a place. The advantages of this approach can be seen in the series 'Le Mémorial des Siècles', published by Albin Michel.

A recent volume, *Saint Louis: roi de France* by the duc de Lévis Mirepoix, brings together modern French translations of a wide variety of sources for the life of Louis IX, including Old French chronicles, letters and Arab accounts of his crusade, with an introduction giving a framework of the main events of the reign, and very useful lists of rulers and the dates of major events. This is an impressive attempt to make the contemporary literature on a popular subject available and comprehensible to an entirely untrained audience, and for the most part it is very successful. The author/editor gives a sense of immediacy and continuity by commentary based on his own Mirepoix family papers, and his account and assessments of Louis's activities are clear and well balanced. Books of this kind deserve to be produced for many characters and events of English history.

Linguistic problems are not the only ones which beset medieval history. It is a subject which has lost its sense of direction. The belief that it should have a sense of direction in the first place runs counter to the attitudes of many medievalists, for whom it is anathema to suggest that their work should be judged by external standards, and not by the intrinsic importance of gaining information about the past. This attitude in itself is unhistorical. History, at least as it is studied in schools and universities today, is a discipline of very recent growth. It evolved out of simple antiquarianism, in the course of the nineteenth century—which is not to deny that there were great precursors. The evolution took place not because a new kind of interest in the past developed as by inspiration but because it came to be believed that history could teach lessons about the present. At the very least, a knowledge of their past would enable men to see where they stood, if it could not direct whither they should go. Bishop Stubbs's sense of scandal that young Englishmen were taught so much more about Greek and Roman antiquity than about their own country's past stands as the epitome of this view. Historians who deny the propriety of asking whether their work has relevance to the present are denying their own founders.

Of course, an insistence on 'relevance' can cover a multitude of intellectual sins. At its worst it degenerates into that narrow philistinism which asserts that only the transient problems of the moment have any interest *sub specie aeternitatis*. The disinterested quest for truth and the delight of discovery are essential to history which is to give profit and pleasure to anyone. But these can coexist with an ability to connect the past with the present. The vein of political and constitutional history which used to provide a sense and a criterion of the importance of the subject as a whole is almost worked out. Some of the greatest monuments to it, the *Oxford History of England* for instance, have reached completion in the past twenty-five years. It is a symptom of the malaise of history in general, and of medieval history in particular, that few new cooperative ventures of a similar scope have been started. Although series of history books of one kind and another remain popular with publishers, their unity of theme is largely factitious, for there is no collective consciousness among authors of what themes ought to be pursued. It is, clearly, high time more thought was given to the overall approach to the Middle Ages we should adopt.

An excellent product of such new thinking is a volume on *Eastern and Western Europe in the Middle Ages* edited by Geoffrey Barraclough in Thames and Hudson's 'Library of European Civilisation'. It is a collection of essays, by five scholars of different nationalities, which sets out to re-examine the framework of Europe geographically and culturally. As the editor says in his introduction, the rise of the Third World has led to an adjustment of our concept of what constitutes Europe. One can no longer think of it as an entity confined to the national states of the West. The authors of these essays have been stimulated by this change of outlook to look again at concepts of Europe in an earlier age, and their common conclusion is that the wider unity of the continent was already coming into existence in a period which has usually been regarded as one of very deep East-West division, along racial and cultural lines.

The five essays discuss the question of links between Eastern and Western Europe from various points of view. F. Graus deals with the racial problems involved, K. Bosl the political, F. Seibt the religious, M. M. Postan the economic, and A. Gieysztor the cultural. The first two essays suffer from the amount of unfamiliar information which has to be compressed into a small space, but the last three are easier reading, and exceptionally interesting. Dr. Seibt demonstrates convincingly that the sheer complexity of the European response to Christianity rules out any straight-forward division on East-West lines, and Professor Gieysztor illustrates most impressively the deep cultural interpenetration between the two halves of the continent.

Professor Postan's survey of the importance of trading links in drawing the continent together is, in many ways, the most thought-provoking essay of all. He argues that the lure of the Orient has led historians to overemphasize the Mediterranean trade of the Middle Ages at the expense of the East-West trade of Northern Europe, and the commercial connexions between North and South. These, he suggests, were in reality more important since they depended on trade in necessities, as opposed to the luxury traffic of the southern route. In all, these essays represent the best kind of 'relevant' history: an inquiry into the past directed by new concerns, but lacking nothing in scholarship.

Another worthwhile way to make history 'relevant' is the publication of books tailored to a specific academic need. In this category comes Maurice Keen's *History of Medieval Europe*. In his preface Mr. Keen acknowledges his scholarly debts to R. W. Southern and E. F. Jacob, and those debts are real and deep. Mr. Keen is an historian in the great central tradition of interpreters of the Middle Ages, for whom the history of Western Christianity, as worked out in the progress of the church, is the basic structure on which all else depends. His book begins with 'the idea of the unity of Christendom' and ends with 'the break with traditional attitudes', and this gives it a strong central theme which is essential if so wide-ranging a survey is not to lose itself in a morass of diffused detail. It is, too, the right theme for an introductory book on the subject: one can easily present the Middle Ages in social or economic terms, but the religious aspect of the age is the one which captures the attention of a modern audience most surely.

Religion, however, is not allowed to swamp everything else. As Mr. Keen traces the emergence of the Middle Ages from the shadow of a greater Rome to a more self-confident identity of its own, he explains that identity largely in economic terms. For him the much-abused 'feudal system' remains a reality, but is expounded not by crude definitions but by delicate socio-economic analysis. He is prepared to admit that some of the broadest movements of the period—

the vast increase of population in the three centuries after 1000 and the episode of the Viking invasions, for instance—remain unexplained and probably unexplainable. When he does set out to explain broad movements, he shows sound judgment in selecting the most crucial and illuminating evidence. One of the best sections in the book is that on the twelfth-century renaissance, and it is particularly pleasing to see Gratian's great work referred to not simply as the '*Decretum*' but also by its original and far more informative title, the *Concordance of the Discordant Canons*. It is also this section which invites the closest comparison with R. W. Southern's great introductory work, *The Making of the Middle Ages*. Almost any book would suffer from that comparison, and it must be said that Mr. Keen does not display the same extraordinary depth of erudition as his mentor; but in some ways his style is more easily comprehensible to the tiro in medieval studies, for whom it is intended.

As the Middle Ages draw nearer to their close, Mr. Keen approaches the home ground of his detailed scholarly work, and his comments are correspondingly more incisive. It is certainly good to be reminded that, even in an age one is prone to think of as overwhelmingly violent, already 'empires were more easily made in the marriage bed than by the sword'. In general, the book unobtrusively corrects some of the more superficial judgments made about the Middle Ages. The Black Death is shown to be quite as important for its psychological effects as its purely economic ones, and the benefits of papal centralization for the church are carefully balanced against the damage it appeared to cause. In some ways the last section is the most interesting of all, for in it Mr. Keen presents the waning of the Middle Ages less in terms of cultural decline than as a function of the growth of nation-states and the decay of the idea of a supreme authority for Christendom.

For all the virtues of books such as these, the rewriting of medieval history in terms suggested by specific problems of the modern world or in books *for* students is too narrow a response to the general crisis facing the subject. What is needed is a conviction that this particular mode of investigating the past can make a significant contribution to perspectives of the present. Most obviously, this is a matter of highlighting differences of thought. Over a surprisingly wide range of topics, the fundamental assumptions of present Western society are utterly unquestioned and largely unexpressed. Controversy may rage over the best means of achieving an ever-expanding gross national product, but the end is taken for granted. It is more than salutary to be made aware that for long periods of history the most intelligent members of society regarded increasing material prosperity as a potential danger and, at worst, a sin. The medievalist, in pointing out contrasts of this kind, is at the same time asserting that the differing viewpoints of his period cannot be dismissed as the products of an alien culture, or a fairy-story world. They are hard facts about a society joined to our own by evolutionary links which often prove to have astonishing strength.

Medieval history, seen in this light, must necessarily continue as an evolving subject. If the study of political and constitutional history is beginning to seem sterile, intellectual and cultural history are still, relatively, in their infancy. The precise forms of difference and the way those differences developed need to be defined and elaborated before they can be appreciated in the present. It is not too arrogant to suggest that the study of medieval history can provide important alternatives for a world short of ideas. This attitude to the subject carries implications for the kind of work to be pursued within it. Medievalists must dare to synthesize. They must try to present serious studies of aspects of an intellectual and cultural world, culled from the mass of discrete research already available. One of the few really great works of medieval history of the past few decades, David Knowles's account of the monastic and religious orders in England, exists as a superb specimen of such a synthesis, and sets a standard for others. Inevitably, the larger the book the larger the chance of error. It must be accepted that error itself is not a disgrace; only carelessness and intellectual dishonesty are that. Errors can be, and will be, corrected; but books must be written in order that it may be. Only if professional medievalists become more willing to publish books of wide scope can the subject as a whole avoid atrophy.

# IO
# THE HORATIAN CREED

SINCE THE ADVENT of the Romantic movement, Horace's *Epistula ad Pisones*—better known as the *Ars Poetica*, and apart from Aristotle's *Poetics* the only general statement on poetic theory to survive from Antiquity—has been, to put it mildly, under something of a cloud. Everything it stands for runs flat counter to the whole trend of post-Coleridgean aesthetics. Those whom the French so delightfully labelled *les amateurs du délire* could not be expected to relish Horace's portrait of the mad poet in action—selfish, dirty, anti-social, clumping over hallowed ground (physically as well as symbolically) with fine irreligious abandon, urinating on his father's grave, an actual drunk and potential suicide, sputtering verses, tumbling into wells, by turns presented as a bear and a leech, grabbing passers-by whom he first 'reads to death' (*occiditque, legendo*), and then drains of their life-blood, the very epitome of what Professor Brink calls 'imagination uncontrolled by reason'. But the whole idea and approach of the *Ars* was equally suspect. Like the *Poetics*, it assumes the existence of a static, not to say hierarchic, scale of aesthetic values; it lays down rules, and believes in their general validity. Inspiration, by and large, it treats as a kind of wild beast, only tolerable when safely hedged about by Greek precedent and the comforting guide-lines of sovereign reason.

Nothing is easier than to go through the *Ars* with an axe to grind and let Horace (though not quite in the way he intended) perform the function of a whetstone. His much-reiterated plea for rational consistency in the arts—a place for everything and everything in its place—can all too readily, like so much else in the *Ars*, be interpreted as a mere frigid academic enshrinement of traditional cliché. He leads off with an introductory section on the visual arts in which he deplores the prospect of horses with human heads, and other such examples of artistic miscegenation: to a generation reared on Picasso

---

C. O. BRINK: *Horace on Poetry: The Ars Poetica*. 563 pp. Cambridge University Press. £8.60.

this argument will have little appeal, and the beast in question cannot but seem a tosh-horse scarcely worth the galloping.

What modern readers may forget, however, is that Horace had plenty to fight against in his own day: chimaeras, centaurs and mermaids were merely the beginning of it. Artists have always felt the urge, if not to reshape creation, at any rate to go one better than the dull existing natural order, which Horace and his like were bent on defending. When we find him protesting at the idea of dolphins in woods or boars at sea, he is not merely picking up a literary figure of speech from Archilochus; what he had in mind are works such as those splendidly grotesque scenes of marine life (from a good Hellenistic tradition, be it noted) which still survive in Pompeian copies, with dolphins, octopi, and fish of every sort taking wing through the empyrean—to the scandal of that down-to-earth architect Vitruvius, among others. *Simplex dumtaxat et unum* was Horace's key motif here: variety, in the last resort, must be subsumed and mastered by unity.

The trouble with the Horatian or Aristotelian formula for aesthetics is that it makes no allowance for natural change or evolution. Here it shares the special disadvantages of ancient political theory (the *polis* cracked long before its intellectual mould did, and nothing could be more hieratic, as a social blue-print, than Plato's *Laws*). Though the notion of the Greeks, and their Roman imitators, as theorists who were virtually incapable of sustained direct observation is a mere popular fallacy—to refute it one needs do no more than leaf through the Hippocratic Corpus—it does nevertheless remain true that observation was always ruthlessly subordinated to the principle, the idea, the system: the reality (from their viewpoint) underlying the appearances. Of the Presocratics it has been well said that they never explained anything without at the same time trying to explain everything, and the habit proved remarkably long-enduring.

The most extraordinary thing about these various Greco-Roman intellectual canons (or dogmas, or shibboleths, according to one's view) is how enormous and indeed tyrannical an influence they exercised, not only over their own civilization, but for countless centuries to come. The emphasis might vary between the medieval and the post-Renaissance periods (Aristotle being large and varied enough to appeal to both); but until the very end of the eighteenth century, and in some respects for even longer, the Greco-Roman 'fixities', to use Coleridge's term, still dominated European thought—

hundreds of years after the rules they propounded had ceased to bear any truly organic relationship to current practice. As Erich Auerbach made clear in *Mimesis*, and C. O. Brink now confirms, with writers such as Dante or Chaucer the line of creative development diverges to a marked degree from the declared adherence to ancient theory which these and other writers profess.

Here, of course, we see a danger that was implicit in the whole approach *ab initio*: the obstinate determination to extrapolate timeless principles without regard for historical or evolutionary change. In one sense (as has often been pointed out) Aristotle's *Poetics* sprang obsolete from his pen, since it sought to impose dramatic norms on a genre—Attic drama—which had been coeval with, and a by-product of, Athens's fifth-century rise to Aegean supremacy, and could not hope in any actively creative sense to survive the destruction of Periclean imperialism. The sort of rules that Aristotle and Horace propound may aim at establishing a pattern *sub specie aeternitatis*; but they more often (to judge from the record) merely build an all-too-solid museum without walls, a rigidly intellectual enshrinement of the past. It is ironic that the famous tag *laudator temporis acti* should have been applied by Horace, in the *Ars*, and by no means as a compliment, to an old man nearing his dotage, when for the modern student it forms so apt a description of Horace himself.

But whether or not we personally like this attitude to life and art, we cannot afford simply to neglect it—as the Romantics rather tended to do, brushing it under the cultural carpet as an unaccountable rationalist aberration. A theory that engaged the minds and passions of innumerable intellectual giants from Plato onwards deserves more than such summary dismissal (the same could be said, in a different way, of early Christian theology). At the very least, we have to recognize that it answers a deep and archetypal need of the human psyche: that ineradicable thirst for order, rule, degree, and pattern which, at one level or another, and in every branch of human activity—from physics to politics, from history to astronomy—demands, and more often than not gets, both intellectual and emotional satisfaction. (How far the pattern is 'true'—i.e. inherent in the nature of things apart from man's concept of them—will of course vary from case to individual case.)

Creative art springs from the very centre of this age-old fundamental instinct, and it would be ludicrous to regard it as in any way immune from the striving after absolute perfection, the rule of truth and knowledge. A. N. Whitehead, in a justly famous aphorism, once described all later Western philosophy as a series of extended foot-notes to Plato; in so far as he had the Theory of Forms in mind, this notion could well be applied to literary theory as well. Professor Flew recently made this very clear when he wrote:

Certainly one large element in the appeal to Plato of his doctrine of Forms was their promise to provide simultaneously both stable, knowable standards of value and ideally perfect exemplars of those values.

The appeal of such a potential yardstick in the shifting and arbitrary-seeming field of creative aesthetics is obviously very great (it need not be purely philosophical, either; a great degree of F. R. Leavis's appeal as a critic can surely be ascribed to the way he stiffens his canons of literary judgment with various built-in moral-cum-sociological criteria). How far Horace succeeded in forging such an instrument with the *Ars*, or even intended to do so, is quite another matter. As Professor Brink reminds us, what we have here is 'a work of the imagination that makes a poetic symbol out of a literary theory'—probably, as he suggests, working from some early Hellenistic model (though the possible influence of Lucilius should not be neglected). Like most creative writers, Horace, when he turned to theory, was largely concerned—whether consciously or not—to vindicate his own methods of composition by equating them with general laws, a tendency which at once casts some doubt on the validity of his poetic testament as a universal witness to the truth. Professor Brink realizes (being a brilliant Latinist with a very acute ear) that 'the principles which he imposes suit above all Virgil's poetry and his own', but—as a lonely latter-day champion of the *Ars*—he shrinks from drawing the obvious inference.

Indeed, one of the few criticisms which can be levelled against this second volume in the series which Professor Brink calls *Horace on Poetry*—a really monumental edition of, and commentary on, the *Ars Poetica* as a whole (the first volume, subtitled 'Prolegomena to the Literary Epistles', was published in 1963)—is that, like its subject, it eschews the historical approach altogether. In well over 500 pages of close-packed annotation (each man, said Wilde, kills the thing he loves, and Professor Brink at times risks burying the 476 lines of the *Ars* under an avalanche of Alexandrian exegesis) it is possible to miss points; but the present reviewer could find nothing on the much-debated identity of the Pisos—who were, after all, the poem's dedicatees—nor even on the date, surely a matter of vital importance, at which the *Ars* was composed or published. Professor Brink, like his subject, clearly prefers to deal with literary theory in a timeless void, and to forget the human progress—against a background of bloody civil war—which led Horace from his position as a 'hog from Epicurus's herd' to that of Augustus's state-subsidized mouthpiece, turning out such things as the *Carmen Saeculare* and the great political Odes in the modest rural comfort of his Sabine farm. These things are not irrelevant to that conservative traditionalism which permeates the *Ars*, nor to the systematic denigration of Italic culture (what Professor Bianchi Bandinelli calls the 'plebeian tradition') and the complementary enskyment of Hellenic models—'vos exemplaria Graeca/nocturna versate manu, versate diurna'—which so irritated writers like Juvenal or the Elder Pliny, and which, as Professor Brink rightly says, constitutes 'the essence of the Horatian, Augustan creed'.

This caveat once made, however, it is hard to find anything but praise for Professor Brink's scholarship, industry and judgment. One would not expect the Cambridge University Press to make rash claims incapable of substantiation, and the statement on the jacket that 'this series of volumes constitutes the only really full scholarly commentary on Horace's critical writings' is no more than the sober truth. As a textual critic Professor Brink is both conservative and sceptical. He does not (unlike most of his predecessors in the field) believe that Horatian manuscripts can be classified, and offers solid arguments for such an assumption, expressed with a pungency that at times recalls an earlier Kennedy Professor, A. E. Housman. He works with a more selective *apparatus criticus* than did Vollmer or Klingner, and stands at the opposite end of the scale, editorially, from a scholar like Peerlkamp, described in 1886 by a rival French savant as 'un hollandais terrible, qui corrige tout, sabre tout, bouleverse tout'.

If Professor Brink has a weakness for *bouleversement*, it takes a rather special negative form. He is much addicted to that supreme gambit of textmanship: obelizing as corrupt a passage which previous editors had blithely assumed (a) that they understood, and (b) was therefore *a fortiori*, textually sound. Unlike Dorothy Sayers's young don in *Gaudy Night*, who had to be carried out of the Hall screaming and kicking because he could not bring himself to say the words 'I don't know', Professor Brink liberally sprinkles his text with the obelizing daggers of ignorance (line 172 is a good case in point), earning himself credit for sound judgment in the process. He even reminds us, tartly, that though we often talk about purple patches, no editor has succeeded in explaining just what Horace's *purpureus pannus* meant (and any enquirer who turns up the relevant section of Professor Brink's commentary expecting to find that *he* has solved the mystery badly mistakes the way this scholar goes about his business, which is warily, like Agag).

Such scrupulousness of judgment (partly dependent on a most sensitive ear for linguistic nuances of every sort) is, in the commentary, allied with exact and wide-ranging scholarship to produce a fundamental and indispensable edition from which all future students in the field will have to begin. Yet—as Professor Brink himself is the first to admit—there is a great deal more to the *Ars* than mere antiquarianism; it raises a number of perennial aesthetic problems that are as pressing today as they were 2,000 years ago. 'I suspect', he remarks demurely, 'my view of the poem depends ultimately on a value-judgment'. Most readers would agree, taking it as axiomatic that Professor Brink's verdict on Horace—'He would be chary of a poetic imagination unaided by a tough intellectual fibre'—also applies to himself.

Professor Brink suggests that a reader's basic reaction to the *Ars* will be dictated by his attitude to *ingenium*—that is, creative talent or inspiration. Those who feel that this quality should be unshackled by tradition (let alone traditionalism) will condemn the *Ars*, he thinks; whereas those who 'can admire originality strengthened, but also limited, by tradition'—a category in which he would clearly include himself—will (if they can understand it) tend to appreciate Horace's achievement. This may sound like a straight showdown between radicals and reactionaries on the aesthetic-principle vote; but, as this book makes clear, it is really more subtle and complex.

Indeed, to put the case in this way suggests that Professor Brink's massive reassessment and vindication of Horace as a literary theorist may be timely: more timely, perhaps, than would appear at first sight. There is still a great deal in the *Ars*, of course, calculated to arouse almost any intellectual's derision or anger: the smugly tidy cultural dogma, the Hellenophile snobbishness, and what Kipling generically labelled as the 'Gods of the Copy-book Headings'. At times one almost feels that the poem might be retitled *Fowler's Ancient Roman Usage*, with its all-pervasive literary nostalgia for a lost Golden Age, and all those sclerotic just-so rules for 'appropriate' diction, style, genre, epithets, character-portrayal, or what-have-you (e.g. the assertion that it is better to rehash the Tale of Troy than invent something new)—although, paradoxically, Horace's obsession with traditional usage, when applied to language (always in a state of Heraclitean flux), leads him into an avant-garde position barely distinguishable from that of the modern comparative linguist. But he makes up for this with his observations on drama. Stick to the five-act rule, he tells us, avoid the *deus ex machina*, and never use more than three actors; if he had lived in an earlier age he would probably have demonstrated in protest when Aeschylus introduced the second actor, or Sophocles the third, rather like that legendary old lady who, at the coming of diesel locomotives, was heard to remark that she liked to see folk riding on the old steam trains, like the Good Lord meant them to. The studied contrast between Greek idealism and Roman money-grubbing hints at that tiresome *odi et amo* cultural inferiority complex which pervades so much of Greco-Roman relationships during the late Republic and the early Empire. Lastly, we cannot fail to be uneasily aware that the rules Horace propounds are closely bound up with just those literary failings—unreality, obscurantism, cliché, and dead bombast—which (though Horace himself pilloried them) afterwards offered critics like Persius, Juvenal, or Petronius a target rather wider than a barn-door.

At the same time there is another side to the debate, and perhaps the time has come for this unfashionable opposition view to get a serious hearing. Horace, of course, does not always help in his own case: violent animadversions against drunken, dirty poets with long hair and untrimmed finger-nails might have been designed for *Daily Telegraph* readers, and there are passages, one fears, in which the *Ars* reads uncomfortably like 'Way of the World' revamped by Malcolm Muggeridge. Yet it is not mere chauvinism to make the point that (in Professor Brink's words) 'not all variety in painting and poetry can be justified by a plea for creative freedom'.

Here we come up against a crucial issue of our time, one which that anything-but stuffy critical bombardier Wyndham Lewis tackled, from much the same standpoint, in *The Demon of Progress in the Arts*. The application of reason, tradition, and craftsmanship to art, the acceptance of at least some constant values or criteria, may in the last resort provide a salutary counter-balance to a creative freedom which (as Horace perceived, with far less justification, in his own day) can all too easily expire in a mindless and patternless welter of anarchic emotionalism. The case should not be allowed to go by default; and we owe Professor Brink a debt of gratitude for reminding us that it is a perennial rather than an exclusively modern phenomenon; that even in Augustan Rome conservative artists could still close ranks against what might be termed the Op. Cit.

# II
# THE MAN WITHIN
## GRAHAM GREENE IN RETROSPECT

GRAHAM GREENE writes in his autobiography, *A Sort of Life*:

If I were to choose an epigraph for all the novels I have written, it would be from *Bishop Bloughram's Apology*:

> 'Our interest's on the dangerous edge of things.
> The honest thief, the tender murderer,
> The superstitious atheist, demi-rep
> That loves and saves her soul in new French books—
> We watch while these in equilibrium keep
> The giddy line midway.'

What reviewer could resist such firm authorial guidance? And especially when the passage does seem to catalogue what is most characteristic in Greene's work—the melodramatic characters and the heightened action on the 'dangerous edge', and the precarious moral equilibrium of the actors, between honesty and thievery, between tenderness and murder. As an epigraph, it will certainly do. The trouble is that it points to qualities in the novels which have been too much noticed. Of course Greene has fixed his imagination upon crime and murder, and of course he can tell a story of dangerous action well; but to say so seems to place him among the gifted story-tellers, somewhere near Ambler and Maugham, and obscures his other and more essential affiliation with James and Conrad and Ford, and the great tradition of the novel as a work of art. This seems an appropriate occasion to note that connexion, and to assert that in fact Greene is the principal English novelist now writing in that tradition; for does he not invite the connexion, by appearing in a Collected Edition with new introductions by the author (as both

---

GRAHAM GREENE: *A Sort of Life*. 215 pp. Bodley Head. £1.80. *Brighton Rock*. 309 pp. £1.75. *The Confidential Agent*. 247 pp. £1.75. *England Made Me*. 255 pp. £1.75. *The Heart of the Matter*. 320 pp. £2. *It's a Battlefield*. 216 pp. £1.75. *Our Man in Havana*. 241 pp. £1.75. *The Power and The Glory*. 266 pp. £1.75. Heinemann and Bodley Head.

James and Conrad did, and Ford wished to do), and by releasing at the same time a memoir of his early years?

Any reader of Greene's *Collected Essays* will have noted another resemblance to James there—the sensitive critic of fiction, interested in technique, almost donnish in his range of literary knowledge, precise and judicious with a careful confidence. Like James, Greene has written best on the novelists of his own tradition: there are several acute essays on James himself, and his appreciations of Ford are simply the best that have been written (though he remains unenlightened on the importance of republishing *Last Post*). And always there is a fine understanding of the craft of fiction, and of the hostility of Englishmen to whatever seems artful; either James or Ford might have written, 'It is dangerous in this country to talk about techniques', but in fact Greene did.

The novels show that his interest in technique is not mere talk. One finds in them the same aesthetic tradition in practice: the manipulations of time and point of view, the discreet voice of the primary author, remote but not removed, the dramatically rendered scenes, the impressionistic touches. Remember how the point of view shifts in *The Heart of the Matter*? How the character of Querry is built up by indirections in *A Burnt-Out Case*? The experiment in stream-of-consciousness in *England Made Me*? The topographical use of London in *It's a Battlefield*? In the new introductions to his novels Greene notes some of the technical problems he has faced, and the importance of recognizing them: 'How dangerous it is', he writes of *England Made Me*, 'for a critic to have no technical awareness of the novel.'

Having claimed Greene for the art-novel tradition, one must add at once that he himself has shied away from that connexion. In an important essay on Mauriac he acknowledges the greatness of Flaubert and James—'the novel was ceasing to be an aesthetic form and they recalled it to the artistic conscience'—but he assigns to Mauriac a greater role:

> M. Mauriac's first importance to an English reader . . . is that he belongs to the company of the great traditional novelists: he is a writer for whom the visible world has not ceased to exist, whose characters have the solidity and importance of men with souls to save or lose, and a writer who claims the traditional and essential right of a novelist, to comment, to express his views.

When an artist praises another artist in such terms, one may assume

that he is describing his own aspirations, and this certainly seems to be true in this case. To Greene, the modern novel has lost the religious sense, 'and with the religious sense went the sense of the importance of the human act'. Like Mauriac, he is concerned to restore that importance and thus to justify the novel in moral as well as in aesthetic terms. This notion is at the centre of Greene's artistic intentions, and for his readers it makes a crucial point: what matters in his novels is not the action, but the moral meaning of the human act—the dangerous edge of things is there.

The right that Greene claims, to comment and to express his views, is one that separates him from the other descendants of James and Conrad. It has made him sometimes didactic, as he admits in his introduction to *Brighton Rock* (which he nevertheless concludes may be the best book he ever wrote); and it has led him to utter the *pensées* that are perhaps the most distinguishable feature of his style, and to incline toward characters who are themselves *penseurs*. Greene has made the standard disclaimer of personal responsibility for the remarks of his characters, but in fact his manner is such that it is sometimes difficult to determine the degree of authorial commitment to voiced thoughts. He and his characters think continually about the importance of human acts, about God and the soul, love and damnation, and speak their thoughts in sentences like these: 'Point me out the happy man and I will point you out either egotism, evil—or else an absolute ignorance': 'The truth . . . has never been of any real value to any human being—it is a symbol for mathematicians and philosophers to pursue'; 'We are all of us resigned to death; it's life we aren't resigned to'. These are all from *The Heart of the Matter*, but are they in the voice of Scobie or of Greene? Are they to be regarded as truths, or only as symptoms? This habit of *pensée*-making is not necessarily a flaw in the novels but it is unsettling to readers and critics unused to the religious sense in fiction.

Greene's didacticism has led to his being identified as a 'Catholic novelist', an identification to which he has many times objected. Against this charge he has quoted Newman—'if Literature is to be made a study of human nature, you cannot have a Christian Literature'—but to little avail (a Catholic in support of a Catholic seems a weak defence). Greene might also have called up Auden, who has said that there can no more be Christian art than there can be Christian cookery, and certainly in Auden's sense Greene's novels are not Christian, but are simply the novels of a rather heterodox Christian man. Still, if there is no such thing as Christian literature, there may still be *Catholic* fiction, and in Greene's case it does seem possible to separate the Catholic books from what one might call the lay books. There is no novel by Greene from which the religious sense is entirely absent, but only a few approach sectarianism. One sign of this quality is the way, in certain novels, a priest is given a strong doctrinal speech at the end (this is true of *Brighton Rock*, *The End of the Affair*, and *The Heart of the Matter*, and, in a rather different way, of *The Power and the Glory*); but this is only one symptom of a more essential peculiarity of those books—the way they all slide off toward abstraction, and away from the felt reality of the visible world, in their final pages. None of these 'Catholic' novels ends as well as it began.

Nevertheless it is these novels that have received most of the critical attention that Greene has got. This is no doubt partly because they have offered easy thematic handles and a certain guaranteed seriousness (a novel about damnation *must* be worth writing about), and partly because Catholic critics have rushed in with Catholic explanations; but some of the responsibility is Greene's, for it is he who first distinguished between his 'novels' and his 'entertainments', and thus encouraged critics to take his best work lightly. His reasons for making the distinction have been various: that the novels were written slowly and the entertainments quickly; that the novels were the products of depressive periods and the entertainments manic; that the entertainments were crime stories, the novels something more. (He has not suggested that the novels are Catholic and the entertainments are lay, though this does seem roughly to be the case). But none of these explanations validates the distinction, and it is gratifying to see that the new edition calls the whole lot novels. Now, perhaps, Greene's critics will begin to see that *A Gun for Sale* is one of the best and most significant novels of the 1930s, and a far more nearly perfect work of art than *Brighton Rock*.

Greene offers a key to the unity of his fiction in a remark in his introduction to *The Confidential Agent*. He says there that when he began to write that novel he had in mind only 'a certain vague ambition to create something legendary out of a contemporary thriller'. This seems always to have been Greene's ambition. If a thriller is a novel containing exciting action and crime, then one might say that he has never written anything else; there is violence in all his novels, and crime in most, and one might argue that what makes the theological back-chat of the heaviest novels endurable is the interwoven elements of the thriller—Ali with his throat cut while Scobie thinks about damnation, Pinky and the vitriol bottle, the knock at the door at the end of *The Power and the Glory*. And even Greene's weakest, dullest novel, *The End of the Affair*, makes miracles tolerable by treating them as unsolved mysteries, almost as crimes.

But the thriller is more than action: it is a set of patterns and conventions as firmly established as those of classical tragedy. Greene mentions some in the passage quoted above: 'the hunted man who becomes in turn the hunter, the peaceful man who turns at bay, the man who has learned to love justice by suffering injustice'. These are the materials of his 'legends', and as in traditional legends they lend a formality to his violences, and lead us to expect a moral meaning (justice will be done, there will be no open endings, life will be ordered, not sliced). Legend is expressive narrative, and what happens in the narrative happens because it carries meaning; in Greene's novels the violence is not there because the world *is* violent, but because violence satisfies 'that moral craving for the just and reasonable expression of human nature left without belief'. It is not surprising, then, to find in the novels episodes of violence that are so formal as to be almost allegorical: the killing of Hale, the gas-mask scene in *A Gun for Sale*, the two deaths of Harry Lime, the murder of Else in *The Confidential Agent*. In this imagined world the action that matters is the eternal spiritual war between good and evil, and the novels are the legends of the battlefield.

The legendary quality of Greene's writing has to some extent been obscured by the particularity of his imagined world. His settings have been so consistently vivid and actual that they have been given a collective name—'Greeneland'—and a descriptive adjective—'seedy'. Greene objects to both the noun and the adjective, but he can scarcely deny that his world *is* consistently seedy, sordid, violent and cruel. These qualities are part of the legend: they describe not an actual environment, but an image of a spiritual condition—a world abandoned by God. Greene is a man with a commitment to a religious tradition which he cannot see as manifested in contemporary society: there is no apparent way of expressing belief with *these* physical, human materials—one can only express the absence of belief. Perhaps the best expression of this sense of the world is in the long passage from Newman which stands as an epigraph to *The*

*Lawless Roads*. In it Newman describes the fearful, suffering condition of men, and concludes:

What shall be said to this heart-piercing, reason-bewildering fact? I can only answer, that either there is no Creator, or this living society of men is in a true sense discarded from His presence . . . *if* there be a God, *since* there is a God, the human race is implicated in some terrible aboriginal calamity.

One might say that in Greene's novels that calamity goes on, a continuing evidence that men have been discarded from God's sight. Hence not only the 'seedy' texture of the novels, and the insistent violence, but also the tone of horror and disgust, a tone which seems to be in excess of the circumstances; for the most important fact about Greene's world is that God has abandoned it, and that fact cannot be represented as a part of the world, but only as an emotion about it. There is, therefore, a correlation between the banality and ugliness of this world and the spiritual emptiness of it, and this correlation is most powerful and emotionally affective when it appears simply as legend—that is in the 'entertainments'.

Greene might perhaps protest that this view of his novels assumes them to be all of a piece, and makes no allowance for differences among them, or for development. One might of course divide the novels into categories—the English novels and the Tropical or Equatorial novels—or into periods—the prewar novels and the postwar novels; and one might note in the later work a creeping benevolence, rising to the comical résumé of his entire career, revisited in the company of his Muse, a raffish old Catholic lady, in *Travels with my Aunt*. But Greene remains a novelist in whom the changes are minor, and the unity overwhelming; the locales of his novels may change, but the imagination has remained a constant from the beginning.

Greene's own theories of the shaping of his mind confirm this reading of his work, for he has always stressed the formative influences of early experience, and the continuity of consciousness. One form of this theory is what Greene calls the 'Judas Complex'—the idea that the cruelties and betrayals of adult lives are born in childhood, that guilts are rooted in innocence. The theory appears in Greene's autobiographical essay, 'The Lost Childhood', where it is epitomized in a quotation from a poem by A. E.:

In the lost boyhood of Judas
Christ was betrayed.

The same theme (with the same quotation) also appears in the story 'The Basement Room', and in a less sombre form it is a principal thesis of *A Sort of Life*, which begins: 'If I had known it, the whole future must have lain all the time along those Berkhamsted streets.'

A curious sub-heading of this theory of childhood is Greene's insistence on the importance of one's early reading. 'Perhaps it is only in childhood that books have any deep influence on our lives', he writes in 'The Lost Childhood', and *A Sort of Life* repeats the thought: 'The influence of early books is profound.' Greene has always been fond of returning to those early books—to Rider Haggard and Anthony Hope and Marjorie Bowen—and has repeatedly testified to their influence on his own work. 'One's life is more formed, I sometimes think, by books than by human beings', he has his character Pulling think in *Travels with my Aunt*; 'it is out of books one learns about love and pain at second hand.'

Greene seems to find comfort in the thought that life is all embryonically there in childhood, and that the images found innocently and accidentally in one's first reading become the defining images of one's vision of experience. As a theory of human psychology this seems very dubious, but as a theory of Greene's own imagination it is revealing. When he says in his essay on the young Dickens that 'the creative writer perceives his world once and for all in childhood and adolescence', Greene is making at most a generalization about his *kind* of writer, and identifying the psychic sources of his own legends, of the hunted man and the peaceful man and the man who has suffered injustice; like Dickens, he has found the images of childhood fears that are never outgrown.

The implications of this theory for Greene's novels are considerable. For one thing, the theory implies a rather special view of character—that it is our origins, and not events, that shape us. 'How little in truth are we changed by events', he writes; 'how romantic and false . . . is a book such as Conrad's *Lord Jim*.' His characters have hearts, not histories (how hollow the psychological explanation of Pinky's evil rings), and the significant changes in his novels are changes of heart. Events can only kill or cure, they cannot save. Plot, therefore, is at best a conventional legendary frame; as Querry says: 'The subject of a novel is not the plot. Who remembers what happened to Lucien de Rubempré in the end?' If neither character nor plot matters, then what does? One is tempted to reply, *souls* do, the shapes and meanings of the religious sense do, changes of heart do, though such a reply seems to return Greene to the simplifications of his co-religionists.

It is consistent with Greene's theory of the imagination that his autobiography should break off in 1932, with the publication of his first success, *Stamboul Train*. For by then the writer had been formed, and the images stored: there was nothing left but the living and the writing. *A Sort of Life* has the virtue of good autobiography: it is frank, honest, and entertaining. As an account of a Georgian boyhood and youth it has value quite apart from the importance of its subject—though one must add that it seems a bit heavier on fear and weakness than your ordinary Georgian boyhood. As a personal record, it adds little that is surprising to what Greene has already written about himself, but it does make his early life rather less melodramatic, by filling in the spaces between the suicide attempts and the Russian roulette. It provides some particular sources for fictional episodes, and it reinforces Greene's theories about the relations between art and life—that is to say between *his* art and *his* life.

Another kind of autobiography emerges from the introductions to the new Collected Edition: the life of Greene-the-Adventurer and Greene-the-Professional, travelling to Sierra Leone, Cuba, and Tabasco, writing his novels, and sometimes judging them. It is interesting to note, after all these years in which Greene has fought against the influence of Conrad, that his introductions are very like Conrad's, and not at all like James's; they are personal and anecdotal, and focus on the occasions of the novels rather than on the creating mind. It is an engrossing story, but the introductions are minor and supplementary, far less important to an understanding of Greene than a few of his essays are. Still, one is glad to have a handsome new edition of the novels to replace Heinemann's old Library Edition, for which the only proper adjective was 'seedy'.

But most of all, the Collected Edition is important as a monument to a major English novelist's achievement. Greene has done what he aimed to do—he has expressed a religious sense, and created a fictive world in which human acts are important. In that world, at least, creative art is a function of the religious mind; Greene would have it that this is always so. His art is perhaps little comfort to the religious, for it offers no confirmation of comfortable words, and if it celebrates, it celebrates minimal virtues. But art has other things to do besides comforting and celebrating; it can feed our imaginative lives by insisting that the religious sense exists, in this world, in Brighton and Tabasco and Indo-China. No one has done that better in fiction than Graham Greene.

# 12

# SARTRE'S FLAUBERT

ON PAGE 96 of Volume 1 of *L'Idiot de la famille*, Jean-Paul Sartre cites a recollection of Flaubert. Some ten years ago, reported the novelist, his father, Achille-Cléophas Flaubert, paid a short visit to a former mistress in Le Havre. Mme Flaubert and the three children waited for him 'à pied dans la rue'. Flaubert concludes this brief anecdote by remarking that his mother felt neither jealous nor in any way spited. This account, says Sartre, calls for some commentary. If Mme Flaubert took matters so calmly, it must be that they were 'customary' and that this *femme-enfant* had been bent to the will of the paterfamilias by a constant routine of submission.

Caroline Flaubert, née Fleuriot, was 'an incarnation of unconditional acquiescence', a child-wife whose pliancy before the 'médecin-philosophe', her husband, made of her less a wife than an 'incestuous daughter'. In 'cohabitation' with her spouse she knew orgasm only via maternal, procreative virtue ('elle jouissait par vertu maternelle'). But seven years of conjugal acquiescence take their toll. Instinctual repressions, unspoken griefs, gagged feelings, produce madness or resentments pitched almost to the point of insanity. The exact parallel, proclaims Sartre, is that of Stalinism and 'de-Stalinization'. Caroline Flaubert has lived seven years of 'stalinisme privé'; the chief surgeon in Rouen has 'une épouse stalinienne'. How else could she and her three offspring have stood waiting in the street—the wait has become 'une longue attente' and it now takes place 'au beau milieu de la rue'—while Achille-Cléophas is upstairs 'rejoining his youth and shedding tears of self-solace'?

Thus the woman who engenders Gustave Flaubert is already 'self-amputated' and *cantonnée* (the current jargon is 'encapsulated') in the absolute essence of the husband. A wife 'par vocation' she had become merely a dutiful mother. She does not babble to baby

---

JEAN-PAUL SARTRE: *L'Idiot de la famille: Gustave Flaubert de 1821–1857*. Volume 1. 1,104 pp. Volume 2. pp. 1,107–2,136. Paris: Gallimard. 110 fr. the set.

Gustave. His nappies are changed deftly but without waste, cherishing motion. The infant finds it difficult to understand 'l'altérité', the 'otherness' of a fragmented objective world. He has made no discovery of self as 'supreme object'. Though well fed and scrupulously cleaned, the baby encounters the world in that bleak and cold substantiality which 'Heidegger has called "nurvorbeilagen" '. He will suck at his mother's breast, *bien sûr*, to the last drop; he is never left hungry. But this very plenitude robs baby Gustave of the chance to impinge actively on reality: he will not be allowed 'de rompre par la révolte le cercle magique de la passivité'.

His attitudes toward *l'Autre* will be 'pathétique'. Pure receptivity ensues in those infants who have not, through their mother's conduct, been compelled to grapple actively with the otherness of the world. Gustave will learn to communicate only haltingly and late because the efficacious but somehow reified, self-alienated care of his mother have given him neither the need nor occasion to do so. In this Heideggerian greyness occurs the all-determining crisis of 'non-valorisation' (baby Gustave arrives at no ontological 'valuation' of his own life, he has been given no unambiguous 'mandate to be'). Unlike the child whom an epiphany of parental love ('une grâce d'amour') impels toward self-realization, Flaubert's daily existence ('temporalisation quotidienne') will have no 'teleological urgency'. From birth, the younger son of Caroline Flaubert is 'deprived of the cardinal categories of *praxis*'. The concerted striving of men will signify no more to him than a 'vain *frisson* on the surface of a dead world'. The only exceptions will be images or impulses of destruction: sadism is a mode of action, perhaps the only mode against 'la Volonté Autre'. Mme Flaubert ought not to have been left waiting 'au beau milieu de la rue'.

But was she? The only source is a casual reminiscence of Flaubert, who, on such points, was often less than precise. Do we know anything of the duration of the alleged rendezvous or of Flaubert senior's conduct (the tears, the quest for lost youth)? Do we have any evidence whatever about the nappying of baby Gustave, about whether or not Mme Flaubert smiled or merely pursed her lips during breast-feeding? Has this prolix edifice of solemn insight any verifiable basis? To all these questions, the answer, of course, is 'No'. But Sartre goes even further. The whole account and analysis (we are on page 139) 'is a fable'. I can imagine, says M. Sartre, that the facts were the exact opposite to those I have *invented*. No matter.

Whatever the true circumstances of the case, and they are presumably irretrievable, the diagnostic terrain, the framework of aetiology, will have to be that of 'the body, and of love'. The first weeks of Gustave Flaubert's psychosomatic existence will determine the fabric of his life. Indeed, says Sartre, in this 'trans-Freudian', Heideggerian attempt to grasp the total phenomenology ('phenomenality') of a human being—'que peut-on savoir d'un homme ?'—our investigation should begin at the pre-natal stage. It is regrettable that we know so little of Gustave's intra-uterine experiences.

On a dark evening in January, 1844, returning from Deauville with brother Achille, Gustave, who was driving the carriage, suddenly let loose the reins and fell down. Taken to a nearby farmhouse, he rapidly recovered from his 'cataleptic' state. The incident is well known to students of Flaubert. Sartre's diagnosis covers about 120 pages; yet even this treatment is characterized as 'merely preliminary'. Gustave's momentary 'falling sickness' represents 'l'option névrotique'. No exhaustive conceptual determination of this 'option' is possible; the levels of 'intentionality' are too manifold and infinitely regressive. Nevertheless, successive levels of explanation are forthcoming. Between the darkness outside (it is a winter evening in Normandy) and the darkness 'within', a tense reciprocity prevails. Gustave experiences the job of driving the horse-carriage as one of 'forced labour' entailing the suffocating totality of his bourgeois future. 'But the night resists' and offers a counterpoise, at once menacing and liberating, to the banal, solar future 'concretized' in Flaubert *père* and in his successor-elect, older brother Achille, the high-flyer, the medical man. Though dialectically interactive, the outward and internal darkness are not the same: 'la nuit du dedans est une médiation pithiatique de la *déchéance* au lieu que celle du dehors est un offre de *mort*'. Gustave's fit signifies, at one introductory level, a refusal of the daylit realities of career and *embourgeoisement* postulated by his family and milieu. His gesture is, however, a premonitory signal ('pithiatisme') rather than a reality. Only quotation will illustrate Sartre's analysis:

Il faut se rappeler que le rapport de l'intention téléologique à la fin qui la définit, chez un agent pratique, se caractérise comme *transcendance*, c'est l'être-hors-de-soi fondamental qui tire sa qualification d'un avenir où il s'engloutira en le réalisant; en même temps, ce rapport est *distanciation*, on la remet à plus tard et ce renvoi est constitutif de l'intention: c'est la position du non-être à réaliser comme terme *médié* d'une temporalisation orientée.

But let us not simplify matters. Gustave's fall involves the intricate aggregate of his conscious and subconscious fraternity. Brother Achille *might* have been driving, in which case 'the internalization of objective structures' would have been radically different. The ontological structure of a fall, moreover, refers us to the metaphysical category of 'negative verticality'. To fall from a driver's seat is to attain a supine state, a posture of quintessential passivity. Beyond the uncertainties of human demise lies the guaranteed finality of the fallen stone. The accident on the Deauville road stems from a symbolic pursuit of petrification: 'Chute et minéralisation ne font qu'un.' What the 'family idiot' has done in January, 1844, is to 'choose his own death'. The choice is a passive one—hence the element of trance, of conscious inertness—but it embodies the resolve 'to live minimally' and to counter the demands of a detested world with a strategy of stasis. Yet even this level of diagnosis does not take us far enough. The carriage accident at Pont-l'Evêque (a telling name) is a symbolic analogue to that earlier fall on the road to Damascus. We are dealing with a conversion 'instantaneous, overwhelming and long-prepared'. By 'willing' his fall, by acquiescing in 'negative verticality', Gustave espouses an invalid condition, an *aliénation* from the requirements and spaces of normal life (medicine, the law). At the price of literal 'downfall'—he lies momentarily at his brother's feet—Gustave secures for himself that economic backing, that long life of invalid ease ('l'infrastructure inerte de son immuabilité') which will make possible the unhurried generation of his art. From his driver's seat Gustave 'falls head-first into property'. He passes through death into the life-in-death of his obsessive vocation.

The foundations for this exegetic flight are again meagre. There is some doubt about the exact date in January of Gustave's seizure. The medical men in the family appear to have treated it fairly lightly, regarding it as a manifestation of hypertension or as a sort of 'false epileptic' attack. There were to be further fits, more or less severe, during the next ten years of the novelist's life. It was not immediately after the event, but only in 1852 that Flaubert, characteristically embroidering, spoke of himself as having given every semblance of death for at least ten minutes. At the time, he wrote to Ernest Chevalier: 'J'ai manqué péter dans les mains de ma famille . . .' Sartre reverts a dozen times to this sentence; he finds in it evidence for Flaubert's experience and consciousness of near-death. But will it sustain this weight of meaning? In fact, the expression is coarsely idiomatic and typical of Flaubert's private parlance. Today one might write 'j'ai manqué crever' (via the image of a rifle exploding in one's hands the one word was already shading into the other in the mid-nineteenth century). Having been bled on his return home, that is just what Flaubert would say. The inference of ontological gravity, of an 'aperception de la mort', is highly inflationary. So is the notion that the twenty-three-year-old *frère cadet* had already fixed, even subconsciously, on a programme of valetudinarian ease. Sartre registers this objection but regards it as ill-founded. The parasitic strategy, the choice of economically buttressed isolation ('un engagement de séquestration') was inherent in Flaubert's condition literally from the moment of conception onward.

Pulling all symbolic strands together, Sartre concludes that Gustave's fit at Pont-l'Evêque was no less than a sub-conscious enactment of parricide. 'The father has slain the son whose death has killed the father.' Henceforth every work by Gustave will have the task of 'renewing imaginatively the initial crisis, i.e., the Passion of the son and the murder of the father'. Like authentic suicides, the mimed suicide of January, 1844, was a thinly-disguised murder. But have we 'dans ce premier examen' (page 1910) come anywhere near exhausting the meanings of the incident? We shall be returning to it often, and notably with reference to the writing of 'St Julien' in 1875. That should be on about page 4000.

How is one to give any general account of these first 2,100 pages? *L'Idiot de la famille* is almost illegible physically. Gallimard, who, one conjectures, received the great man's opus *la mort au coeur*, have produced a stifling page, poorly inked and murderous to the eye. Sartre writes in mastodontic paragraphs. With a regularity which is infuriating, characteristically French, and which renders the vast apparatus of theoretic solemnity even more suspect, the appearance of a foreign name or idiom signals massacre. Poor Enid Sterkie, wretched Cottfried Benn. A new movement in art emerges: *l'act-painting*, and so on. These two lumbering tomes breathe the melancholy conviction that no one, including proof-readers, will ever do more than skim them or quarry for modish bits (what reviews have appeared so far in the general press in France pay an all-too-manifest tribute to the brevity of human life and the excellence of the blurb).

Yet a number of coherent themes do unfold or, more exactly,

they can be pieced together from this formidably opaque mosiac. Perhaps 'mosaic' isn't right either (one finds oneself writing like Sartre): imagine a spiral wound within a spiral, but key bits of which have fallen into the centre where they form a dense tangle.

The external armature, as it were, is a socio-psychological investigation of the bourgeois family. Though there are occasional and oddly superficial forays into the actual circumstances of provincial bourgeois mores and beliefs in the 1830s and 1840s, Sartre's focus is more abstract. What he is after is a typology of bourgeois life crystallized in the structure—at once objective and symbolic—of family relations. This structure determines or 'over-determines' (*sur-détermination* is a key term) the psychic dispositions of the individual. 'To be Gustave Flaubert' is to be the younger son of a senior medical officer at the Hôtel-Dieu in Rouen, whose brother Achille is, in turn, 'determined' by his status as first-born, and so forth in a formally unbounded regression of social, economic, conventional particularity.

This exhaustive mapping could apply to *any* child engendered under comparable biosociological conditions. This, in large measure, is Sartre's point. The 'fact of Flaubert' is methodologically contingent, almost distorting. Yet, simultaneously, the aim of gnosis which Sartre has set himself—'que peut-on savoir d'un homme?'—calls for analytic specificity. At the last the *données* must add up to produce, to localize diacritically, one Gustave Flaubert. What necessarily emerges from reconstructive intellection, says Sartre, is the insight 'that a man is never an individual', but rather 'un universal singulier: totalisé et, par là même, universalisé par son époque, il la retotalise en se reproduisant en elle comme singularité'. This is a very important idea, as is the correlative notion that the study of a man's life demands a simultaneous study of 'singular' and 'universal'. As Sartre himself acknowledges, it is not certain whether the methodological and substantive means for so total a 'science of man' or, more properly, 'science of a man' exist.

The realities of Flaubert's birth and infancy make for 'passive activity'. The great ennui, which underlies so much of the genius and barbaric potential of the nineteenth century, is the natural context of Gustave's nascent perceptions. As there has been no 'valorisation' of the self (Sartre is being thoroughly Eriksonian at this point), Gustave stands in a relation of dubiety or estrangement towards his own Ego ('la réalité même de son Moi lui demeure étrangère').

Henceforth, when he says 'I', Flaubert 'is never sincere, he plays a game, he manipulates'. This void at the centre and the angst which it entails will determine the decisive postures of Flaubert's sensibility: his horror of paternity, his masturbatory preferences, the precautionary, sequestered style of existence at Croisset. Above all, it will shape his attitude toward language. Emanating from him (from his 'moindre-être' and 'non-valeur') words will lack reality; yet in so far as they are external to him, as they possess undoubted public energies and authority, they will take on a fantastic autonomous substance. Flaubert's style (not that Sartre touches on it except with anticipatory obliqueness in these opening volumes) will result from a dialectical motion between subjective doubt or passivity and a compulsive reification of the word as object.

Baby Gustave's relations to his mother have robbed him of 'affirmative power' and corrupted his relations with the Logos ('ses rapports au Verbe et à la vérité'). The younger son's relations with his father have taken from him the sense of reality. There is only one possible exit from this psychic trap: in order to 'become real' the boy must 'become another'. By trying to be an actor and then a writer, young Gustave projects himself outward into a reality whose very 'outsideness' is a guarantor of his own being. Sartre's formulation is obscure but crucial: 'Il s'offre autre à un témoin qui n'est autre que lui-même; en d'autres termes il s'incorpore à la matérialité du graphème, et à défaut de réalité, il se donnera la pesanteur matérielle en se faisant objet autre à ses propres yeux.' Flaubert writes for a reader who is his own self in its sole incarnate reality. Hence the famous obsessive character of Flaubert's later *métier*, the need to make of language a total 'counter-creation' in the absence of which the Ego would remain vacant and the world an intolerable *altérité*.

In the course of 1839, Flaubert makes the key discovery that his business lies not with poetry and inspiration, but with art and will. He is the first, says Sartre, to grasp the ontological implications of 'artisanship'. The poem, and the romantic poem in particular, is the enactment of the self; the work of art, as Flaubert will define it, absorbs the Ego as one of its almost technical constituents. The subjectivity of the creator may be discerned in the finished work, but that work does not translate or manifest it. From this model of impersonality it is only a short logical step to the concept of art as an absolute, as an autonomous concentrate of form which does not serve men but is served by them. Genius becomes will or, as Buffon had put it, 'une longue patience' (a long patience, a long suffering).

The work of the true artist is quintessentially *critical*; it takes place against life, against the contingencies and disorders of the living ('contre le vécu'). Language is most decidedly contrapuntal to life when it seeks to invest with objective, grammatical forms those realities of sensuous experience which are, initially, most subjective and least communicable. The written sentence not only 'ingests' the multitudinous aspects of taste, sound, light, touch, somatic perception, but gives them an intensity greater than any they possess 'in reality'. Baudelaire to a lesser degree, Flaubert with complete methodological awareness, create 'une antiphysis du langage', a verbal semiology capable of conveying 'ces sur-communications silencieuses qui ne transmettent aucune signification conceptuelle'. (Indebted to Husserl, Heidegger and Jacques Derrida, Sartre's idiom is, throughout this vital phase of the argument, nearly untranslatable.) Style must atomize reality before it can become a surrogate for it and, ultimately, a creator of worlds more coherent, more ramified than 'the world' because in them the 'unsayable' can be expressed and apprehended, 'Le style transmet l'indisable par l'irréalisation du langage.' This tactic makes of Flaubert the true begetter of modern literature and the novelist whose work 'embodies all the literary problems of today'.

Stemming from the failure of Flaubert's voluminous juvenilia and from the prophetic strengths of 'Novembre', these insights, obscurely realized, and the need to escape from the vertigo of ennui—albeit by entering into, by appropriating that vertigo—have taken 'the idiot of the family' to the threshold of *Madame Bovary*. (In fact, Sartre's treatment is by no means chronological. The bulk of these first 2,000 pages is concerned with Gustave's family milieu, infancy and early adolescence. The other period treated in some detail goes from 1838 to 1845. Nothing is said, for instance, of the crucial phase immediately preceding the beginning of the composition of *Madame Bovary*.)

There are few clearings along the taxing way, few vistas past the minute examination, often over a hundred pages or more, of some conjectural construct of attitude or juvenile piece of fiction—'L'Anneau du prieur', 'Smarh'—which even the most assiduous 'Flaubertians' have, until now, passed over lightly. Yet on occasion Sartre's genius allows itself free play. There is an aphorism about the difference between falsehood and insincerity: the latter abuses us by means of truth. An inspired footnote argues that Balzac and George Sand write during the night when sleep annihilates society, whereas Stendhal is a man of morning and, therefore, of the eighteenth century and its concordant view of art and polis. There is a summary but acute excursus on Flaubert and Kafka and a comparison between Flaubert's and Proust's doctrines of remembrance (Flaubert insists on the imaginary substance of memories, Proust on their intemporal reality). That life is but a tale told by an idiot, full of sound and fury, is not Shakespeare's last word, but it is Flaubert's; and Sartre says interesting things of the 'pre-cognitions' with which Flaubert reads *Macbeth* or reads Montaigne. But such breathing-spaces are few and there is, so far, no index for the *flâneur*.

Regrettably, the most significant thing about this book is why it should have been written at all. Why should Jean-Paul Sartre have given up the promised second volume of the *Critique de la raison dialectique*, why leave off at mid-point in his study of Tintoretto or not carry forward from the inspired beginnings of autobiography in *Les Mots*? Where is the treatise on ethics promised in *L'Etre et le Néant* (a damaging hiatus in the entirety of existentialism)? What can account for an obsessive immersion in Flaubert which has already absorbed ten years of work, three or four drafts, a complete revision in 1968–70, and which will probably demand years to come (Sartre speaks of two or more tomes yet to be completed)? Most of *Les Mots* seems to have existed in an early version and Sartre needed only three months in 1963 to prepare the text for publication. As he himself says, since *Les Séquestrés d'Altona* Flaubert has been his exclusive concern.

What is going on here?

Given Sartre's stature and the 'enormity' of the enterprise, it is unlikely that any single answer will do. The aim is to 'know a man, to determine the limits of such knowledge in a concrete instance—for example, Flaubert'. That *par exemple* is a wry figure of speech. Sartre has been involved with Gustave Flaubert from the time he first read him in childhood and re-read him closely at the Ecole Normale. He studied *L'Education sentimentale* during the 1930s, experiencing a sharp antipathy for the author 'who is himself at once sadist and masochist'. As early as 1943, Sartre seems to have resolved that he would one day do a book on Flaubert. The immediate instigation was his reading of the *Correspondance*. Like many before him, Sartre found in Flaubert's letters the most detailed, lucid record we have of the pathological condition of a human being whose centres of reality and 'lived life' are located in the written word. At the close of the chapter on existential psychoanalysis in *L'Etre et le Néant*, Sartre actually announces a future study of the author of *Madame Bovary*. His dislike of the man and of his style is undisguised in *Qu'est-ce que la littérature?* Flaubert's sentences, we are told, 'surround an object, seize it, immobilize it and break its backbone'. His determinism 'substitutes for human action the uniform responses of automata'.

Overtly Sartre did not concern himself with Flaubert again until 1954 when Roger Garaudy suggested a joint experiment in 'total biography' using, respectively, a Marxist and an existentialist methodology. Sartre chose Flaubert and had written roughly a thousand pages which he broke off in mid-1955. This incompletion, one of several, continued to preoccupy him until he plunged fully into the vast opus in 1960 or 1961. With hindsight, however, one can see the referential or hostile proximity of Flaubert to many of Sartre's key works. There is more than a hint of the *Trois Contes*, especially of 'Saint Julien', and also of the *Tentation de Saint Antoine* in *Le Diable et le Bon Dieu*; *Les Séquestrés d'Altona* is like a variant on Sartre's inquiry into the Flaubert household and into the novelist's self-banishment from the world; *Les Mots* takes on a new, compelling resonance when we see in it an attempt to differentiate the author's childhood from that of Flaubert and to determine his own 'word-pathology' in the light of Flaubert's *Correspondance*. As for the notion of 'total penetrative portrayal', it is already inherent in *Saint Genet* (so Flaubertian a title) and explicitly outlined in *Question de méthode*.

Though the term is germane, 'love-hatred' is far too crass a piece of shorthand to cover so complex and lasting an affinity. In a lengthy interview published in *Le Monde* (May 4, 1971), Sartre claims that Flaubert is thoroughly unlike him: 'Je l'ai choisi aussi parce que, précisément, il est loin de moi.' His childhood was the antithesis of Flaubert's: 'From this point of view, I am wholly the opposite of Flaubert. At bottom, I have it in for Caroline because I was well loved.' It is plain, nevertheless, that Sartre is radically implicated in Flaubert, that he is *using* the compelling hazard of Flaubert's existence to give to his own the complex visibility of an objective, opaquely resistant 'otherness'. Serge Doubrovsky puts it concisely:

Le voilà, *entier*: tous ses langages théoriques, rappelés du fond du passé, cohabitent et coexistent. Le penseur, vite rejoint par le moraliste, se ressoude au romancier; fausse homosexualité de Gustave, et *l'Enfance d'un chef* ressuscité; Roquentin se rattrape avec Flaubert de la biographie de Rollebon, abandonnée dans *la Nausée*. Ici une théorie de la lecture; là, de la névrose. Saynètes, sermons, boutades, formules lapidaires, philosophie politique, littérature, critique: trente ans d'écriture tournoyant comme un soleil. C'est tout Sartre.

But this is to over-simplify. The Sartre of *L'Idiot de la famille* writes *badly*. Though there are numerous patches of baroque verve and though there are pages instinct with a marvellous vehemence of thought, the production as a whole is turgid, wilfully repetitive and linguistically contorted. Why? Because, declares Sartre, 'I chose not to take pains . . . as to style, that belongs to Flaubert. . . . I wrote the book at a go, as it came. . . . Why take time to construct beautiful sentences?' There is, undoubtedly, a parodistic tactic at work here: the notion of writing badly about Flaubert, for whom beauty of language was the valid object of fanatical labour, is of itself an ironic, critical means of achieving distance.

But this intent of stylistic 'contrariety' would not account for the monstrous prolixity of Sartre's treatment, for a functional relation which, as one critic in France ventured to observe, sets one thousand lines of Sartre against ten of Flaubert. *Length* is a complicated psychological and formal category to which far too little attention is paid (the history of musical statement from Haydn to Mahler and Bruckner is, in essential ways, one of magnification). If Sartre carries on in the present exponential form, his commentary on *Madame Bovary* would run to three volumes each of about one thousand pages. One suspects that a certain element of scarcely controlled facility is involved, an ability, perhaps a need, to write incessantly, to turn the torrential pressure of thought and self-address into stable form (*Saint Genet* suffered from the same choking abundance).

Yet Sartre can be, as we know from *Les Mots*, a master of sparsity. The gigantism of this monograph points deeper. On the one hand, there is the pursuit—it has a maniacal stress—of 'totality', the proclaimed aim to circumscribe, to 'ingest' into reason, the entirety of Flaubert. It is Flaubert's vengeance on his self-elected anatomist that the very charge Sartre brought against the prose of *Madame Bovary*—the sentences are a boa-constrictor crushing life out of the object they enfold—can now be cited against Sartre himself. In a way which sometimes reminds one of Péguy (but lacking Péguy's unfailing ear and inner music), Sartre is using repetition, circularity, incantation to hammer his way nearer and nearer the truth, nearer and nearer the buried core of the matter. But on the other hand, he is using these massive instrumentalities in order to raze the terrain, to break clear. Paradoxically, there is a violent 'minimalism', a programmatic pursuit of emptiness in the dense torrent of Sartre's treatise. The violence of penetration, of appropriation through rational discourse is unmistakable and has a profoundly ambivalent effect, Sartre is 'finishing off' Flaubert, the bourgeoisie, the 'fausse situation' of the artist in the nineteenth century ('ces écrivains sont tous plus ou moins névrosés'). He will, literally, talk them to death.

But the stakes are, one feels, even higher. *Les Mots*, says Sartre, 'were a farewell to literature'. Today 'in any case, there is no more literature' (French syntax allows a gruffer dismissal: 'de toute façon, il n'y en a plus de littérature!'). All speech and writing, indeed all thought, is 'a material act' to be studied in part through historical materialism, in part through psychology. 'Creation' has no privileged zone, no apartness from the socio-biological configuration of man. Yet art and letters, in however vulnerable, 'consumerized' a vein, do continue to lead a distinct existence. They persist in generating mythologies of 'value-free' status. It is clear that Sartre loathes this factitiousness and its atavisms in his own sensibility. In 'ingesting' Flaubert—he himself compares such an endeavour at total knowledge with the omniscient psychology of God—he is probing at the stubborn roots of literature and language itself. Externalized, these will never again pretend to a mystery of transcendent worth.

Thus the parodistic intention reaches far beyond the provocative instance of Flaubert's style and *art pour art*. It seeks out the heart of the whole suspect enterprise of literature, of literary scholarship, of criticism. It would subvert no less than the whole, perhaps inhuman, perhaps lunatic, world of words about words, of language parasitic on language, in which Sartre grew up and of which he has been a troubled, increasingly self-contemptuous master. There is a terrible letter of A. E. Housman, though perhaps meant ironically, in which he writes to Arthur Platt: 'If you prefer Aeschylus to Manilius you are no true scholar; you must be deeply tainted with literature.' Housman loved Aeschylus above all other poets, and gave thirty years of his life to the aridities of Manilius. A comparable suicidal mock characterizes Sartre's long immersion in

Flaubert, a similar defence against the deeply felt but ultimately anarchic, spiritually and socially ambiguous solicitations of art.

Sartre must know that the only readers this work will reach, by virtue of its price and difficulty alone, are the very scholars, *littérateurs*, reviewers and bourgeois mandarins who make up the despised, spurious establishment of a waning culture. That culture has, however, proved far more resistant to political revolution, to the indictments of socialism, to idealistic corrosion, than Sartre himself had supposed. It is he who now stands *en fausse situation* between a middle-class civilization and high literacy which he despises but to which he ineluctably belongs, and a *gauchisme* which has long passed him by and to which these esoteric tomes will only be a vaguely insulting fossil. 'If I were fifty today', says Sartre, 'I would not begin this *Flaubert*'. The prodigal violence of the book suggests deep displeasures of self-consciousness.

And what of Gustave Flaubert, creator of *Madame Bovary* and *L'Education sentimentale*? So far he stands intact. The very mass of Sartre's knowledge falls ironically short of explaining how *this* neurotic, bored young man, this 'family idiot' suffocating in the mendacities of the mid-nineteenth-century bourgeois order, should have composed *Madame Bovary* and created the modern novel. There is, says Sartre, both utter defeat and total victory in that achievement. Until now, the weight of his diagnosis has borne almost exclusively on the logic of defeat. The 'quantum jump' to victory lies ahead. The question whether Jean-Paul Sartre, so bitterly wary of the concept of literature, so intransigent about the sham aspects of art, will be able to conceptualize the insolent wonder of Flaubert's actual creations, is as yet open. It is a question of more than bookish interest.

# 13

# *THE WASTE LAND* REVISITED

It is impossible to say just what I mean!
But as if a magic lantern threw the nerves in patterns on a screen . . .

THUS, with suddenly dishevelled desperation, speaks J. Alfred Prufrock at the end of the poem which T. S. Eliot gave to him under the sardonic description, 'Love Song'. And there is reason to think that this description by Prufrock of what it is like for him to speak may stand also as a description by Prufrock's creator of what it was like for him to make poems. That is to say, one may see—or read, or 'decode'—a poem by Eliot as if it were a kind of gridded pattern projected on to the world 'out there', by a magic lantern at the back of the poet's skull. In that case, the seemingly 'out there' in an Eliot poem is of no interest for its own sake, but merely as providing a screen on to which is projected the meshed design of the poet's sensibility, his 'nerves'.

Something like this seems to be what Eliot himself asked for more than once, and notably in a statement which Valerie Eliot places as a conspicuous epigraph to this long-awaited edition of *The Waste Land* drafts:

> Various critics have done me the honour to interpret the poem in terms of criticism of the contemporary world, have considered it, indeed, as an important bit of social criticism. To me it was only the relief of a personal and wholly insignificant grouse against life; it is just a piece of rhythmical grumbling.

This is a singularly ungracious communication, at once deprecating and impatiently arrogant. (As often when Eliot's tone is 'off', he speaks to us as *plus anglais que les Anglais.*) Yet Valerie Eliot is

---

T. S. ELIOT: *The Waste Land: A facsimile and transcript of the original drafts including the annotations of Ezra Pound.* Edited by Valerie Eliot. xxx plus 149 pp. Faber and Faber. £5.

probably right to force it on our attention, for it affords the only firm basis on which to defend *The Waste Land* against the attacks from two directions which are now levelled, often with startling virulence, against a poem that for so long was taken to be virtually above any criticism at all.

Our second thoughts about it have been all the more rancorous for being so long delayed; and the drafts will not allay the rancour—quite the contrary. Critics of the poem either contend that it gives an incomplete and perversely slanted account of the world 'out there' which it offers to deal with; or else they complain that the emotion which the poem expresses is 'immature' or 'unhealthy' or 'life-denying'. But Eliot seems to say that in his sort of poetry, as in J. Alfred Prufrock's sort of talking, on the one hand the world, the 'out there', is not being criticized nor accounted for at all; that, on the other hand, the emotion felt by the poet or the talker is equally 'insignificant'. The point of interest is neither the emotion felt and expressed, nor the 'out there' which appears (misleadingly) to provoke or to focus that emotion; the point of interest which determines the poem's structure is somewhere between the emotion and its apparent object or provocation—it is 'the nerves in patterns'.

What goes wrong when we take *The Waste Land* as a poem about the 'out there' may be illustrated from some recent comments by Ian Hamilton (in the symposium, *Eliot in Perspective*) about some lines near the opening of the poem:

> And when we were children, staying at the archduke's,
> My cousin's, he took me out on a sled,
> And I was frightened. He said, Marie,
> Marie, hold on tight. And down we went.
> In the mountains, there you feel free.
> I read, much of the night, and go south in the winter.

Mr. Hamilton asks us to conjure up, as the speaker of these lines,

> someone middle-aged, female, of cosmopolitan background, someone neurotically clinging to remembered fragments of childhood experience, someone anxious to assert her aristocratic origins ('the archduke's/My cousin's': an over-eager parenthesis), someone rather desperate and rather boring.

But these remarks, like the tediously many of late which go on about Eliot's alleged antisemitism, assume that this poem and others by him direct our attention on to the world that we experience in our daily encounters, in which every voice we hear is spoken by some person, that person socially conditioned and with some design upon us. But the voice of Countess Marie Larisch (who was a niece of the Empress of Austria and hence in fact a cousin of the Archduke) is a voice that sounds not in society, not even 'in the poet's head', but specifically in *a poem*, and in a poem which is haughtily indifferent to any society at all, whether that of London in 1920 or of Vienna before 1914.

Some of Ezra Pound's annotations suggest that he apprehended Eliot's devious and peculiar intention no better than Mr. Hamilton was to do. Marginal queries about Joyce and (more surprisingly) at one point about William Blake are among several which suggest that Pound saw Eliot doing for London what Joyce's *Ulysses* had done, in the more expansive and cumulative mode of prose, for the city of Dublin. We may wish that this indeed had been Eliot's intention; and certainly the excisions which Pound demanded have made *The Waste Land* far more a poem about London than it looked like being when in draft. Yet Eliot's imagination was, even so early, Virgilian rather than (like Joyce's and Pound's) Homeric. And the existence in draft of passages later excised make it quite clear that Eliot at no time was concerned to register the 'out there' of London and London life at a specific epoch. In particular the drafts begin with a very lame passage of 55 lines which seem to establish a squalidly Irish-American milieu. Instead of this, what we have in the final poem is the superbly taut passage of London pub-talk for which Eliot gave credit to Ellen Kellond, a maid in the Eliot household, though the drafts suggest that the first Mrs. Eliot deserves credit too.

Yet Eliot seems to have thought, when he sent the drafts to Pound, that there was room in the poem for that and for the Irish-American passage no less, as also for a passage about mishaps at sea off the New England coast. Moreover, on the same page of the draft as the London pub-scene there is a flurry of annotations by Pound against 'the closed carriage at four', asking whether this reference does not date the milieu as of 1880 rather than 1920; and this question Eliot ignores. A specific locality and a particular date were the last things he was concerned with. For the 'out there' was of interest to him only as a necessary screen on to which he might project something else.

And what was to be projected was not 'an emotion'. The clearest proof of this is another of the excisions suggested by Pound and accepted by Eliot—of more than 100 lines of pastiche heroic couplets.

To some reviewers Pound's objection to this has seemed conclusive. According to Eliot himself in his introduction to the *Selected Poems* of Pound in 1928, Pound had

> induced me to destroy what I thought an excellent set of couplets; for, said he, 'Pope has done this so well that you cannot do it better; and if you mean this as a burlesque, you had better suppress it, for you cannot parody Pope unless you can write better verse than Pope—and you can't.'

This is fair comment on the first 35 lines of the pastiche. For these, as Valerie Eliot points out, are a laborious imitation of *The Rape of the Lock*. (Some of them nevertheless Pound at one stage seems to have thought might be salvaged.) However, the pastiche later mounts to a greater intensity, to a point where the model seems to be no longer *The Rape of the Lock* but the more pungently colloquial Pope of the Moral Epistle, 'On the Characters of Women':

> Fresca! in other time or place had been
> A meek and lowly weeping Magdalene;
> More sinned against than sinning, bruised and marred,
> The lazy laughing Jenny of the bard.
> (The same eternal and consuming itch
> Can make martyr, or plain simple bitch);
> Or prudent sly domestic puss puss cat,
> Now autumn's favourite in a furnished flat,
> Or strolling slattern in a tawdry gown,
> A doorstep dunged by every dog in town.
> For varying forms, one definition's right;
> Unreal emotions, and real appetite.

If we take it for granted that these couplets would have been given a final polish before being printed, it is not unreasonable—though it is doubtless rash—to think that they measure up to their great original, and are not damned by the comparison which they presumptuously challenge. Moreover, there are places where Eliot moves out of Pope's range altogether and writes with a direct ferocity that recalls rather Swift's scatological poems or, more pertinently still, Dryden, in his memorable translation of Juvenal's Sixth Satire, 'On Women':

> This ended, to the steaming bath she moves,
> Her tresses fanned by little flutt'ring Loves;
> Odours, confected by the artful French,
> Disguise the good old hearty female stench.

The calculated slapdash of the four epithets in the last line strikes Dryden's tone quite magnificently.

These passages make it plain that those readers, from I. A. Richards to Randall Jarrell and beyond, who have seen the emotional impetus behind *The Waste Land* as hatred and fear of sex, will find their suspicions confirmed more completely than they could have hoped. But this certainly does not mean that this is the 'real' subject of the poem, that the drafts have revealed what the published poem has half-concealed all this while. For the excision of the eighteenth-century pastiche means that this emotion remains *behind* the poem, not in it. Undoubtedly this makes the poem more obscure; if we had in *The Waste Land* some of the couplets about Fresca, we should be better placed to know how to respond to Mrs. Porter and her daughter, to the typist who is seduced by the 'young man carbuncular', and to that sad wraith, the girl whom Highbury bore and Richmond and Kew undid:

> Trams and dusty trees.
> Highbury bore me. Richmond and Kew
> Undid me. By Richmond I raised my knees
> Supine on the floor of a narrow canoe.

And indeed one sequence of verses which appears in the drafts, perhaps every reader will regret not to find in the poem:

> Highbury bore me. Highbury's children
> Played under green trees and in the dusty Park.
> Mine were humble people and conservative
> As neither the rich nor the working class know.
> My father had a small business, somewhere in the city
> A small business, an anxious business, providing only
> The house in Highbury, and three weeks at Shanklin.

But the excision, which seems to have been made on Eliot's own initiative without prompting from Pound, is plainly justified in terms of the intended design, however lamentable in terms of humanity; Eliot does not want sympathy for any of his ruined women, he wants to arouse no sympathies at all, nor antipathies either, for in his poem there are no people, only voices.

And so it is more instructive to ask why Eliot agreed to suppress the couplets which hate women, than to inquire why Pound asked him to suppress them (if indeed Pound did). And the answer to that question should be clear: the emotion which prompted the poem was, as regards the final structure of the poem, 'insignificant'. We are to be directed by the poem not towards the state of mind of a man who hates and fears women, but towards the difference which that sort of obsession makes to a man's sensibility when it is directed on quite other matters, for instance on the recorded history of Western culture. The 'pattern of the nerves' is what we are concerned with; not with the emotional compulsion behind that pattern, any more than with the world in which the agent, thus compelled, may be required to act. Eliot was not Pound's puppet. He used, he exploited, the miraculously tuned literary sensibility that Pound then was. He used it; he was not used, nor manipulated, by it.

In any case, among the surprisingly many matters on which the 1970s are more squeamish and more mealy-mouthed than the 1920s (not to speak of earlier centuries), misogyny must figure large. In the post-Lawrentian, post-Freudian 1970s, the years of Women's Liberation, what should we have done with a poem which explicitly aligned itself with the ancient tradition of Juvenal and Dryden, Pope and Swift, the poems written by men against women, and against the sexual enslavement to which the mere fact of Woman condemns most men? It is the scandalous, the forbidden topic, the subject that *must not be entertained*, the thing that is unutterable. Yesterday it was sexual appetite, today it is sexual satiety. Fortunately Eliot, not in the least so as to save or pander to our susceptibilities but strictly for artistic reasons, chose not to present us with the challenge in his poem. If this publication of the drafts presents us with it, well and good—let us come to terms, as best we can, with the fact that the most influential English poem of our time was impelled by a hatred and fear (oh yes, that much we have learnt—hatred, and therefore fear) of woman as a sexual partner. It could be the occasion for a quite momentous clearing of our minds of cant.

Unfortunately, this will not happen, the occasion will not be seized—and this not because we are pusillanimous and muddle-headed on this issue, though doubtless we are, men and women alike. There is, so one understands, a testamentary disposition by the poet which prevents his widow from giving us, in her introduction, more than the baldest chronological record of the poet's relations with John Quinn, relations which culminated in the giving of these drafts to Quinn—with bibliographical consequences that were explained in the *TLS* (November 7, 1968) by Donald Gallup when the documents turned up in the possession of the New York Public Library.

However this may be, the end-result is disastrous. What was wrong with Eliot, that took him to a clinic in Lausanne where most of *The Waste Land* was written? More to the point, what was wrong with

Vivien Eliot, his English wife? Already there is one book, Roger Sencourt's *T. S. Eliot, a Memoir*, which appears to have ducked under the testamentary ban on biographical revelations; and there is no lack of hearsay and gossip, nor of persons who are ready to testify authoritatively on the basis of this word-of-mouth information. One sympathizes with Valerie Eliot in her predicament, unable to divulge information which would have decisively changed the picture. Nevertheless, the situation must be faced: that until the facts of Eliot's predicament are revealed, we have a picture of Pound and Quinn being sponged upon quite shamelessly, by whining hypochondriacs—Joyce on the one hand, Eliot on the other. And until the facts can be divulged, this image will persist, giving every handle to those who want to discredit Eliot as poet to discredit him first as a man and as a friend.

The poetry, we like to say, speaks for itself. But it can do so only when what it speaks can no longer give offence. Eliot's poetry gives offence to many people—as it seems, to more and more as the years go by. And so long as it continues to offend, those who are offended by it will continue to take cover behind the confessedly partial and partisan reticence of the biographical record. What is there to hide? Whatever it is, it cannot be worse than what is commonly alleged in whispers. Eliot the poet cannot challenge and disconcert us as he should, until Eliot the man is made to emerge from the shadows amid which he concealed himself. In the meanwhile, the publication of this finely produced and meticulously edited facsimile does not reveal, as many have thought and still think, a poet slavishly dependent on the good opinion of his chosen master, but on the contrary a poet who knows the peculiar thing he has vowed himself to do, and who will not be diverted from that objective.

*Letters arising out of this review were printed in* T.L.S. *on December 17 and 31, 1971 and throughout January 1972.*

# 14

# POETRY OF 1971

## (*a*) TED HUGHES

### *Crow*

AFTER *Lupercal*, Ted Hughes's bestiary seemed to be complete, and there was much wondering at the time (though more in private than in print) about where this gifted poet would go next. Beastless, would Hughes allow the fevered, apocalyptic rhetoric that had been ominously omnipresent in his first book, *A Hawk in the Rain*, to reassert itself, or would he try to develop the naive, generalizing commentaries on human conduct ('With man it is otherwise') that were inserted here and there in *Lupercal*? The justified suspicion was that, in a period of tame, chatty, effortfully rationalistic verse, it was rather easy to overrate a poet who possessed even the beginnings of linguistic vigour; to mistake, in Hughes's case, a souped-up, ripplingly muscular neo-Georgianism for something much more wise and novel than it really was.

At the same time, though, there was a general unwillingness among critics and reviewers to blur the advent of 'a poet of the first importance' (A. Alvarez) by making too much of such qualms; for example, by examining too closely the considerable discrepancy between the delicacy of Hughes's eye and the crudity of most of his ideas; by pointing out, in short, that if this poet were to apply to

---

(*a*) TED HUGHES: *Crow*. 80 pp. Faber and Faber. £1.

(*b*) GEOFFREY HILL: *Mercian Hymns*. Unnumbered pages. André Deutsch. £1.75 (paperback, £1).

(*c*) THOM GUNN: *Moly*. 55 pp. Faber and Faber. £1.

(*d*) JOHN WIENERS: *Nerves*. Unnumbered pages. Cape Goliard, £1.50.

JAMES DICKEY: *The Eye-Beaters, Blood, Victory, Madness, Buckhead and Mercy*. 63 pp. Hamish Hamilton. £1.25.

RICHARD WILBUR: *Walking to Sleep*. 79 pp. Faber and Faber. £1.50.

(*e*) STEPHEN SPENDER: *The Generous Days*. 47 pp. Faber and Faber. £1.

(*f*) SYLVIA PLATH: *Crossing the Water*. 64 pp. £1.25. *Winter Trees* 55 pp. £1. Faber and Faber.

human beings even a fraction of the fond exactitude he brought to bear on animal behaviour he would not find it possible to deal, as in *Lupercal* he almost exclusively did deal, in cartoons rather than in characters (the pimply clerk, the Mafeking Colonel, the prize village boozer, and so on)—cartoons employed, moreover, to support a vague, simple-mindedly asserted preference for the primitive, the brutal and the sudden, as against (need one bother to trot out the hoary antitheses?) the cerebral, the sophisticated, the hesitant.

The absence from Hughes's work of any complex or subtle human personality continued to be worrying throughout the ambiguously aimed *Earth-Owl and Other Moon People* and the somewhat thrown-together package of stories, drama and verse entitled *Wodwo*. In both books, Hughes's gift for fierce and thrilling natural observations was intermittently in evidence, but so too were his most striking faults; the flailingly portentous verbiage, the indulged relish for the violent and the painful, the deep authorial evasiveness, the skimped and shallow dealings with the human world, and so on. The problem of not having any more animals to write about he sinisterly solved by, quite simply, inventing imaginary ones or (in 'Second Glance at a Jaguar') revamping an old favourite. The horrific nursery frieze assembled in *Earth-Owl* was not just a marginal departure; it was a sketch of things to come, and the bursts of Gothickry that kept cropping up in *Wodwo* confirmed that intimation, suggesting as they did that Hughes—far from looking for a way of directing his linguistic gifts back to the human world (where, admittedly, they would need to have been refined, made more tentative, less self-admiring)—was indeed seeking an area in which those gifts could be exercised even more randomly than hitherto. He was seeking, in short, a territory and a device which would enable him to unload his obsessions without requiring that he test them out, in any precise way, against reality.

The device and territory of *Crow* are perfectly chosen for this purpose. Crow's naturalistic presence, so far as he has one, allows some scope for Hughes's old bestiarizing gifts; his theological presence—he is simultaneously God's partner, God's victim, God's godless Man—is vague and immense enough to permit unlimited portentousness; his human stance—tough, sardonic, blood-soaked, I've-seen-it-all-but-I'm-still-here—is so deliberately (and fashionably) cartoon-like for it to seem soppy to complain that it is wholly superficial.

The world that Crow moves in and is an emblem for, is drenched in blood, racked with agony, devastated by numerous varieties of violence; he views it with an eye proprietorial, laconically appalled yet also sadistically gratified. Standing for nothing, he can stand for anything, and moves effortlessly from God's right hand, through the Garden of Eden, to battlefields and blacknesses both old and new. The agent of evil or the principle of enduring, suffering humanity; the villain or the victim? Well, both of course, for are they separable? Once this malleable symbolic function has been grasped, the reader can settle down to enjoy the creature's grisly travels; enjoy, indeed, a cosy, unperplexing wallow.

The majority of the poems in *Crow* are built on the catalogue, and sometimes the crescendo, principle; the formula is simple and utterly hospitable. Take a phrase, like, for example: 'Black was the . . .' and invent resonant attachments to it. 'Black was the heart/Black the liver', 'Black the blood in its loud tunnel', 'Black the bowels packed in furnace/Black, too, the muscles'. When the human anatomy is exhausted, move on to abundant Mother Nature: 'Black is the rock', 'Black is the wet otter's head'. Another method is the question and answer session, with either question or answer remaining constant throughout:

> Who owns these scrawny little feet?
>   *Death*
> Who owns this bristly scorched-looking face?
>   *Death*
> Who owns these still-working lungs?
>   *Death*
> Who owns this utility coat of muscles?
>   *Death.*
> Who owns these unspeakable guts?
>   *Death.*

—or—

> Where is the Black Beast?
> Crow, like an owl, swivelled his head.
> Where is the Black Beast?
> Crow hid in its bed, to ambush it.

Or, more sophisticated, there is the 'When the . . . then the' strategy:

> When the owl sailed clear of tomorrow's conscience
> And the sparrow preened himself of yesterday's promises
> And the heron laboured clear of the Bessemer upglare
> And the bluetit zipped clear of lace panties
> And the woodpecker drummed clear of the rotovator and the rose farm
> And the peewit tumbled clear of the laundromat

When the bullfinch plumped in the apple bud
And the goldfinch bulbed in the sun
And the wryneck crooked in the moon
And the dipper peered from the dewball
Crow spraddled headdown in the beach-garbage, guzzling a dropped ice cream.

What these techniques have in common is that they grant total licence to the poet's freewheeling inventiveness; when he runs out of ingredients, the cake is baked. It is true to say of Hughes's list-poems in this book that each of them could be half-a-dozen lines shorter or half-a-dozen lines longer without being seriously damaged or enhanced; the formula depends on a mechanical, drugging repetition, and the last thing we are asked to do is respond to or examine the relevance and accuracy of individual components. Similarly, we need not look for any rhythmic subtlety, nor any pondered or incisive line-breaks; the liturgical scaffolding takes care of all that.

Just as we are not invited to make severe formal or rhythmic demands of these poems, similarly much of the actual language hardly bears examination. By employing rigid structural formulas and by making the most of Crow's own deflatingly ironic disposition (though how cumbersome so many of his ironies in fact are), Hughes manages to contain some of his rhetorical belligerence, but there can be no disguising the fact that the central energies of this book are, in their eager pursuit of blood and thunder, only minimally tempered by poetic caution—that caution which insists on trying to connect words to their full meanings. Take, as a sample of the book's bludgeoning behaviour, this (not exhaustive) list of blood-images and ask yourself if their progenitor need ever have seen anybody bleed; not, admittedly, a clinching test but one well worth applying to a work which has been credited with affording us *new* insights into our bloody selves: 'God bled, but with men's blood'; 'Blood blasts from the crown of his head in a column'; 'Blood was too like water'; 'Shock-severed eyes watched blood/Squandering as from a drain-pipe/Into the blanks between stars'; 'Screaming for Blood'; 'All this messy blood'; 'Black is the gall lying on the bed of the blood'; 'As he drowned in his own blood'; 'Blood her breasts her palms her brow all wept blood'; 'He stands trousered in blood and log-splits/The lolling body, bifurcates it/Top to bottom, kicks away the entrails—/Steps out of the blood-wallow'; 'His wife and children lie in their blood'; 'The suddenly dropped, heavily dropped/Star of blood on the fat leaf'; 'Drinking Beowulf's blood, and wrapped in his hide'; 'Smiles that went off with a mouthful of blood'; 'The pavement and the air and the light/Confined all the jumping blood/No better than a paper bag'.

One could compile a similar, similarly oppressive and similarly undisturbing, list involving Death or Disease (facile play with 'tattered guts', 'shattered brains' and 'death's mouldy tits' abounds), and one could point also the book's key violent-verbs—stabbing, smashing, screaming, writhing, and so on. The measure of the sensibility behind the language is to be discovered in the way most of these words are mechanically chucked in, lazily relished, insultingly (to actual suffering) exploited.

One of the most significant poems in *Crow* is called 'Lovesong'; the described lovers are vampiric, gluttonous, destructive, bent on a brutal, absolute possession of each other. The significance of the poem is not in the black view it takes of human love (though this, as we have seen, is hardly insignificant), but in the way it (gluttonously, vampirically) piles blackness upon blackness, the way it seems—after the first dozen lines or so—to have moved far beyond any real gravity or wisdom into a horror-comic realm of barely controllable fascination with its own subject-matter. An important quality for poets is knowing exactly where to stop; this poem, like so many others in this book, not only doesn't know but doesn't care. It flogs on until it's drained, replete.

## (*b*) GEOFFREY HILL

### *Mercian Hymns*

SEEKING TO NUDGE ITS WAY out of the diminishing circle of direct personal experience, English poetry seems to have taken a recent turn towards myth, folk-tale and legend. We have had Thom Gunn's *Moly*, Stuart Montgomery's *Circe*, Patrick Creagh's *To Abel and others*, Christopher Logue's experiments with Homer and, in rather different vein, Jon Silkin's recent reflections on a nineteenth-century Durham mining settlement; and now we have Mercian legends from Geoffrey Hill.

'Myth' and 'legend', loose and largely intertwined as the terms are, suggest rather different emphases. Examining modern experience through myth, in the case of poets like Gunn, Creagh and Montgomery, takes the form of timeless universalizations through symbol and archetype; 'legend' works in an opposite direction, excavating the specific substance of a time and place remote from ours, salvaging it for reinhabitation. Variations of stylistic technique have reflected these alternative approaches; the frail, elusive, weightless diction of Creagh or Montgomery, as against the gnarled, myopically particular materialism of Silkin. The first mode threatens to evaporate, the second to bury, its subject out of sight. Behind this modern duality, maybe, stands a more decisive historical confrontation: that between Eliot and Pound. The line from Pound to Bunting is obvious enough; the relations between *Briggflatts* and *Mercian Hymns* much less apparent, but, vestigially, perhaps just as significant.

One strength of Mr. Hill's new cycle of prose-poems is its firm regulation of the tension between 'myth' and 'legend'. The poems reconstruct the career of the historical (but also legendary) Mercian king, Offa: they progress from his naming and crowning, through his childhood, law-giving and political government, to the extended ritual of his death. Offa is presented, at one level, as a mythical type: as the 'presiding genius of the West Midlands' whose dominion stretches into the twentieth century. So the historical legend interacts mythically with modern experience:

> Cohorts of charabancs fanfared Offa's province and his concern, negotiating the by-ways from Teme to Trent. Their windshields dripped butterflies. Stranded on hilltops they signalled with plumes of steam. Twilight menaced the land. The young women wept and surrendered.

Myth in this universalizing sense, however, is a fairly minor element: the real interlocking between ancient and modern in the poem lies in the direction of archaic materials by a distinctively contemporary intelligence. Most of the attention is given over to re-creating the feel of an alien culture, material and specific yet also formally elaborated:

> Their spades grafted through the variably-resistant soil. They clove to the hoard. They ransacked epiphanies, vertebrae of the chimera, armour of wild bees' larvae. They struck the fire-dragon's faceted skin. . . .
>
> It is autumn. Chestnut-boughs clash their inflamed leaves. The gardens fester for attention: telluric cultures enriched with shards, corms, nodules, the sunk solids of gravity. I have accrued a golden and stinking blaze.

These brilliantly exact verbal organizations are typical of the book: the activities of Mercia—coining, hammering, carving—are, first of all, the qualities of Mr. Hill's own poetic technique, so that style matches theme in a striking congruency. Each prose-poem is an achieved construct of trimmed, interlocking units, polished without glossiness (both 'kempt and jutting', like Offa's head on a coin), tense but unstrained, calculatively wrought without seeming synthetic. Within these rigorously compressed verbal structures, immense pressure is thrown on to the impact of single epithets; yet the diction just succeeds in not obtruding. The poem hoards its words frugally, with the sparseness of a primitive economy, thus forcing each phrase to flex its potential to the full. The loss entailed by this stringency is a drastic shrinking of tonal diversity—a kind of tight-lipped, poker-faced emotional anonymity which, one guesses, would weary if the book was not as brief as it is.

## (*c*) THOM GUNN

### *Moly*

FROM *Fighting Terms* onward, Thom Gunn's poetry has been concerned with discovering a kind of poise—a knack, mask or posture—which would preserve the self's intactness from the invasion of a gloomy Sartrean *néant*. What that involves, to adopt Gunn's own description of his work in a recent bulletin of the Poetry Book Society, is a capacity to 'live experience through in detail' yet always to be able to extract oneself from it; and this quest for an achieved balance, where the poet is simultaneously subjected to and in control of his subject-matter, has reflected itself continuously in a problem of technique.

Gunn's earlier oscillation between tortuously rigorous iambics and probing, tentative syllabics expressed the moral dilemma as simple dichotomy: either the poet as sharply separate perceiver, processing and controlling his starkly defined object to the point where the poem stood up as an arthritically joined, cerebrally reverberating structure from which most of the felt life had been squeezed out: or a more relaxed, syllabic submission to the rhythms of an experience which, even in a poem as fine as 'Considering the Snail', tended to limit the kinds of complex moral statement which Gunn at his best is capable of making.

Gunn's latest two volumes, however, reveal an interesting development. In *Touch*, the impulse towards an edgy, defensive hardening of the self underwent some sardonic questioning, as images of melting, dissolution and momentary merging began to creep in. In *Moly*, that tendency has become considerably more affirmative: and one reason for this is that Gunn's sense of what sustaining 'poise' involves seems to have been significantly modified. The surf-riders in San Francisco bay keep their balance, but they do so by moving with, not against, natural forces:

Their pale feet curl, they poise their weight
  With a learn'd skill.
It is the wave they imitate
  Keeps them so still.

The sharp disjunctions between controlling mind and chaotic matter of the early volumes are here superseded: it is by rooting himself responsively in the flow of natural forces, not by fending them off, that man can master them. And so, whereas Gunn's previous use of such images as the werewolf suggested a clumsy, potentially tragic discontinuity between man and Nature, the imagery of man-beast metamorphosis in *Moly* seems, while preserving something of this attitude, to express a more generous sense of some organic, ecological *rapport* between man and the forces among which he moves. On the one hand, the Circe myth to which the volume's title refers underscores the need for a vigilant self-awareness which allows man to master and transcend the bestial; but a series of 'centaur' poems in the book seem to view the frontier between man and beast as being in any case blurred and indefinite, a merging rather than a dividing:

light is in the pupil
                    luminous seed
and light is in the mind
                    crossing
in an instant
          passage between the two
seamless
          imperceptible transition
skin melting downward into hide
at the centaur's waist. . . .

The moly plant, whose black roots shade upwards into a white flower, itself images this division-within-unity. Human consciousness sinks its tentacular roots into the earth ('Through breast and calf I feel it vined,/And rooted in the death-rich earth'), and at its most intensified (some of the poems were written under L.S.D.) it acknowledges the dependency of its sharpened perceptions on an amorphous undertow of mindless natural merging:

> On the stream at full
> A flurry, where the mind rides separate!
> But this brief cresting, sharpened and exact,
> Is fluid too, is open to the pull
> And on the underside twined deep with it.

This emergent trend in Gunn's development is not, however, thematic. The perceptual relation between knower and known, mind and Nature, has always been an ambivalently moral and aesthetic issue for Gunn, defining a way of writing as well as an ethic. The moral values of *My Sad Captains*, for example, are obviously enough underpinned by the rigorous epistemological doctrine of a poem like "Waking in a Newly Built House"; and a similar interaction can be traced in Moly:

> In looking for the words, I found
> Bright tendrils, round which that sharp outline faltered:
> Limber detail, no bloom disclosed
> I was still separate on the shadow's ground
> But, charged with growth, was being altered
> Composing uncomposed.

Separateness is preserved in art and perception—it is only in sexuality here as in *Touch*, that it is momentarily lost—but preserved within an organic interchange between perceiver and perceived, a mutual nourishing which can image the relation between an animal and its young as exactly as the stance of the poet to his object:

> The brown fur oozes milk for the young one. He,
> Hatched into separation, beaks his fill.
> If you could see through darkness you could see
> One breaking outline that includes the two.

At both moral and aesthetic levels, then, Gunn seems in this new volume to have broken beyond his former implication that the only alternative to a blank, existential alienation was a dangerously undermining empathy. Vigilant separateness and outgoing responsiveness can now be embraced within a single outline: and this is true at the technical, as well as the thematic, level:

His body makes to imitate the flower,
Kneeling, with splayed toes pushing at the soil,
  The source, crude, granular, and sour.
His stillness answers like a looking glass
The flower's, it is repose of unblown flame
  That nests within the glow of grass.

The language here imitates the fusion of separateness and harmony which it describes: a spare, precise verbal economy is maintained, but a complex sensuousness is allowed to emerge through it, so that the objects are at once separately 'placed' and experienced as an emotional unity. *Moly* lacks much of the metaphysical drama of the earlier Gunn; but it represents a mature distillation of some of the major issues which he has pursued so ambitiously throughout his work.

## (*d*) JOHN WIENERS

*Nerves*

## JAMES DICKEY

*The Eye-Beaters, Blood, Victory, Madness, Buckhead and Mercy*

## RICHARD WILBUR

*Walking to Sleep*

THE MODERN MOVEMENT in American poetry has been coloured from the start by an impulse to subvert the establishment; but particularly since the 'beat poets' made their impact on the cultural scene in the United States, poetry has become a popgun for the young to aim at the supposedly fixed orders of family and society. Recitations in which the poet's life style matters more than the style of his work have grown commonplace. Even when the verse is not set to music, the meaning of the lines seems of less interest to the Vietnam generation than the evocative tone of the words or the shock effect of the imagery. It is ironical that a tent revivalist preaching the religion they despise could serve as the model for what these listeners often admire.

This condition would be less tiresome if it affected only the spontaneous poets and their friends. But there is an ecology of literary talent; and when the environment fails, the talent withers. What American poets need today is the sense of an audience. Too many genuine, modest poets feel they are delivering their lines to an empty theatre. Yet the readers do exist, even if one excludes from that category the editors, reviewers, and others for whom poetry is part of a job. But the readers are also thinly dispersed over a continent. Some of them seldom meet anybody who shares their taste. In university towns they are less anomalous, but there they live in the shadow of scholars and students whose special subject is literature—and to them poetry is something to be examined on.

A stable body of judicious, sympathetic readers is something else again. For many writers it is indispensable to their survival. The size of the body has nothing to do with its effectiveness. Half-a-dozen true readers would be ample, so long as they make the poet feel his work refreshes their life, so long as they palpably believe in the value of poetry. The Fugitives operated in this way for John Crowe Ransom; Black Mountain College offered a haven to Robert Creeley.

Unfortunately, the sense of an audience is independent of the other attributes of a writer. Today the poorest talents in America may root themselves in the richest loam. So numerous are the aspirants to quasi-literary (or radical-activist) distinction that simply by exchanging opportunities for coming out in print, or by opening their little magazines to one another, they create the impression of a thriving literary movement. Anyone who hears much poetry read by the under-forties must find new point in the tag from Juvenal: *Semper ego auditor tantum? numquamne reponam?*

The man of talents droops in this climate unless his self-confidence approaches arrogance. The listeners he needs are harder than ever for him to feel in touch with, since they are scattered among those who neither see the felicities of a writer nor follow his sense. If he still wishes to practise his art, he turns costive, falls back upon preciosity, self-imitation, translation. What he wants besides talent is the ambition that compels a circle to form itself around him. His work must reverberate constantly from a familiar sounding board. Wallace Stevens could create all the machinery within his mind, and much of his poetry deals with it. But the poet of a more genial cast wants at least the illusion that his chosen few are volunteers, or that his poems, like those of Pindar and Thomas Gray, are *phonanta synetoisin.*

The books by Richard Wilbur, James Dickey, and John Wieners may illustrate this argument better than they illustrate the value of poetry. *Nerves* will provoke agreeable reveries in those who get a psychedelic jolt from phrases like 'afternoon's patience for drank twilight to halo drawn's root cart'. Life has let Mr. Wieners down; love has brought him desolation. 'All the men I wanted were married to others', he writes. As he keeps harping on thwarted perversities against a backdrop of decaying cities, one begins to think of urban sprawl as a sexual pun.

But the appeal of these poems on the level of language remains valid. Mr. Wieners has several shrewd ways of tormenting syntax: referring pronouns far back to forgotten antecedents, failing to repeat key words in parallel expressions, playing on the dirty or drug-culture meaning of common words, modulating from flat and easy speech near the opening of a poem to gaudy, tantalizing incoherence towards the end. Poets better endowed than Mr. Wieners might enjoy playing with some of his devices.

The most enviable feature of his work is its assurance. Mr. Wieners clearly knows whom he is writing for; he is used to the kind of appreciation that one friend gives him on the wrapper of this book and other friends have published elsewhere. With their backing he can indulge in his fantasies of martyrdom and sound convinced if not convincing. His book has drive, character, life (or life-in-death); and no poetry can reach far without these attributes. Unfortunately, it is also a pool of banal emotions.

In *The Eye-Beaters*, Mr. Dickey displays a style that seems daring or difficult while lacking invention. It is founded on the exclamatory sentence, treated with an expansiveness that makes one long for Whitman and a violence that makes one wince for Hopkins. To suggest intensity of feeling, he repeats words often and erratically, as if in a stammer of ecstasy. This does not mean that the words are carefully chosen. To distract one from his lack of grace, Mr. Dickey makes a showy distribution of words on the page, to look like elaborate stanza forms, with touches of concrete poetry. Since these shapes have little foundation in rhythm, they are largely arbitrary. But Mr. Dickey often likes to end lines so as to break normal syntactic bonds: 'made/up', 'middle/Age' 'over/Other houses'. Sometimes this habit becomes expressive.

In effect, Mr. Dickey tramples on the slogan of 'fit audience though few' and reveals a degree of ambition that would raise a claque for him in an underground station. The loudest, most visible effects, clearly designed to gather the biggest, most miscellaneous audience, are the standard elements of his work. He has no sense of the ludicrous to warn him against lines like, 'O parents great things can be released/From your left-handed son's left hand!' His greed for heroic postures leads him to deal with themes that are both sensational and grotesque. In an eagerness to retain every possible listener, he cannot relax his noisy, panting style but treats each experience as climactic. What looks like confidence that he is carrying his audience with him is really a fear that he may be losing touch.

If great poets require great audiences, a good poet depends peculiarly on a good audience. When a man who got strong, well-earned praise at the start of his career falters at the age that should produce his deepest work, what he wants is discriminating praise from loyal readers. Modesty can hardly cure his malaise; more likely, it is the cause. During the years of self-doubt his minor temptation is to pursue the current of fashionable taste, however hostile to his genius. His major temptation is to feel contempt for his work and give it up. Only if he can resist these dangers, cling to his innate character, drive himself to write abundantly about what moves and impresses him, can he rise from a slump into a kind of prosperity.

Mr. Wilbur, in *Walking to Sleep*, reveals talent of a quite different order from that of Mr. Wieners or Mr. Dickey. He has exquisite control of verbal patterns, the sounds of words, the rhythms of speech; he has intelligence, learning, and moral wisdom. But to these he must still add something like the ambition and self-assurance of his inferiors.

The truth is that Mr. Wilbur has never allowed his gifts the freedom they deserve. He has shortened the leash whenever the creatures ran too near the onlooker. An instinct for simile, unobtrusive though precise, is applied to a boy feeding himself as he reads: 'The left hand, like a mother-bird in flight/Brings him a sandwich.' It also reaches the sound of tanks approaching a city in wartime, 'like the clearing of a monstrous throat'. But neither image snaps at the reader. Mr. Wilbur's tact would not let it. Just as accurately and expressively, he represents the leaves of thyme as 'a green countlessness' and the heavenly constellations as 'grand, kept appointments of the air'. But his brilliant descriptive powers are never stretched so far as to indulge the poet at the risk of tiring the reader. Perhaps they might be. Mr. Wilbur's humour (two attempts at satire fail) irradiates his wit and word play. In 'Seed Leaves', a poem that Herrick could not improve, it gives the most benign humanity to the birth of a plant. But sometimes wit should run wild. These hints are not meant to say that the poet should transform himself into another person. Rather they mean he should be more himself. He should let his audience find him, whoever he decides to be.

## (*e*) STEPHEN SPENDER

### *The Generous Days*

'REDEEMING THE WORLD by introspection': Louis MacNeice's phrase (from his autobiographical sketch, *The Strings Are False*) about Stephen Spender in the late 1920s could serve as an epigraph to the whole body of Spender's poetic work as well. Indeed, it makes much better sense to look at the poems in this way, as attempts at redemptive and quasi-religious self-searching, than it ever did to see them as coming primarily from social or political concerns. Express trains, pylons, the unemployed at street corners, the burning of the Reichstag or the Spanish Civil War—all were merely grit for Spender's insatiably self-regarding oyster. But for some years the question has been about the quality of the pearls produced.

The strikingly handsome and wayward poet who emerged at Oxford has become legendary, in such memoirs as Christopher Isherwood's *Lions and Shadows*, Arthur Calder-Marshall's *The Magic of My Youth*, MacNeice's book already mentioned, and not least in Spender's own autobiography, *World Within World*—arguably his best book. This is the perpetual 'young poet', 'the Rupert Brooke of the Depression' as Norman Cameron wittily characterized him. What all his memorialists, including Spender himself, settle on, apart from his appearance ('a towering angel not sure if he was fallen', 'a great scarlet poppy-face, wild frizzy hair, and eyes the violent colour of bluebells'), is his intense, dramatic, often embarrassing self-absorption, tormented, blundering, confessional to the point of absurdity: 'the most rapidly self-revealing person I had ever met', as John Lehmann put it. One gets an impression of some sort of holy fool.

Yet the early poems both support and belie this. 'My parents kept me from children who were rough' incurred the scorn of a Thom

Gunn poem which appeared to see such a statement as a sign of incorrigible wetness and weakness. It is true that weakness, impotence, the incapacity to act—and, as a consequence, pity—are all themes in Spender's first book. But they are handled with an instinctive firm skill, a sureness of cadence that is entirely individual:

What I expected was
Thunder, fighting,
Long struggles with men
And climbing.
After continual straining
I should grow strong;
Then the rocks would shake
And I should rest long . . .

He will watch the hawk with an indifferent eye
  Or pitifully;
Nor on those eagles that so feared him, now
  Will strain his brow:
Weapons men use, stone, sling and strong-thewed bow
  He will not know.
This aristocrat, superb of all instinct,
  With death close linked
Had paced the enormous cloud, almost had won
  War on the sun;
Till now, like Icarus mid-ocean-drowned,
  Hands, wings, are found.

Admiration for the force and achievement of the perfected will, and for the hero figure who personifies that will, is tempered by equally romantic notions of the inevitability of failure, death, darkness: 'And all those other 'I's' who long for "We dying".' The first-person of these early poems—and they are very much poems of the first-person—seems to be an amalgam of the majestic arch-creator Beethoven ('What else is iron but he?') and the slobbering scapegoat, Van Der Lubbe ('I laugh because my laughter/Is like justice, twisted by a howitzer'). The frequent images of the imprisoned self, painfully trying to communicate through vulnerable senses its need to love and be loved, suggests something almost autistic, certainly solipsist. They seem the last gasp of the stricken deer, the wounded romantic artist.

These early Spender poems are demonstrations of a critical distinction he made much later, in the Berkeley lectures in the late 1950s which became *The Struggle of the Modern*, between 'moderns' and 'contemporaries'. The moderns explore and are dynamic, trying to make broad relations between fragmented areas of life: the contemporaries document, analyse, but are essentially static rather than dynamic. Spender is very much a modern, sometimes yoking together disparates so violently that he becomes absurd:

> When we touched hands
> I felt the whole rebel, feared mutiny
> And turned away,
> Thinking, if these were tricklings through a dam,
> I must have love enough to run a factory on,
> Or give a city power, or drive a train.

(One feels, perhaps unfairly, that it was mere chance that prevented Spender from being drawn by the chime into making that last word 'tram', which would have pushed the absurdity even further.) Yet it is the dynamism, the nervous energy and dangerously pent-up force of the early poems, that give them their peculiar distinction. MacNeice's documentation is sharper, Auden's analysis is far more intelligent, but as an explorer of the psyche Spender is beyond them both. He is Isherwood's 'truly weak man', and his weakness liberates him.

But to be 'most remarkable for weakness' requires an effort against distractions if the 'modern' poet is not to become as static as the 'contemporaries'; and in this began Spender's decline as a poet. In *World Within World* he has described with startling honesty his rapid fame and what it did to him. He knew the attractions of being a public figure; himself the product of a political and public family, he knew the dangers, too. The poem from which he took the epigraph to *World Within World* catches him at the point of balance:

> To break out of the chaos of my darkness
> Into a lucid day, is all my will.
> My words like eyes through night, strain to seek
> Some centre for their light: and acts that throw me
> To distant places through impatient violence
> Yet join together to curve a path of stone
> Out of my darkness into a lucid day.
>
> Yet, equally, to avoid that lucid day,
> And to conserve that darkness, is all my will.
> My words like eyes that flinch from light, avoid
> The light, and seek their night; my acts
> Cast to their opposites by impatient violence
> Shatter the sequent path. They move
> On a circumference to avoid the centre. . . .

And in the autobiography itself there is a passage about himself and his attitude to his work at this time (when he was living in Germany) which one must quote in full:

At this time my prevalent social attitude was one of pity. This, and sympathy with weakness, showed in my work and behaviour. These were attitudes of what Yeats calls 'passive suffering'. They were the projections of a mixture of strength and weakness: strength, to the extent to which I was master of my own kingdom of the creative imagination, my own work wherein I might create as I chose. Within this inner world even weakness could become a kind of strength. It isolated me and disqualified me from other kinds of work than poetic writing. I needed only the strength of my own weakness to say that I had no other responsibilities than simply to exist in order to write. It enlarged my sympathies by leading me down paths where people were insulted, oppressed, or vicious. It saved me from having to judge them by conventional rules of conduct, since I did not observe these myself.

That a poet's sole *raison d'être* can be the exploration of his own inner perspectives was no new idea; but the times in which Spender lived and the pressures of his own public self gradually forced him to make compromises with what was essentially a nineteenth-century Romantic stance. His experience of the Spanish Civil War, his membership of the Communist Party, his readiness to be a literary and journalistic pundit, stirred up cross-currents of feelings which sapped more than they invigorated:

Circumstances combined to make me attach too much importance to my opinions. For my views as critic, as journalistic observer, and as amateur politician, were all in demand. . . . I found that my own views, however strongly held, bored me as soon as they were uttered. I realized that they concerned things which other people could express better, or that they arose out of the irritation of the moment, like an angry telegram. The effect of publishing too many opinions was like an inflation of the currency of my reputation, not only before others, but—which was more serious—to myself.

The poems Spender wrote as a result of his experiences during the Spanish Civil War are almost the last in which he managed, perhaps almost unknowingly, to fuse his own 'passive sufferings' successfully with those of others: his own emotional involvement at a thoroughly personal level (gone into with naked frankness in *World Within World*), together with his recoil from the waste of the only war he had seen at first-hand, combined to give the impetus to many of the poems in *The Still Centre* (1939): 'Ultima Ratio Regum', 'Two

Armies', 'The Room Above the Square', 'A Stopwatch and an Ordnance Map'. In all these poems the objective correlative was utterly unsatisfactory from any partisan political point of view—they must, indeed, have been an embarrassment to any loyal Communist—yet they create their own authentic world, verify it, and add to the sum of experience rather than simply notating or qualifying it.

This was not to happen much during the years of the Second World War. 'Passive suffering' continued, but there seemed to be no personal insight to cope with it: only the decorative, Edith Sitwellian plangencies of 'Air Raid Across the Bay' ('In the fields the corn/ Sways, with metallic clicks./Man hammers nails in Man,/High on his crucifix') or the sub-Hardy of 'June 1940' ('Twinned with our lives was our doom/Our killer at our birth, from the same womb'). The tone became more uncertain, the language more eclectic and more diffuse. The self-centredness which had seemed so transparent and winsome at twenty now looked merely gauche at thirty-five, in those immediately postwar poems in memory of Margaret Spender:

> Of what use is my weeping?
> It does not carry a surgeon's knife
> To cut the wrongly-multiplying cells
> At the root of your life.
> All it can prove
> Is that extremities of love
> Reach the Arctic Pole of the white bone
> Where panic fills the night in which we are alone.

Now even private grief seemed muddied and inflated by a public self who was no longer simply critic, journalistic observer and amateur politician but an international figure, *conférencier* in chief, and soon to be founding editor of an international politico-literary periodical, *Encounter*. When Spender's *Collected Poems* appeared in 1955, Edwin Muir's comment that 'section ten, which contains his latest poetry, contains also his best' had the smell of hopeful generosity rather than well-judged insight.

Apart from the handful of new work towards the end of the *Collected Poems*, Spender's most recent book of verse until the other day was *The Edge of Being* (1949). *The Generous Days* therefore draws, potentially, on the products of more than twenty years. But it is a slim offering for such a time span.

Some of the poems look like re-workings of old ones, perhaps products of a wartime notebook; others are marginal notes, either variations on someone else's themes (such as the 'Four Sketches for Herbert Read') or—like 'Bagatelles'—half-hearted epigrams or memorabilia; and there is the persistent feeling of poems being grubbed up from 'occasions', such as 'Central Heating System', which, with an uneasy mixture of imagism and expressionism, attempts to memorialize what was evidently a long night of the soul spent in Storrs, Connecticut. The most direct is a hasty character-sketch called 'Art Student', clumsily and rawly done, but the clumsiness and rawness might be justified by arguing that, after all, they embody what the poem is about. For the rest, there are some wan and rather abstract love poems, and a title-poem which speaks with a formal rhetoric unfamiliar in Spender and very difficult to follow:

> Body soul—soul body—are his breath
> —Or light or shadow cast before his will
> In these, his generous days. They prove
> His utmost being simply is to give.
> Wholly to die, or wholly, else, to live!
> If the cause ask for death, then let it kill.
> If the blood ask for life, then let it love.
> Giving is all to life or all to death.

One feels that a text is being offered here, if one could only grasp it: the concept of giving, of generosity, has always been a strong one in Spender (perhaps in some odd way his own surname has had something to do with that), and yet constantly playing against it has been the deeply self-centred, ungiving, unsharing impulse from which his best poems seem to have sprung. The search for unity, for fulfilment of the self in the selves of others, meets its obdurate barriers, is diverted and leaks away:

> Beholders of the promised dawn of truth
> The explorers of immense and simple lines,
> Here is our goal, men cried, but it was lost
> Amongst the mountain mists and mountain pines.
> So with this face of love, whose breathings are
> A mystery shadowed on the desert floor:
> The promise hangs, this swarm of stars and flowers,
> And then there comes the shutting of a door.

The dangerous vagueness of this early poem is circumvented by the pressure of assurance sensed behind the words and the cadences: what G. S. Fraser once neatly characterized as Spender's 'stumbling eloquence' steers it through the clichés of promised dawns and mountains, the ready-made images of stars and flowers, towards the flatness, bareness and mysteriousness of 'the shutting of a door'. It is this quality of painful inward search, of obsessive but momentarily lightened self-questioning, which is missing from the poems in *The Generous Days*. The introspection is still there but it redeems nothing: it seems fitful, distracted, a mood of perfunctory force, observing little, remembering less.

Towards the end of *World Within World*, at a point where he is making a series of alternative summaries of what his life has shown him, Spender writes:

Strictly speaking, one never *is*, one is only moving. The ideal is the conception of a goal shared by others which unites separately existing individuals within shared values. The goal is the highest conception of the group towards which the individual, from his separate moment, moves. It is the tension between past acceptance and future endeavour, between the isolated individual and the community, between material and form, which is the impulse, the direction, the movement, the closest approximation towards what really *is*.

This is cloudily seen and expressed, but it indicates the tension which has always underpinned Spender's work, at its best giving purely personal impulses a firmer stamp and wider currency, at its worst being inert and lacking substance but at least escaping the gnomic arrogance of bad Auden, the urban superciliousness of bad MacNeice, or the moral fatuity of bad Day Lewis. Self-knowledge, Spender says, can never be a goal, because the self never stays still; and yet Spender's best poems are those in which, momentarily, apparently unwilled, almost in a state of trance, his self suddenly swims into focus and is caught. At these moments, paradoxically, he has spoken most clearly of himself and of others; but they have been rare moments. In a poem in *The Generous Days*, he remembers 'Three undergraduates standing talking in/A college quad'—MacNeice, Bernard Spencer and himself:

Their lives are now those poems that were
Pointers to the poems to be their lives.
We read there in the college quad. Each poem
Is still a new beginning. If
They had been finished though they would have died
Before they died. Being alive
Is when each moment's a new start, with past
And future shuffled between fingers

For a new game.
                    I'm dealing out
My hand to them, one more new botched beginning,
Here, where we still stand talking in the quad.

It is a poignant moment in an otherwise largely unsatisfactory book: the young man among other young men—two of them now dead—poised on the brink of a world which they did not, and could not, redeem.

## (*f*) SYLVIA PLATH

### *Crossing the Water* and *Winter Trees*

THE POSTHUMOUS PUBLICATION of Sylvia Plath's poems has been an oddly ill-organized affair. Forty poems went into *Ariel*; now, with the publication of these two volumes, we have a further fifty-two, plus the radio play, *Three Women*, which appears in *Winter Trees*. Of these, thirty-four—collected in *Crossing the Water*—are said to have been 'written . . . in the transitional period between *The Colossus* and *Ariel*'. How many poems are yet to come, and from which period, is anybody's guess: but perhaps it's time to forget publishing logistics and produce a definitive, chronologically ordered collection.

In any case we should be grateful for small deliveries. The latest poems, like those in *Ariel*, were written at a time when Sylvia Plath had stepped away from the traceable influences of her first book into a discovery of a style—more specifically, a vocabulary—which, in the earlier work, was always on the verge of being liberated. One of the most noticeable aspects of that vocabulary is the way in which it enables discrete images to assume an internal relevance: never glossed by abstraction, but obviating the narrative shifts which would have left the poems limply polemical:

The Sunday lamb cracks in its fat.
The fat
Sacrifices its opacity . . .
A window, holy gold,
The fire makes it precious,
The same fire
Melting the tallow heretics,
Ousting the Jews . . .
                    ('Mary's Song')

The effect there is not one of comparison but of a progression made logical by a metamorphosis which brings the poet to the centre of things:

> It is a heart,
> This holocaust I walk in . . .

The particular value of this permeable vocabulary, and what made it inevitable—even instinctive—for Plath, is the manner in which it incorporates into a private mythology those external events most likely to serve it. The references to concentration camps, pogroms, Hiroshima and so on (often regarded as common currency in Plath's work, though a good deal less frequent than sometimes supposed) are not conscious attempts at empathy so much as an involuntary garnering of metaphors.

The bare bones of this process can be seen in the way in which similar events produce similar images (in fact, a line from 'The Surgeon at 2 a.m.' is used more or less unchanged in 'Three Women'); but it would be wrong to suggest that the poems were written by some irresistible osmotic force. It is the precise control over language which sustains the idiosyncratic, perfectly balanced tone: a symbiotic relationship between lyricism and a carefully judged version of common speech. The startling thing about the poems is that the control over language scarcely ever falters, though if examples of relative failure were to be looked for, 'The Tour', a poem from *Crossing the Water*, might be indicted as an example of the tone tending to become frantic and dissipative. Most often, though, the poems produce a seemingly effortless, though overwhelmingly powerful, congruity of language and content:

> Over one bed in the ward, a small blue light
> Announces a new soul. The bed is blue.
> Tonight, for this person, blue is a beautiful colour.
> The angels of morphia have borne him up.
> He floats an inch from the ceiling,
> Smelling the dawn draughts.
> I walk among the sleepers in gauze sarcophagi.
> The red night lights are flat moons.
> They are dull with blood.
> I am the sun, in my white coat,
> Grey faces, shuttered by drugs, follow me like flowers.
> ('The Surgeon at 2 a.m.')

A poem like the one just quoted, coming out of a hospital visit, demonstrates the extent to which Plath's sensitivities worked on an external event. The persona of the surgeon is never twisted by simile or bald statement into a gratuitous system of emotional equivalents; if anything, he is committed to a world of exclusive artifact, a singular vision:

> It is a garden I have to do with—tubers and fruits
> Oozing their jammy substances,
> A mat of roots. My assistants hook them back.
> Stenches and colour assail me.
> This is the lung-tree.
> These orchids are splendid. They spot and coil like snakes.
> The heart is a red-bell-bloom, in distress. . . .

But the strength and depth of the poet's perception, together with the persuasive universality of the violent imagery, endow the poem with an importance and a perspective well beyond the limitations of a piece of brilliant, if grotesque, description. In the same way, small quotidian occurrences—a cut, a bruise, a child's restlessness at night—conspire to attract, as a magnet attracts metal filings, a perfectly tuned vocabulary: the perennial external horrors, by some almost casual correlative process, have become indivisible from the most intense internal pressures; and the language, miraculously, encompasses them both.

In a poetry where events and objects relate directly to conditions there is no possibility of constancy. The world constructed by these poems is a mutable one, amorphous almost; a world in which, behind the apparent permanency of natural objects, things are breaking up; what makes it compelling is the shock of surprise which comes with recognition—the way in which deeply personal themes are transmuted into poems which look intuitively outward for their effect. These last poems map out a territory which is unique, harrowing, yet always controllable; and which breeds its own distinctive landscapes: 'The wet dawn inks are doing their blue dissolve.' Fixed temporally, that line could be the product of 'that still blue, almost eternal hour before the baby's cry, before the glassy music of the milkman, settling his bottles'; but it is also an emotional landscape: an inescapable affinity. For Sylvia Plath, discovering that landscape must have been like coming home.

# 15

# THE SCIENCE SIDE

## (*a*) THE 'KAMMERER SCANDAL'

IT WAS TIME, after nearly half a century, for the old 'Kammerer scandal' to be taken out again and examined afresh in the light of our present biology, which has become less passionately concerned with the questions it raises. It is a subject very well suited to Arthur Koestler's combination of a novelist's interest in human motivation with the intellectual acumen of a well-read and diligent non-professional student of science. The main part of *The Case of the Midwife Toad* is as fascinating reading as any of the detective stories to which its rather flippant title makes allusion. Some of the appendixes are rather heavy going, but they undoubtedly add to the quite considerable weight of Mr. Koestler's argument.

The story is briefly this. In the early years of this century, a brilliant young man, one of the dashing, elegant, music-loving society of Vienna in the last days of the Austrian Empire, began a series of experiments with several species of amphibia—salamanders, toads, and others. Paul Kammerer was fascinated by these animals, and was able to keep living and breeding in captivity species which other zoologists found unacceptably delicate and impossible to maintain.

After several years' work, in which he had reared a succession of generations of some of his animals, Kammerer found himself driven to a conclusion running contrary to a doctrine which was rapidly becoming accepted as orthodox. Kammerer claimed that his evidence showed that, if an animal is forced to live under circumstances which are stressful to it, but to which it can make physiological adaptations, and if under these circumstances it succeeds in breeding,

---

(*a*) ARTHUR KOESTLER: *The Case of the Midwife Toad*. 187 pp. Hutchinson. £2.

(*b*) JACQUES MONOD: *Le Hasard et la nécessité: Essai sur la philosophie naturelle de la biologie moderne*. 197 pp. Paris: Le Seuil. 19.50 fr.

FRANÇOIS JACOB: *La Logique du vivant: Une histoire de l'hérédité*. 354 pp. Paris: Gallimard. 32 fr.

(*c*) I. BERNARD COHEN: *Introduction to Newton's 'Principia'*. 380 pp. Cambridge University Press. £13.

then the adaptations will appear more easily in its offspring, and may even appear in them if they are reared in a non-stressful environment.

This is, of course, the doctrine of 'the inheritance of acquired characters', first made fashionable in evolutionary theory by Lamarck in the eighteenth century and accepted for a time by Darwin himself. Since the rediscovery of Mendel's laws of inheritance at the beginning of this century, it rapidly became less acceptable to those who were struggling to lay the foundations of the new science of 'genetics'. By the 1920s, when Kammerer visited London and exhibited his evidence, William Bateson, the main champion of genetics and the inventor of the word, declared it anathema, and almost openly expressed the opinion that Kammerer was a charlatan.

Bateson skilfully and fiercely directed his polemics on to an ever-narrowing front, finally concentrating the whole issue in one experiment, involving the appearance of thickened and darkened lumps of horny skin on the hands of the males of the Midwife Toad. The experiments, which lasted many years, had been completed before the First World War. By the 1920s only one preserved specimen showing the crucial skin-pads still survived, pickled in a jar. The few biologists who tried to repeat the experiment gave up in despair when their animals died or refused to breed.

Bateson concentrated his whole attack on finding fault with this one poor pickled toad, brushing aside Kammerer's statements that he regarded this experiment as rather a side issue, and not his main evidence at all. So the toad was brought out of its jar in 1923 and inspected carefully by the assembled savants in Cambridge and London—but not by Bateson, who thus preserved his freedom of manoeuvre. But if no fault could be found with it in 1923, the situation was changed in 1926. A young American biologist, G. K. Noble, visited Vienna, got permission to inspect the famous toad, and proved conclusively, within minutes of seeing it, that Indian ink had been injected into the places where there were supposed to be naturally darkened pads of skin. Six weeks later, Kammerer shot himself.

So, was Kammerer a faker? It is considered unfair to reveal the secrets of a whodunit, but one may hint at the general character of the sequel by quoting a single sentence: 'Paul Kammerer broke the record by falling in love successively with the five famous Wiesenthal sisters.' There let us leave him under Mr. Koestler's quizzical eye.

To the student of science, however, there are some more general questions raised by this story. The issue certainly appeared real enough to the biologists of the 1920s, but would we now take it as such; and if not, how did it come to be accepted? And supposing the issue were real, how does one explain the almost unscrupulous vehemence of Bateson's advocacy? Is such bloody-mindedness endemic to the learned world, as some of the fashionable anti-rational school of today would suggest (and Mr. Koestler sometimes seems to wave a friendly hand in their general direction)?

The question whether we would now accept the issues as real breaks down into two questions: would we be upset if it were proved that the environment in which an animal grew up changed the hereditary endowment which it passed on to its offspring? and: did Kammerer's experiments look like proving that?

On the first question, the answer is that today we should certainly be very surprised indeed—quite incredulous in fact—if anyone claimed to show that environment could change the basic *qualitative character* of an animal's heredity; but it is realized more and more that there are quantitative aspects which might well be changed in a relatively long-lasting way. Animals, for instance, do not always contain only one representative of each gene for each chromosome, but often have a group of several, or even several tens, of nearly but perhaps not completely identical examples. Again they have some hereditary particles not in the chromosomes in the one and only nucleus of the cell but in other cellular particles, such as mitochondria, of which the cell contains many, again probably not quite identical, representatives.

We know very little about the rates of multiplication of the slightly variant forms of quasi-identical chromosomal or mitochondrial genes, or about the effects on this of demands on the cell's metabolism made by environmental factors. If any awkward facts about 'the inheritance of acquired characters' turned up, there is plenty of room here to hypothesize—and test—theories based on changes in the proportions of closely related genes before we should be forced to the very difficult proposition that alterations had been made in the primary genetic information.

Even so, do Kammerer's experiments look now as though they even began to raise this issue? The answer is certainly, No. In all his experiments—those with colour patterns in salamanders, as well as those with the toad on which Bateson concentrated his fire—began with fairly large numbers of animals, of which only a very few left offspring throughout a series of generations; and in all cases, the 'funny appearances' which looked like being 'acquired characters' were appearances which closely related animals were known to be able to produce 'naturally'.

For instance, most toads of the Midwife Toad species do not have the thickened pads of skin, but a very few sometimes do; the ability to produce these pads is already available in the 'gene pool' of the toad population. We have now become so used to thinking of evolution in terms not of individual animals but of whole populations that we should hardly be tempted to ask whether the environment of one individual can affect the heredity endowment of its offspring. We naturally pose the question: does the environment of a parental *population* affect the heredity of its offspring *population.* And, of course, it obviously does, by leading to the *selection* of suitable individual parents to leave more offspring than others. That certainly seems to be what happened in Kammerer's experiments. They all involved very strong selection, which led to 'genetic assimilation', a well established and quite orthodox phenomenon.

This is a remarkably clear example of what T. S. Kuhn has called a change of 'paradigm'. But why did biologists in the 1920s see evolutionary genetics in terms of individuals, whereas we see it in terms of populations? The answer illuminates the other question of the unusual virulence of the attacks on Kammerer. The emphasis on framing genetic questions in terms of individuals was in fact a reaction against a still earlier paradigm which had stressed populations.

At the time Mendelism was rediscovered, the orthodox theory of inheritance was derived from hereditary processes within populations, deduced by statistical analyses by authors such as Galton and Pearson. When Bateson started talking modern, Mendelian genetics he found himself heavily attacked by a 'population paradigm' orthodoxy. In fact, the attacks became at least as fierce and polemical as anything that Kammerer had to suffer, a whole journal—*Questions of the Day and of the Fray*—was launched by the scientific establishment, and Bateson had his contributions refused publication by the prestigeful periodical *Nature*. It was by such bitter infighting that he eventually established his 'individual paradigm'.

This pre-1914 history, which Mr. Koestler only briefly refers to, makes it easier to understand why Bateson in the 1920s had such peculiar ideas of the standards of decent scientific controversy, and also why he was so immovably wedded to his 'individual paradigm' that he could not begin to see that Kammerer's results would have appeared merely interesting, but not so shattering as to be incredible, if only they were seen from the perspective of a 'population paradigm'. Probably we are being equally blind today to something which will be obvious in twenty years' time—if only we knew, now, what it is.

## (*b*) VITAL HYPOTHESES

THESE TWO books are the most important discussions yet published of the implications of the recent advances in molecular biology for the philosophy of the life sciences; and since Man is in some sense a biological organism, and the authors are not afraid to discuss the ways in which he differs from other animals, their arguments demand consideration by anyone interested in the problems of general philosophy today. Both authors are, of course, among the most eminent of living biologists. They shared the Nobel Prize for Medicine in 1965, which was awarded for work carried out in close collaboration at the Institut Pasteur in Paris in one of the most critical areas of molecular biology. Not only are their technical qualifications as professional biologists of this unassailable character, they each show clearly that they are inheritors of the best French traditions of historical and philosophic culture.

It would be otiose for a review of these books to take the form of a catalogue of their outstanding excellences, which need no further advertisement. It is more interesting to consider, first, one point of agreement between the authors, which may seem surprising to some, and then to discuss the very interesting differences in their philosophical outlooks. The point of agreement is that neither Monod nor Jacob is disposed to write of DNA as 'the secret of life', as so many popularizers of recent biology have done.

They both see the invariance of genetic endowment, which the DNA of the genes maintains, as only one among several major properties of living systems. Professor Monod lists three such properties: 'téléonomie, morphogénèse autonome, invariance reproductive.' Professor Jacob agrees about the first of these when he writes 'on ne peut plus faire de biologie sans se référer constamment au "projet" des organismes, au "sens" que donne leur existence même à leurs structures et leurs fonctions'. And, since the 'projets' have been brought into being by, and are themselves the target of, natural selection, he continues: 'Mais quel que soit le niveau étudié, qu'il s'agisse de molécules, de cellules, d'organismes ou de populations, l'histoire est posée comme perspective nécessaire et la succession comme principe d'explication. . . . Pour lui (le biologiste), c'est seulement du jour où il donne prise à la sélection naturelle qu'un objet mérite le nom "organisme".' He agrees also on Professor Monod's second property: 'C'est par l'assemblage spontané des constituants que se forment les êtres vivants.'

So much for the agreement, which will seem surprising only to those who have accepted too easily the popular notion that the whole secret of life is the DNA double-helix. But there are interesting differences in the approaches of the two authors. Simplifying and exaggerating, one might say that Professor Monod is a 'hard-liner', Professor Jacob less exigent, and often less explicit since his book is cast in the mould of a history of biological ideas whereas Professor Monod's is a close argument about ideas in the form in which they are important in modern thought.

Professor Monod's toughness appears, for instance, in its most appealing form in his criticisms of Teilhard de Chardin and 'General Systems Theory', when he expresses himself as 'choqué par le manque de rigueur et d'austérité intellectuelle'.

It may be questioned, though, whether he is not himself in some instances in danger of paying the penalty of too great austerity, the penalty of aridity. Consider how our two authors deal with the question of morphogenesis by self-assembly. Professor Jacob is content to make the general statement quoted above; Professor Monod sets out to describe how the self-assembly operates. He begins his discussion of morphogenesis (the word is used in the general sense usual in France) by adopting a widely accepted 'hard-headed' theory, that of *information*, in the sense of Shannon and Weaver. This immediately leads him into a tricky situation; he concludes that we need to estimate, in terms of information theory, the degree of complexity of the phenotype as it is offered to natural selection, but he has to admit that 'Cette grandeur théorétiquement définissable n'est pas mesurable en pratique'.

One wonders, however, whether the statement that such a measure of complexity is definable in theory is any more than a bare assertion. The addition of one new chemical compound to a developing system may cause the most profound changes; for instance, thyroxin to a salamander larva or ecdysone to an insect. Are the mathematical rigours of information theory in any way applicable to such cases? Should one not be content with the 'softer' outlines of algorithm or programming theory, which is prepared to admit that it has as yet no way of defining or predicting the degree of complexity which may be engendered by the interactions of a number of programmes? Professor Monod, in fact, is forced to settle for a very similar situation: that 'la biosphère ne contient pas une classe prévisible d'objets ou de phénomènes, mais constitue un événement particulier, compatible certes avec les premiers principes, mais non déductible de ces principes. Donc essentiellement imprévisible'.

Here we come near to the central point of debate between the hard and soft liners. These 'premiers principes'—do we know them all already, or, perhaps better, do we already know them quite fully? Hard-line thinkers, in the sense that expression has been used in here, are those who are mainly concerned to preserve the already accepted primary principles undiluted and clearly defined. Professor Monod, for instance, describes the great recent advances in our exploration of the extent to which protein units may assemble themselves into many-membered complexes by the formation of stereo-specific bonds. This undoubtedly provides one mechanism by which biological entities larger than individual molecules may be formed. Professor Monod would like us to believe that it is the only mechanism:

> Il faudra l'enrichir d'hypothèses cinétiques, analogues peut-être à celles qui permettent d'interpréter les interactions allostériques. Mais je demeure convaincu, pour ma part, que seules les propriétés associatives stéréo-spécifiques des protéines pourront, en dernière analyse, donner la clé de ces phénomènes.

Again, he is very concerned to identify the 'basic causes' of phenomena:

> L'*ultima ratio* de toutes les structures et performances téléonomiques des êtres vivants est donc enfermée dans les séquences de radicaux des fibres polypeptidiques, 'embryons' de ces démons de Maxwell biologiques que sont les protéines globulaires.

A soft-line thinker, on the other hand, would be more concerned to discover if there are processes of form generation which depend on different principles than those already known, as for example in the 'gradient' or 'field' phenomena which have recently evoked new interest in the work of biologists such as Turing, Wolpert, Goodwin, Cohen and others. These cannot, without unduly straining the concepts, be reduced to self-assembly of protein sub-units. As Professor Jacob writes: 'Que l'hérédité puisse aujourd'hui s'interpréter en termes de molécules, ce n'est là ni une fin, ni la preuve que désormais toute la biologie doive devenir moléculaire.' He admits that the world of phenomena, and in particular the living world, reveals a succession of 'levels', for which he coins the word 'intégron':

Un intégron se forme par l'assemblage d'intégrons de niveau inférieur; il participe à la construction d'un intégron de niveau supérieur. . . . Avec chaque niveau d'organisation apparaissent des nouveautés, tant propriétés, que de logiques. . . . Les concepts de démocratie, de propriété, de salaire sont aussi dépourvus de signification pour une cellule ou un organisme que ceux de reproduction ou de sélection naturelle pour une molécule isolée.

This point of view emphasizes that a study of phenomena in 'higher levels', which are compatible but not deduceable from primary principles, may teach us something we did not know before about those primary principles. Does it mean much to say that the *ultima ratio* of the proteins is their primary sequence? Is not the *ultima ratio* of that, in its turn, the properties of the individual atoms of which the chain is composed? What is important, surely, is that it was a real discovery, unforeseeable, or at least unforeseen by the chemistry of forty years ago, that atoms can combine into amino-acids which can link up into polypeptide chains, which can fold themselves up into globular proteins which can exhibit the remarkable properties of stereo-specific non-covalent bonding and allostery, on which Professor Monod rightly lays such emphasis. The 'primary principles', or concepts, of the atom to which we have thus been led are richer and fuller than the earlier-held principles with which the phenomena are compatible, but from which they could not be, or were not, predicted.

Professor Monod's cast of thought is, of course, profoundly Cartesian. In fact, he explicitly accepts that the Cartesian dualism of mind and matter 'conserve en somme sa vérité opérationelle'. This leads him, in his final chapter, to find that 'le mal de l'âme moderne' arises from the conflict between science which is based on completely objective knowledge, and all the previously dominant philosophies, which he regards as based on myths and categorizes as 'animist'.

S'il est vrai que le besoin d'une explication entière est inné . . . si pour paraître vraie, signifiante, apaisante, l'explication doit se fondre dans la longue tradition animiste, on comprend alors pourquoi il fallut tant de millénaires pour que paraisse dans le royaume des idées celle de la connaissance objective comme *seule* source de vérité authentique.

Modern society, he claims, is in crisis because it remains 'désespérément attachée, pour justifier ses valeurs, à la tradition animiste, tout en l'abandonnant comme source de connaissance, de vérité'.

The solution he proposes is based on the idea that 'il est évident que de poser le postulat d'objectivité comme condition de la connaissance vraie *constitue un choix éthique* . . .'. Science, as 'objective knowledge', is in fact a 'myth', in which one can choose to believe, as people in the past have believed in the myths which Professor Monod calls animist. This is a point of view which has been expressed by Anglo-Saxon writers, such as Julian Huxley and C. H. Waddington, some decades ago; it probably appears less satisfying to most people today.

Professor Jacob does not discuss the matter explicitly enough to show how a soft-line thinker would approach it, but his argument might well start from Professor Monod's point that 'jugements de connaissance et jugements de valeur . . . sont inévitablement associées dans l'action, y compris le discours'. But he would proceed to argue that we cannot achieve complete objectivity about either type of judgment; our knowledge of atoms was incomplete, that is, not fully objective, until Professors Jacob and Monod discovered that, united in certain ways, they could build up compounds exhibiting allostery. Man, the argument would go, is always attempting to bring his actions into some optimum conformity (which may be defined in terms of biological natural selection or of cultural evolution) with the constraining forces of non-human nature. In this endeavour, he modifies both his knowledge and his values, but it may seem presumptuous to suppose that he ever attains complete objectivity in the one or complete wisdom in the other realm.

## (*c*) NEWTON'S PROGRESS

In 1955 the late Alexandre Koyré, professor at the Sorbonne and for the next decade a most influential figure among historians of science, published an article by which he intended to

montrer sur un exemple précis les enseignements que l'on peut tirer d'un examen comparatif des trois éditions des *Principia* et de plaider pour une édition critique de l'oeuvre maîtresse de Newton.

As Koyré remarked, it was the republication in facsimile of the first edition of Isaac Newton's *Philosophiae naturalis principia mathematica* (1687) that had enabled him shortly before—as it also permitted his future collaborator in Newtonian studies, I. Bernard Cohen—to perceive the changes that Newton had introduced into the more accessible, later editions of 1713 and 1726; for the days when Maynard Keynes had picked up a first edition from David's Cambridge bookstall for 4s 6d were long past.

In 1955 Professors Koyré and Cohen, in common with most historians of science, had very little notion of the manuscript treasury that Newton had left behind him, although a fair catalogue of the portion of it preserved in Cambridge had been in print since 1888, and the remainder had become well known to dealers and collectors through its sale at auction in 1936 (for which Sotheby's prepared an excellent catalogue). Moreover, no attentive reader of the nineteenth-century writings on Newton should have remained long in ignorance of the necessity for manuscript investigation. But before 1955 virtually no one thought it worth the trouble.

By contrast, in the past dozen years the fruit of three major enterprises based on Newton's heritage has begun to appear from the Cambridge University Press. The late H. W. Turnbull, whose patient work had long gone unnoticed, issued in 1959 the first volume of Newton's *Correspondence*; recently D. T. Whiteside has given resplendent life to Newton's mathematical researches; and now we have the long-heralded variorum edition of the *Principia* begun by Professors Koyré and Cohen, and completed by the latter alone since his collaborator's death in 1964. Or rather, since the veils are not yet lifted from the edition itself, we have the introductory volume to it.

There is perhaps some embarrassment in reviewing the introduction to a vast work of scholarship (even when the introduction itself is proportionately massive) while the work itself is still inaccessible. Several points about the forthcoming text of what is, by universal consent, the greatest single volume in the history of science are nevertheless clear. The editors evidently decided pretty soon to abandon the plan of simply piecing together the variant readings of the three printed editions, useful as this would be. They resolved to bring in the manuscript evidence as well. Now there is more manuscript material extant bearing on the *Principia* than, perhaps, on any other book except the Bible; besides the printer's copy there is an almost complete antecedent version, in addition to a preliminary sketch; there are interleaved, corrected copies of the first and second editions; there are endless notes of other people about Newton's notions for improving his book; and above all there are masses of Newton's own drafts and correspondence.

The collaborators drew up rules to prevent their enlarged design being quite submerged under a sea of paper, but obviously there is no logical reason why any manuscript note should be excluded from consideration once one steps beyond the three printings. And in fact in this *Introduction* Professor Cohen does refer to many manuscripts related to the *Principia* outside the corpus chosen to provide the variant readings.

While the utility of a text from which the reader may follow an author's changes of mind through successive printings requires no argument, the significance of manuscript variants may seem less obvious. For printed texts are, in general, the best authorities for an author's meaning at the time of their appearance, unless manuscript evidence must be used to correct a corrupt or obscure edition. However, manuscripts may also permit one to follow the course of a writer's thought between successive editions, and, of course, before a first edition.

In the case of Newton, a quarter of a century elapsed between the first and second editions of the *Principia mathematica,* though the book is said to have become scarce within a few years of publication. During this interval Newton discovered many errors in the 1687 printing, and others were pointed out to him; critics attacked the theory of gravitation and other aspects of his work on general grounds; Newton himself had new ideas to which he sought to give expression. Moreover, *Opticks* had been released at last, and disputes with Leibniz and the Continental mathematicians had broken out.

For twenty-five years Newton wrote and talked about a new edition of his masterpiece; it is therefore certainly of interest to see how this second (and all but final) version of the *Principia* took shape, the more so because some thoughts that were recorded for, but in the end rejected from, the second edition (such as Newton's essay on the atomism of the ancients and a long paper on the theory of matter) show us aspects of Newton of which we might otherwise be ignorant.

This *Introduction*, then, deals essentially with two topics. The first is an account of the origin of this edition in collaboration with Alexandre Koyré, of its organization, and of the other publications in connexion with it that are to appear in the future, notably a *Commentary* on the *Principia* text and a revised English translation. Throughout the *Introduction* Professor Cohen illustrates the usefulness of the variant readings he has collected and of much other material, largely manuscript, bearing on the development of Newton's book. Some of this leads into odd byways.

For example, Professor Cohen twice explains how the obscure *Historia cycloidis* (1701) of a certain Jakob Groening, to which was appended a list of corrigenda in the 1687 *Principia* (most of them noted by Newton himself, though Groening did not say so), not only permits certain changes to the first edition to be dated, but demonstrates the still lively interest in Newton's book—which Groening, however, did not mean to praise. Much of such material, relating as it must to the minutiae of textual changes, cannot be of overwhelming interest to the general student of the development of the sciences despite the fascination of Professor Cohen's detective work, but the bulk of the *Introduction* can also be read in a different and more broadly interesting way as providing a general account of the development of one of the most important, which is also one of the best-documented, of books.

Strictly speaking, Professor Cohen does not deal with the origin of the *Principia* in the years of Newton's scientific preparation from 1664 to 1684, a topic already discussed by John Herivel and D. T. Whiteside among others and one to which Professor Cohen may well return elsewhere; it would be a mistake, however, for a reader of this *Introduction* to infer that Newton had virtually nothing of the future *Principia* in his closet when he received that famous visit from Edmond Halley in (probably) August, 1684. Indeed, one might well argue of Newton (as analogously of others) that the most significant period of his life was not that in which he wrote the *Principia* but that in which he made himself the one man who could write it.

Professor Cohen shows with great learning how the first printed *Principia* was written, not without outside criticism (perhaps from Halley) to which he draws attention for the first time. Having brought the book into existence—and even the wording of the first law of motion did not come to Newton easily—Professor Cohen then traces from its initial reception by the learned world the slow progress towards a second edition, finally reaching fruition with Richard Bentley in 1708.

It is not to be expected that Professor Cohen's narrative should alter the broad outline of these events, but he has filled in many previously sketchy points and revealed innumerable strange subtleties of Newton's thought and action. If Newton's ambivalent attitude towards his would-be editors, David Gregory and Fatio de Duillier, remains as enigmatic as before, we can now be quite certain that the so-called *Systema Mundi* was indeed the original second book of the *Principia* (that is, the precursor of the present Book Three) and that the manuscripts of the Lucasian lectures are pious frauds.

Thus the *Introduction* may be read by itself as the summary and present culmination of a scholarly tradition more than a century old devoted to the *Principia.* Professor Cohen has had not a few predecessors in this part of his task, but none has been more devoted than he, none has done more to display Newton's endlessly fascinating tergiversations as an author. For Professor Cohen's interpretation of the thinking which Newton struggled thus painfully and long to define in print we must await his future volumes. While recognizing that the danger nowadays is not so much of neglect of Newton as of burying him within a grandiose sepulchre of learning, all who are interested in the course of thought must be grateful for the erudition that Professor Cohen has bestowed upon Isaac Newton.

# 16

# HOGARTH'S TRUE MEANING

SIX YEARS AGO W. S. Lewis, in an aside which may have surprised those who noticed it, described Hogarth as 'a sub-continent of the eighteenth century that is relatively unexplored'. It is a strange and shameful thing that the literature on an artist whose importance no one doubted for 150 years at least should have been so repetitive and complacent as to conceal that there was anything to explore. The observation with which Ronald Paulson prefaces his remarkable book is no more than just. Only two biographies of Hogarth have ever been 'researched'—the *Biographical Anecdotes* compiled from his notes by John Nichols and George Stevens within fifteen years of his death, and the life by Austin Dobson.

Soon after Dobson's final edition was published, in 1907, the trend of artistic taste obscured the significance of Hogarth. Indeed a large tract of the eighteenth-century achievement has been *terra incognita* in recent times. Basil Taylor reminds us that Stubbs was not so much as mentioned in Roger Fry's survey of British painting in 1934. Though Fry's superior reference to Hogarth's 'extraordinary lack of feeling for formal relations' has become notorious, the dismissal was not unusual. An age which fostered a lack of feeling of its own for whole areas of the meaning that the past had to offer bore particularly hard on an artist whose meaning was social and moral.

We have still far to go (and not in historiography alone) before we realize how largely the imaginative achievement of art and literature is wrought on and through society, and there will be need of many expeditions of rediscovery, of the kind that Mr. Paulson has mounted on behalf of Hogarth, before some subjects are liberated

---

RONALD PAULSON: *Hogarth: His Life, Art and Times.* Volume 1: 558 pp. Volume 2: 557 pp. Yale University Press for the Paul Mellon Centre for Studies in British Art. £17.50 the set.

WILLIAM GAUNT: *The Great Century of British Painting: Hogarth to Turner.* 240 pp. Phaidon. £6.

BASIL TAYLOR: *Stubbs.* 220 pp. Phaidon. £6.

CONSTANCE-ANNE PARKER: *Mr Stubbs the Horse Painter.* 203 pp. J. A. Allen. £5.25.

from the lazy *idées reçues* that have served. But, whereas understanding of other artists may be more or less incomplete without factual knowledge of the social aspect of their work, with Hogarth there is hardly anything else to know. Not only his themes and his message were social; the innovation with which he confronted society concerned the sociology of art. If Hogarth is not seen as rooted in his time, he amounts to hardly more than the aesthetic critics thought.

It is in just this respect that the accepted view of him is not only incomplete but biased. Nichols and Stevens transmitted a caricature which was based on Hogarth's own despair in the last months of his life. It persuaded the writers who followed to share his own ultimate conviction of defeat, and this, rather than anything that happened to Hogarth himself, was the real tragedy. It obscured his profound significance, paranoia and all, to Britain and to Europe and his veritable triumph.

The need was thus not merely academic. The true estimate of a great and enigmatic artist and the understanding of highly significant relationships between visual art, literature and society at large have both awaited more and better biographic information about Hogarth. It can be said at once that Mr. Paulson supplies this need as fully and thoroughly as we could hope. He has clearly made an exhaustive search of the sources—'a task', as he notes with candour, 'inexplicably never before undertaken'.

The present biography is the first attempt to establish the facts of Hogarth's life from a large range of primary sources: public records (rate books, baptismal and burial registers), records of banks and insurance companies, memoirs and letters of contemporaries, and notices in contemporary newspapers and magazines (including his own advertisements).

Mr. Paulson has tackled these sources omnivorously. It has been no secret; some of us have dined on his crumbs. (It is likely, for example, that knowledge of the elder Hogarth's imprisonment in the Fleet, betrayed in a front-page review in the *TLS* on February 9, 1967, of Mr. Paulson's catalogue of *Hogarth's Graphic Works*, was inadvertently derived from his generous conversation.) Now we have the feast, and it is certain that Hogarth studies will never be so undernourished again. Every turn of the story is enriched. Much is revealed for the first time; the background and upbringing, for example, are quite clearly reconstructed. The relation to Thornhill and the eclipse of the English Baroque style, the sources, the attitudes and observations, the friendships, among them those that turned to enmity, and the highly significant jokes—all these are documented in detail for the first time.

Yet the resulting book is quite unlike the customary archival study that an earlier generation devoted to British artists and might, if taste had not been so lily-livered, have given to Hogarth. Mr. Paulson is not only the first writer on him willing and able to sift the sources. He is also the first who has brought to Hogarth a serious knowledge of Fielding and Sterne. Understanding that neither archival nor critical work dispenses with the necessity for the other, indeed that they are eventually inter-dependent, seems to be commoner in English studies than among historians of British art. Mr. Paulson commands the critical equipment that has been evolved to deal with the beginnings of the English novel, and he applies it unsparingly.

This is the aspect of his study that may prove controversial; it is certainly salutary. We are ready enough for far-fetched iconology, provided the art in question is not too near home, but it is another thing to take seriously Hogarth's unambiguous announcement, 'My subjects I considered as writers do'. There is in fact some solid knowledge as well as much speculation about how Fielding and his circle considered such things, and Mr. Paulson extracts all that is to his purpose from both. And more, perhaps; occasionally one of his interpretations has a touch of the fantastication against which students of art history are customarily warned. This has nevertheless an undoubted value; now that the question has been opened there will be time enough for sober measurement of the iconographic and moral affinities and differences between painter and writer.

At the moment the basic discrepancy between visual and literary terms of reference remains unresolved. References to the Choice of Hercules are detected as an overtone, like a barely audible descant to *Joseph Andrews*, but an unvarying determination to read them into every threesome in Hogarth is ultimately more suggestive of King Charles's head. Occasionally an image (and in particular the imagery within it) reads more naturally and easily than Mr. Paulson sees, and it is not certain that the fondness for 'shows of all sorts', which Hogarth proclaimed his starting point, and the patterns of characterization, which he seems to have borrowed from them, have been given their full weight.

Nevertheless the central point is made and it must be taken. Hogarth's modern moral subjects continued the aims and the methods of history painting, and it was in this context that they were understood. Fielding said as much when he called them 'the Works of a Comic History-Painter'—though a habitual and uncharacteristic misquotation deprives Mr. Paulson of some of the support the words in fact give him; the hyphen shows that it was a history-painter and a comic one, not merely a painter of comic narratives, that Fielding had in mind.

This is the context in which the life, the art, and their significance to Hogarth's times are reconsidered, and it is an illuminating one. The commentary on successive works is continuously revealing. At the start one can hardly imagine that anyone can bring the 'Hudibras' plates, which sometimes look uncommonly dusty, to life, but Mr. Paulson's sensitivity to the force of the mock-heroic idiom manages it. He is equally good on 'The Beggar's Opera'—no one but a literary historian should ever have written on such works. But does the picture quite support the conclusion that it is 'an extraordinarily complex study of the nature of reality'? It would be a very great picture if it did, but it appears that the actual reference is limited to the stratified nature of satiric meaning. When 'reality' is invoked, a stereotype of our own has supervened. And so on; it is hard to think of another study on this scale (in the neighbourhood of half a million words) with so few longueurs.

Add to this the fact that Mr. Paulson has lately also produced a useful revision of the admirable *Graphic Works*, first published no more than six years ago, and it will be clear that this represents a personal achievement of quite exceptional calibre. It would be reasonable if the author had some help, in addition to the plainly enviable conditions of American academic life, and indeed someone has worked on the description of 'Marriage à la Mode' who thinks the husband of a Countess is a Count, a view gainsaid on other pages.

If—without detracting in the slightest from one's gratitude for the single book in this field that the twentieth century has produced which is wholly original, quite indispensable and certain to remain so —one is aware of any disappointment, it concerns the discussion of one special class of document, the paintings.

It may be that Mr. Paulson has not fully realized how vital the art-historical equivalent to the establishment of a textual canon is in the understanding of an artist; the outlines of the oeuvre are the very contours of the artistic personality.

The frontispiece here is the 'Mackinnon Children' from Dublin, a charming picture, but one in which the heads are constructed on conventional lines quite different from the burgeoning protuberance of modelling invariable in the undoubted works. Only one other work shows anything like this construction, an alleged self-portrait formerly in the Kinnaird collection which Mr. Paulson also accepts with insufficient discussion. The early authentication seems more positive regarding the likeness than the authorship. If either picture is supposed to be by Hogarth, the consequences for his stylistic development require full elucidation in a study on this scale. If early authentication is to be credited, the case for the 'Paviour's Signboard', and thus for the other putative early pictures supposed, rightly or wrongly, to depend from it, is worth extended examination.

The biographical importance of this question is obvious, and an author who really could not make up his mind on it would hardly be ready to write a life at all. If, as seems likely, these pictures are indeed Hogarth's delayed juvenilia, then the popular direction of his style at fifty becomes comprehensible as the resurgence of an element that had been in abeyance since his twenties. Charles Catton is treated as if his work as a coach painter made his testimony less respectable; he was in fact an interesting figure. Several of the painters who flit through these notes were a good deal more substantial than they appear; Kneller himself is oddly undervalued, making the genesis of Hogarth's portrait style hard to understand. The belief that 'The Four Times of Day' were painted for Jonathan Tyers remains as unexplained as Mr. Paulson's doubts about 'The Fairies'. The chronological outline of the development also requires clarification at some points. If there is evidence that the scandalous portrait of Sir Francis Dashwood (here assigned to the 1750s) was not commissioned by the 2nd Viscount Boyne, who died in 1746, it should be quoted. The activities of the Dilettanti in the 1750s would have been repugnant to Hogarth and, though it is pleasant to read about Medmenham, there is no apparent relevance to the matter in hand.

The dating of the crucial turn of events in Hogarth's artistic life, the thunderous change of mood reflected in the later states of prints like 'The Rake's Arrest', remains uncertain. It is hardly to the point whether the third state should be dated 'before 27 September 1762' or 'ca. 1763?', as it is on successive pages, still less whether the thunderbolt is 'very like' one in 'The Ascension' (1756)—it is just as much like one in 'The Tempest' nearly thirty years before. The third state of the print no more than underlined the change of mood recorded in the second. It is the second state that we need to date, and it is a pity that the rather confused account in the *Graphic Works* cannot yet be finally clarified. If the obsessive pessimism was peculiar to Hogarth's last years, the paranoid fury certainly was not.

*Hogarth: His Life, Art and Times* belongs, in fact, to the select class of book that offers one the equipment to disagree with it. Its essential rightness, invariable usefulness, and lasting value are never in doubt. The printers, who served the *Graphic Works* rather poorly, have now risen to the occasion. Marvellous illustrations of the engravings show with minute but total legibility the whole of the inscription on every sheet. The price, all things considered, is most reasonable. Henceforward no one working in any field that Hogarth touched can afford not to begin with Mr. Paulson's splendid book.

Mr. Taylor, who tells us that he 'has pursued his subject for twenty-five years', cannot be called a prolific writer, but in estimating the calibre of his achievement it must be remembered that it is in large part due to his direction of the Paul Mellon Foundation until 1969 that books like Mr. Paulson's appear as they do. The restrained and concentrated essay that he has supplied to this volume of Stubbs plates is the best piece that has been written on the artist—and not merely because it is almost the first (only preceded by Geoffrey Grigson) to show any interest in the general nature of the activity described as art. One can only wish Mr. Taylor well with the big book that is surely in store, and repress a feeling that is close to envy for the inviting lines of investigation that this essay opens up. It will be exciting to discover who was seriously concerned with the geometry of picture-making in the London of 1760. Is it possible that Giles Hussey was the source that Mr. Taylor is looking for?

The lack of any serviceable material on Stubbs gives a special importance to the plates. The quality is good, but most unfortunately the illustrations of the nine most important works have been carried across the fold of the book, reducing their use either for enjoyment or study. One may guess at or remember the unity of these pictures but one certainly cannot observe it here. In the circumstances the adequate plates which accompany *Mr. Stubbs the Horse Painter*, a compendious and chatty digest of the known (but none too accessible) sources by Constance-Anne Parker, the Assistant Librarian of the Royal Academy, are particularly valuable. For general libraries, where the primary need is for solid information, this book may be the more useful buy.

The text of William Gaunt's book (like Mr. Taylor's) is printed like tasteful publicity on coloured paper twice the thickness of the plates. It is rather thin and far from perceptive. How can anyone regard de Loutherbourg's 'Methodist Preacher' as 'a sober eye-witness statement carrying conviction that this is just how everything appeared'? It is an eclectic collection of flagrant caricatures, interesting in its reflection of the painter's connexions with Rowlandson. Lawrence's characterization of Payne Knight, described as 'strong', is simply his standard expression, with no more individual differentiation than usual. The stereotypes that inform this kind of criticism are conventional indeed, and it is most unsatisfactory to bleed a plate (mutilating drastically two figures in 'Calais Gate') simply to make blocks big enough for us on the dust jacket. A purchaser of both the Phaidon books might have a complaint; Mr. Gaunt's plate 63 is Mr. Taylor's plate 31, while Mr. Taylor's dustcover reappears as Mr. Gaunt's frontispiece.

# 17

# RUSSIA'S CHRONICLER

SOLZHENITSYN HAS A HABIT of upstaging his critics, commentators and interpreters. Acclaim him for his brilliant story *A Day in the Life of Ivan Denisovich* and he advances from *skaz* to a full-length novel; praise the poignant story of Matryona with its echoes of Turgenev and Leskov and he counters with the Tolstoyan edifice of *The First Circle*; concentrate on his adroit handling of character and situation in his novels and one overlooks the delicate filigree of the *krokhotki*, his 'prose poems'. Calling him a novelist is to forget his poems, his plays and a film-script; labelling him a realist is to ignore the symbolism of cancer, the first circle of Hell, Vega, or the *uryuk* tree blossoming in a Tashkent courtyard. What other writer would debate literature by expert reference to multi-dimensional mathematics, as Solzhenitsyn does?

Every literary work can be seen as a bunch of surfaces. This bunch of surfaces intersects at one point. You choose this point according to your bias, your life history, your superior knowledge.

Small wonder that Sophie Laffitte, when asked to contribute an article to the French Solzhenitsyn collection published by L'Herne, replied to the editors with a firm refusal:

To my mind the time has not yet come to speak as I would like to have done about a great writer who has still only half travelled his road. Could one have judged Dostoevsky before the publication of his last works? Could one have judged Tolstoy fairly after the publication of his first novels?

Nevertheless, Solzhenitsyn's latest novel, *August 1914* (or literally, 'August of [the year] fourteen') falls squarely within the framework of its author's *weltanschauung* and his estimate of his own stature.

---

ALEKSANDR SOLZHENITSYN: *Avgust chetyrnadtsatogo*. 573 pp. Paris: Y.M.C.A. Press. 35 fr.

GEORGES NIVAT and MICHEL AUCOUTURIER (Editors): *Soljénitsyne*. 519 pp. Paris: L'Herne. 64 fr.

LEOPOLD LABEDZ (Editor): *Solzhenitsyn: A Documentary Record.* 182 pp. Allen Lane The Penguin Press. £1.50.

Between 1962 and the present Solzhenitsyn's output has been considerable. No longer a young man, he has made up for his years of enforced silence with prodigious and savage fluency. His literary labours have brought him a Nobel Prize, an accolade which is both a reinforcement and a measure of his moral stance. No other Soviet writer has called so eloquently for the abolition of censorship, for freedom from the KGB and for the rehabilitation of those writers eliminated in body and in name under Stalin. With every year Solzhenitsyn has grown in conviction and assurance. He appears to view himself as a successor to Tolstoy and Pushkin. *August 1914* is as much an outgrowth of Pushkin's studies of Petrine Russia as it is heir to Tolstoy's theory of history and its apotheosis in *War and Peace.*

Solzhenitsyn's legacy of personal suffering through illness and imprisonment has been reformulated as *Cancer Ward*, 'The Right Hand', and *Ivan Denisovich*, *The First Circle*, *The Tenderfoot and the Tramp*, while more recent memories are treated in the prose poems, 'Matryona's House', 'For the Good of the Cause' and 'Zakhar-Kalita'. Only the 'cybernetic' morality play *A Candle in the Wind* ventures outside the framework of autobiographical reference. To say this is in no sense a justification of the Soviet criticism that Solzhenitsyn is 'obsessed' with his own past. Yet in a way it does begin to define Solzhenitsyn's horizons as a writer. Anna Akhmatova once suggested that he might lack great imaginative vision. A scientist by training, his powers of observation, memory and cross-reference are outstanding. Hence the power of scenes like Volodin's first night in the Lubyanka, or Rusanov's admission to hospital.

Somehow his grim moral conviction, born of grievous experience, seems to have deprived him of his sense of humour and his optimism. What humour there is in his writing is wry and ironic—the 'trial' of Prince Igor for treason in *The First Circle*, or the 'liberation' of Polonsky in 'The Ashes of a Poet', while Zakhar the custodian of Kulikovo, with his 'I'll go straight to Furtseva', has little of the hilarity of Steinbeck's down-and-outs. Is there not then a consistent logic in Solzhenitsyn's resort not to the present or the future but to the past history of Russia in his desire to analyse and understand her fate?

*August 1914* is the work of a scientist-novelist. Solzhenitsyn has become a chronicler, while pursuing his long-standing literary and moral aims. It is reported that he once told an interviewer:

What is the most interesting genre for me? The polyphonic novel with precise indication of time and place. The novel without a principal hero. . . . How do I understand polyphony? Each character becomes the principal character on entering the field of action. The author must then be responsible for thirty-five heroes. He does not give preference to any one of them. He must understand and motivate them all.

Both *The First Circle* and *Cancer Ward* are polyphonic by this definition. They possess in addition a powerful tension which gives them cohesion and holds the reader's interest. In *The First Circle* this tension rests in the polarity between liberty and imprisonment and is sustained by the ironic reminder that the first circle of Dante's Hell was reserved for the privileged, the philosophers and the intellectuals. The pyramidal hierarchy of the Stalinist *apparat* is reconstructed with great care within the context of the conflict between freedom and un-freedom. The engineer Bobynin is shown to be freer stripped of dignity and possessions in prison than the security chief Abakumov and even Stalin himself at the very apex of the power structure.

In *Cancer Ward* the dominant tension is between the living and the dying, and the point is hammered home by the presence of Tolstoy's *What Do People Live By?* in the very ward where the hideous symptoms of the patients' imminent death are catalogued with meticulous accuracy. Each work has a classical unity of action and setting which still permits the author his multiplanar treatment. It is significant that Solzhenitsyn regards *Cancer Ward* not as a novel, but as a 'tale' (*povest*)—a term which suggests less concentration on characterization and more concern for incident.

Certainly *August 1914* is in the same mode, its polyphony founded once again on a broad array of characters. The non-Russian reader may well find the book less impressive than the earlier novels, if only because its theme is historical rather than universal. Its title is devoid of symbolic overtones and its moral concern is to establish responsibility for Russia's defeat by the Germans in the battle of Tannenberg at the outbreak of the First World War. By this token it is Solzhenitsyn's most dramatic novel, contrasting markedly with the much more static concept of *The First Circle* and *Cancer Ward*, where the basic events are the arrest and imprisonment of a diplomat because of a technical discovery made in a prison scientific laboratory, and the admission of men to hospital, their treatment for cancer and subsequent discharge.

The plan to write this novel has been with Solzhenitsyn for a long time and is not totally devoid of its autobiographical side. As he has himself admitted,

> East Prussia [is] a region linked with my destiny in a remarkable way. As early as 1937, as a first-year student, I chose to write an essay on 'the Samsonov disaster' of 1914 in East Prussia, and in 1945 myself went to this area.

Since the late 1930s, the author claims in his afterword, he has never lost sight of his original plan, diverting his energies into other books only as a result of the 'quirks of biography and the wealth of contemporary impressions'. He calls the book the 'First Fascicle' of a three-volume cycle which will take him twenty years to complete.

*August 1914*, limiting itself to the opening two weeks of the war, describes with close attention to historical facts the Russian offensive into East Prussia aimed at Königsberg and eventually Berlin. The offensive resulted in the encirclement and defeat of General Alexander Samsonov's Second Army by Hindenberg and Ludendorff at Tannenberg. This basic theme is filled out by the inclusion of a great cross-section of characters, both fictitious and historic, from every walk of Russian life. Since the catastrophe of Tannenberg exemplified the shortcomings of the Tsarist state and hastened its downfall, Solzhenitsyn has been at pains to reconstruct the command structure of the Army, the Staff and the War Ministry so that blame can be apportioned in due measure. He manages to cover these different areas through the viewpoint of his creation Vorotyntsev, a young staff colonel who is something of a 'Decembrist' in his attitude to the system in which he is obliged to act. Solzhenitsyn gives a sympathetic portrait of Samsonov himself. The manner in which he fell victim to planning blunders and personality clashes outside his control is convincingly detailed, and ends with a poetic description of his suicide in defeat.

Woven into the factual matter is a wealth of heartfelt discussion about Tolstoy's philosophy of Christian love and history, as well as of religion and Marxism. Solzhenitsyn recognizes that at this stage in history Germany was superior to Russia both as a civilization and as a fighting force, and he dismisses the Tsarist Pan-Slavism which led Russia into a war that culminated in two revolutions and a civil war. All this material is organized in a manner which is a new departure for Solzhenitsyn. *August 1914* contains sixty-four brief chapters without titles. They comprise his own reconstruction of the events he describes, supplemented by montages of newspaper cuttings and quotations in full from German army despatches. These are then punctuated by trenchant aphorisms, linked by daily summaries of the military situation and lent an impressionistic colour by the inclusion of a number of what Solzhenitsyn calls 'cinematic' episodes. The author's language, sounding at times distinctly post-revolutionary, remains for him a primary artistic concern, and there are many passages of great beauty and power conveyed in Solzhenitsyn's polished, innovatory and distinctive style.

*August 1914* is an impressive work, and its true place will doubtless emerge when the other two volumes of the series are complete. In writing it Solzhenitsyn once again outstripped the literary critics who were busy assessing the importance of his Nobel Prize. The L'Herne volume, *Soljénitsyne*, compiled by Georges Nivat and Michel Aucouturier, is, as they point out, a homage to Solzhenitsyn. It is one of the first attempts in a language other than Russian to provide an anthology of excerpts from Solzhenitsyn's writing, with the addition of critical commentary, documents, biographical material and a bibliography. Readers of Russian will doubtless already be familiar with the Possev Verlag six-volume *Complete Works of Solzhenitsyn* and a number of well-known Slavists have collaborated on this French volume. In addition to the editors' own work there are contributions from C. Frioux, G. Katkov, H. Zamoyska and J. de Proyart, with a *samizdat* essay by L. Kopelev and R. Orlova to provide a little balance.

The collection falls into three parts and is preceded by a brief chronology which introduces some hitherto unpublished comments attributed to Solzhenitsyn. No authorized account of Solzhenitsyn's biography has appeared in print yet, apart from the author's own letter to the Nobel Committee for the 1970 Yearbook (not included here). Four separate studies—by Michael Scammell, Patricia Blake, David Burg and George Feifer, and the late Arkadi Belinkov—have yet to appear. Consequently this chronology is important in itself by appearing to be authoritative and yet giving no source for a remark like:

> It was only immediately before the war, when I came to Central Russia, that I discovered that region which for me is utterly unique, and thanks to which I was to become not just a writer in general, but a Russian writer,

a comment which echoes the beginning of 'Matryona's House'. The chronology has some unspectacular omissions; it does not for example mention Solzhenitsyn's period of forced labour on Moscow building-sites immediately after the war in 1945, a factor which connects up with the story of Nerzhin in *The First Circle*. Otherwise it should prove useful to those interested in following the course of Solzhenitsyn's life and the manner in which it is reflected in his writing.

The first section contains three stories: 'Zakhar-Kalita', 'The Right Hand' and 'The Easter Procession', as well as the first published translation of *A Candle in the Wind* and the already much-translated prose-poems. The French versions appear to be faithful to the original, though 'L'Inconnu de Krechetkova', a translation used elsewhere in the text, is hardly an apt rendering of the Russian *Sluchai na stantsii Krechetovka* and loses much of the irony of the original title.

This section is followed by an excellent collection of documents on the 'Solzhenitsyn Affair'. Many of these have not been included in *Solzhenitsyn: A Documentary Record* and can be found only in separate Western publications like Patricia Blake's *Khrushchev and the Arts*, Abraham Brumberg's *In Quest of Justice*, or *Survey*, *Problems of Communism* and the Soviet press. Even volume six of the *Complete Works* does not attempt such an ambitious coverage. Most of the standard documents by and about Solzhenitsyn are contained in this section: his famous open letters from 1967 onwards, letters in his support from other writers, reports of Writers' Union meetings leading to his expulsion in 1969 and a final brief reference to the Nobel Prize award, an event which came too late to be covered by the editors. It should be noted that in the L'Herne version the text of the detailed discussion of *Cancer Ward* by the Moscow Section of the Writers' Union in November, 1966, in which Solzhenitsyn played a leading part, differs markedly from other texts available in Russian and English. Once again no source is given, but it may well have been provided by Belinkov, whose own perceptive comments at this very same meeting have inexplicably been omitted here.

*Solzhenitsyn: A Documentary Record* is a far less ambitious book, produced on the premise that 'a documentary record of the Solzhenitsyn case . . . may help the reader to understand [the background of his life, of his fate as an individual and a writer]'. This is a hastily assembled, in some instances woodenly translated and clumsily edited, collection of numerous essential documents on the 'Solzhenitsyn Affair'. There is no attempt to provide anything more than a superficial assessment of Solzhenitsyn's literary worth. In the scramble to publish as soon as possible after the Nobel Prize award and thereby secure a market for a budget-priced popular book much of importance was lost. The result is that English readers who are not experts in Soviet affairs, speak no Russian, but are interested in Solzhenitsyn purely as a literary figure, will turn to this volume as a reputable source. They would do well to consult L'Herne first, if not in preference.

A glance at the extremely thorough and valuable 'bio-bibliographie' at the end of the L'Herne collection is enough to convince anyone that an enormous amount has been written about Solzhenitsyn. The Soviet critic V. I. Lakshin in his 1964 article for *Novy mir*, 'Aleksandr Solzhenitsyn, His Friends and Enemies', already made the vital distinction between normative and analytical criticism of Solzhenitsyn's writing. It was on this issue that the *TLS's* Commentary column aroused a heated debate at the turn of the year when it asked for clarification and justification of the Nobel Prize Committee's motives in awarding Solzhenitsyn the Literary Prize.

Though Vinokur may write on Solzhenitsyn's language, Belinkov on the synecdoche of good and evil in Solzhenitsyn's work, Mihajlov on *Ivan Denisovich* and Dostoevsky's *Notes from the House of the Dead*, Lukács on Thomas Mann's *Der Zauberberg*, Solzhenitsyn and Socialist Realism, Solzhenitsyn will continue to write and elude definitions. But no doubt everybody's view will be changed after the next Solzhenitsyn 'sensation'.

# 18

# FICTION OF 1971

## (*f*) NADINE GORDIMER

### *A Guest of Honour*

ALTHOUGH SHE FIRST BECAME KNOWN (through the *New Yorker*) as a short-story writer, Nadine Gordimer has always seemed to belong in the spacious, solid, conscientious tradition of novelists we associate with the nineteenth century—a sterner discipline than the sort of fiction nowadays described as 'documentary'. Her cool camera eye observed details of white and black behaviour—Scenes from Johannesburg Life. Her first novel, tracing the upbringing of a middle-class white South African girl and the awakening of her liberal conscience, recorded experience with the sort of spontaneous honesty that inspires us all to think we too might be novelists—ignoring the imaginative transmutation and skill beneath the easy Yes-I-know-that-feeling manner. There have been other novels and collections of stories since then, sometimes appearing more passionately committed, occasionally too effortlessly fluent and clever, but gradually extending Miss Gordimer's reputation as a writer inescapably haunted by the South African situation and reinforcing an impression that, without overt didacticism or distortion, she was a profoundly moral and political writer no longer content merely to observe.

Now at last, with *A Guest of Honour*, Miss Gordimer has consolidated all her achievements in a long, weighty, and magnificent novel which not only reflects the mature political awareness that has always been implicit, but which also shows her special gift of patient and painstaking honesty as a writer to its fullest advantage. Its

---

(*f*) NADINE GORDIMER: *A Guest of Honour*. 504 pp. Cape. £2.50.

(*g*) ANTHONY POWELL: *Books Do Furnish a Room*. 240 pp. Heinemann. £1.75.

(*h*) PHILIP ROTH: *Our Gang* (*Starring Tricky and His Friends*). 200 pp. Cape. £1.75.

(*i*) IVY COMPTON-BURNETT: *The Last and the First*. 159 pp. Gollancz. £1.40. *Dolores*. 330 pp. William Blackwood. £1.50.

(*j*) JAMES PURDY: *Jeremy's Version*. 308 pp. Cape. £1.85.

authenticity is so powerful that one might almost say this is 'the novel as history'—not at all the same thing as an 'historical novel'; moreover, its very setting and subject, the first days of a newly independent East African state, are a logical consequence of Miss Gordimer's South African experience—the liberal daydream confronting the Third World as it actually is; no longer an idealistic vision but a painful, problematical society which risks wrecking the very freedoms fought for. Her protagonist, though in no sense a crude symbol, is carefully chosen to represent the paradox of the white liberal situation in such a state. A former D.C., forced out for being too pro-African, Bray is now in his fifties but still the tall, handsome, civilized English colonel. Trying to define why he has left his peaceful retirement and his wife Olivia to return, not only as a guest at the independence celebrations, but to stay on, at the confident request of his old friend Mweta, now President, and prepare a survey on educational needs, he hesitantly admits that he is aware of his symbolic importance to his African friends:

> I was . . . something that never happened in Africa: a voluntary relinquishment in friendship and light all round, of white intransigeance that can only be met with black intransigeance. I represented something that all Africans yearned for—even while they were talking about driving white people into the sea—a situation where they wouldn't have had to base the dynamic of *their* power on bitterness.

In Gala, his old district, he lives a haphazard bachelor life again—no curtains, monotonous meals devotedly cooked by his old houseboy, only the tawdry, pathetic imitations of European luxury hotels and comforts touchingly maintained by African owners, the same few white settlers drinking and complaining and getting out fast, the same anxious struggle for Western educational talismans, the same dreadful poverty and bewilderment, expecting him, as a figure of authority, to solve insoluble problems overnight.

And yet, it is not the same, and it is not—at least to start with—a depressing return 'home' for Bray. Full of confidence and immensely popular, Mweta seems a splendid President, his enthusiasm infectious, and his plans intelligent. In Bray's old Residence, cheery, plump Aleke and his sprawling family seem competently at home: a white girl, Rebecca, whose husband is off making money in the South, becomes Aleke's secretary. She also becomes Bray's mistress, at first in gentle, almost anonymous fellow-feeling: she is young and healthy, he wrily and detachedly thinks of her as his 'final kick of the prostate', and is grateful for pure pleasure. But under the surface political turmoil is building up: Shinza, the ruffianly, bearded old guru of Mweta's youth, a dedicated socialist and cunning politician, as well as a close friend of Bray's, has been excluded from the Cabinet. Bray, visiting his remote and primitive hide-out, is disquieted by Shinza's evidence of secret arrests, torture and corruption. There is trouble in the mines, rumour of gun-running across the border by dissident exiles, Mweta announces a State of Emergency, and imposes his choice on Congress against the growing discontent of Shinza and union leaders. Bray finds he must choose between loyalty to the regime and faith in the old revolutionary, and his political choice is paralleled by a reluctant awareness that he has also 'chosen' Rebecca—his wife seems a stranger in another world, his emotional involvement with the girl too strong to resist. He even has a sudden flash of awareness—Olivia and Mweta are linked, individuals who no longer touch the things he believes in.

It is inevitable that Bray should become the innocent victim of his beliefs, although Miss Gordimer builds up the tension in her narrative with such skill and sense of danger that the climax remains a shock and should not be revealed here. In the aftermath of tragedy, Rebecca's decision to leave her husband offers a comment on what Bray represents—he has made it impossible for her to live with a man who exploits Africa to 'make his pile'. With tragic irony, Bray is dismissed by a militantly pro-African young woman as 'one of those nice white liberals getting mixed up in things they don't understand'.

One can't do justice to the scope of *A Guest of Honour*. Warned that there are many pages of Congress speeches reported in full, discussions of union problems, of how to reconcile independent socialism with the need for Western capital investment, the reader may balk at having to make the unaccustomed effort of political involvement. Yet because Miss Gordimer still retains her clear and witty eye and ear for detail, the images of African life provide a superbly entertaining background—almost a film documentary to lend force to the ideas discussed. She fixes certain scenes and smells indelibly even on a memory ignorant of her beloved continent—the Greek café with its 'staple frontiersman diet' and synthetic juices churning brightly in containers, where Shinza prepares his campaign, the still forest lake with baobab and white sandy beach, the backroom crowded with children, card-players, the silent old barefoot black woman enthroned on her commode while the eager politicians argue and the radio plays. Among the huge cast of characters, white and black, are some splendidly satirical sketches—Loulou, the glamorous wide-boy, with his retinue of frizzy-pigtailed 'petites folies' and stock of tourish junk; old Dando, the disgruntled white lawyer refusing to change his manners or drinking habits even if he is Mweta's Attorney General; the anxious Dane who runs the Silver Rhino Hotel, and his truculent, pretty daughter who elopes with a supercilious African media man—all these we see through Bray's eyes, yet without preconception or distortion.

It is part of Miss Gordimer's talent to have used as her camera, her symbolic hero-victim and spokesman, a man like Bray who has a private dignity and no personal axe to grind; because he is so obviously a good man, despite being white, liberal, vulnerable, and imperfect, we can accept his commitment to the ideal of Free Africa without questioning Miss Gordimer's imaginative integrity and this is perhaps, most of all, why her novel deserves to be read carefully and widely by those whom the problem concerns.

## (*g*) ANTHONY POWELL

### *Books Do Furnish a Room*

ANTHONY POWELL'S GREAT SEQUENCE OF NOVELS now begins to reach a point in the narrative—the immediate postwar years—not far short of the moment at which the whole scheme was conceived; that key passage at the beginning of *A Question of Upbringing* where Jenkins stands rapt in contemplation of mortality, aware suddenly of the patterns in which human beings dance around him to the music of time, must have described an experience belonging to the late 1940s. Those early pages set a scheme and an atmosphere for the whole series which Mr. Powell has sustained with an extraordinary determination and consistency over twenty years' writing. At the same time, it would be equally extraordinary if so intelligent and pertinacious a writer, having so profound a control of his means, had not developed his art within such a period—allowed, perhaps, some significant sea-change to occur as the series nears its completion (the novel under review is the tenth of the author's projected twelve).

*Books Do Furnish a Room* does, in fact, extend certain processes which had begun in the war novels and become pronounced in the last of them, *The Military Philosophers*: life is seen less to repeat itself than to move in a developing sequence of events, its formal patterns modified to permit a more realistic untidiness. But whereas a bewildering array of characters and episodes in the war novels threatened at points to submerge the design, this first novel of a peacetime trilogy splendidly restores the equilibrium. Although necessarily and unmistakably part of his wider scheme, it is probably the most self-contained novel Mr. Powell has written since the sequence was started, a witty, sinister and original evocation of the postwar years, their oddly unfruitful literary life in particular.

For one thing, the author's gift for the long, subtly detailed comic episode and the development in depth of entirely new characters has returned to him. Erridge is dead. Conventional relatives and old left-wing cronies (including the rising Labour backbencher, Widmerpool) mingle weirdly at a funeral which combines the comic and the alarming with great brilliance—and culminates in Mrs. Widmerpool (née Pamela Flitton) vomiting into a vase of dubious value in a corridor: maintaining the talent for causing trouble which she showed as a child of six by being sick in the font at Stringham's wedding. 'She seemed an appropriate attendant on death', Jenkins comments as she irrupts into Erridge's funeral service; and it is clear that Mrs. Widmerpool as an agent of destruction now commands her creator's imagination as thoroughly as her husband dominated it in the earlier books as a representative of striving and impregnable vanity. She has already destroyed Templer, in the last novel; here she ruins Mr. Powell's newest character, and a fine creation indeed, the bizarrely talented writer X. Trapnel, author of *Camel Ride to the Tomb*, a kind of outcast, unpolitical Orwell. She is the most striking guise assumed by mortality at a stage in Jenkins's life when youth is past, when friends and habits are being gloomily reshuffled, when it is a painful effort to recover identity after the upheavals of war, and when Melancholy—in all the forms listed and elaborated by Robert Burton (whom Jenkins is studying as his creator studied John Aubrey)—seems increasingly to waylay human effort and hopefulness. As always, Mr. Powell's observations of the particular melancholy of love-madness, which Mrs. Widmerpool inflicts with such arbitrariness, are unerring—a blend of detached exactitude and sardonic sympathy.

One need go no farther than the concept of melancholy to find the theme which characterizes the later novels of *The Music of Time* and introduces into the comedy a seriousness not altogether promised by the original programme: in such a way, perhaps, have twenty years' work, developing the ideas which obsessed him at the start, led now to a finer, wiser, ultimately more serene view of human progress through the vicissitudes of existence. Sillery, the don intent on the power game he plays through his more influential students, is now a peer of the realm, publishing his ineffectual memoirs. Jenkins accords him not patronage, but a sort of genuinely affectionate pity. J. G. Quiggin, Howard Craggs (of the Vox Populi Press, and Boggis and Stone) and the new Bagshaw (whose nickname is the title of the novel) join together to launch a left-wing publishing house and an up-to-date literary magazine. The hopes expire in a welter of personal conflicts, prosecutions and general mediocrity. But the atmosphere generated is one of a wise sadness rather than mockery or satire. Jenkins goes on a visit to his school and meets Le Bas, now well over eighty and acting as librarian. There is something of a feeling of wonder and respect at his sheer endurance, outlasting so many transient lives and fashions: Stringham's and Templer's lives in particular. Le Bas has even lived to see a son of the mysterious Akworth, disgraced by Widmerpool and expelled, coming to the school. Time has added a dimension of compassion to the theme which has in no way diminished the comic sharpness and resource; if anything, the new novel is a more finished, inventive and entertaining book on the purely comic level than several that have gone before, sustaining its humour through a series of scenes which rival in subtlety and surprise almost anything Mr. Powell has ever written. And the sea-change in his approach is possibly the most gratifying and heartening one that could have occurred: his comedy has become a high, serene art, increasingly able to encompass and interpret the gravest subjects, achieving and transcending the objectives he set himself at the beginning.

## (*h*) PHILIP ROTH

### *Our Gang*

THE UGLY PIETIES of current political rhetoric provide the ample target for Philip Roth's satirical venom in *Our Gang*, and he bespatters it with shots aimed both cunningly and casually. The trouble is, though, that he could hardly fail to miss. The chief object of Roth's assault is one Trick E. Dixon, President of the United States (and successor to such familiar stalwarts as John F. Charisma and Lyin' B. Johnson). Tricky, as the nation knows him, is everything we are now used to hearing American Presidents described as—ignorant, opportunistic, dishonest, unstable, blood-thirsty, and so on. His chief guiding impulse is a simple lust for as much power as he can lay his hands on, and his most potent instrument for achieving this objective is a genius-sized gift for cloaking dire deeds with comfy clichés. Tricky's linguistic treachery is boundless; he takes a connoisseur's delight in seeing just how much distance he can put between words and their true meanings. Rivals he has certainly; but they are men whose lies, though of staggering proportions, are never quite of the calibre and magnitude to outstrip his. And he is lucky to have a Vice-President who talks exclusively in alliteration:

> the hairy, the half-cocked if you know what I mean, the hammer-and-sickle supporters, the hard-core pornographers, the hedonists, the Hell's Angels, those whom God won't help because they won't help themselves, the hermaphrodites, the highbrows, the hijackers, the hippies, the Hisses, the homos, the hoodlums of all races, the heroin pushers, the hypocrites. . . .

For Tricky, this kind of thing is kid's stuff. His rhetoric rarely lacks the virtue of balancing his own dark ends against his audience's bright expectations—as he keeps telling everyone, that's what comes of a legal education.

The book opens with Tricky being questioned by a citizen on a key anti-abortion speech, a speech in which he has come out firmly on the side of 'the sanctity of human life—including the life of the yet unborn. For, surely, the unborn have rights also, recognized in law, recognized even in principles expounded by the United Nations.' The citizen wants to know how Tricky squares this courageous stand with his attitude to Lieutenant Calley's murder of twenty-two Vietnamese civilians.

It's not that the citizen is worried about the fate of the twenty-two *as such*; what really bothers him is the possibility that one of them might have been a pregnant woman: 'I am seriously troubled by the possibility that Lieutenant Calley may have committed an abortion.' Tricky is more than equal to the challenge and there ensues a long and brilliantly funny disputation on the Swiftian model with the force of our amusement and horror deriving from the disputants' simple refusal to admit into their argument the one element that would make ugly nonsense of both sides. Once the twenty-two deaths are taken for granted, humanitarian zeal can have a rhetorical field day. It is worth quoting a typical exchange:

CITIZEN: I hate to say this, Mr. President, but I am seriously troubled when I think that one of those twenty-two Vietnamese civilians Lieutenant Calley killed may have been a pregnant woman.

TRICKY: Now just one minute. We have a tradition in the courts of this land that a man is innocent until he is proven guilty. There were babies in that ditch at My Lai, and we know that there were women of all *ages* but I have not seen a single document that suggests the ditch at My Lai contained a *pregnant* woman.

CITIZEN: But what *if*, sir—what *if* one of the twenty-two was a pregnant woman? Suppose that were to come to light in your judicial review of the lieutenant's conviction. In that you personally believe in the sanctity of human life, including the life of the yet unborn, couldn't such a fact seriously prejudice you against Lieutenant Calley's appeal? I have to admit that as an opponent of abortion, it would have a profound effect upon me.

TRICKY: Well, it's very honest of you to admit it. But as a trained lawyer, I think I might be able to go at the matter in a somewhat less emotional manner. First off, I would have to ask whether Lieutenant Calley was *aware* of the fact that the woman in question was pregnant *before* he killed her....

And so it goes on. Was she 'showing', was she in the middle, early or late stages of pregnancy? Tricky even manages to sidetrack the discussion into the hypothesis that perhaps the woman *wanted* an abortion: 'Let's be perfectly frank; you cannot die of an abortion, if you don't go looking for the abortion to begin with. If you have not gotten yourself in an abortion *predicament* to begin with. Surely that's perfectly clear.' It is all managed by Roth with great delicacy and wit, and establishes a standard which the rest of the novel only intermittently lives up to.

Having provided Tricky's credentials, Roth pitches him into a grotesque chain-reaction of decision-making. The President's stand for the unborn is developed into a major electioneering plank, with Tricky proposing to extend the franchise to foetuses ('here at long last, we have a great bloc of voters who simply are not going to be taken in by the lop-sided and distorted versions of the truth that are presented to the American public through the various media'). This master-stroke backfires, provoking a Boy Scouts Revolution in which Tricky is branded as an advocate of fornication. A crisis meeting held in the blast-proof underground locker-room (with Tricky dressed in his thinking suit, the spanking new 'football uniform he wore during his four years on the bench at Prissier College') produces the decision to retaliate against the Boy Scouts with armed force and to foist the blame for the uprising on a conspiracy organized by a Black baseball star who had recently defected to Denmark, kingdom of pornography. The Scouts are crushed (there's a very funny sequence in which Tricky, on television to explain himself, displays the various blades of the Boy Scout knife, thus establishing the Army's need to answer force with force), and Tricky simultaneously launches an invasion of Denmark, on the pretext of restoring Elsinore to English-speaking hands. This invasion eventually escalates into a nuclear attack.

Needless to say, thoughout all this Tricky maintains his usual level of explanatory rhetoric, though it must be said that Roth sets himself a much less taxing and subtle task here than in the book's opening chapter. Tricky's absurd speeches go on far too long, and the satirical analogies are too frequently merely laborious and crude. The Denmark joke, once it is registered, is simply not apt or surprising enough to be dragged out for more than a page or two, but Roth gives it virtually a whole chapter. The mimicry is accurate, no doubt, but we don't really need to have it proved to us that, on top of everything else, Presidents are boring.

Much of the same charge can be laid against the book's closing scenes, in which we are plunged into the hubbub of lies, counter-lies and counter-counter-lies provoked by Tricky's assassination (he is discovered, in a foetal position, in a plastic bag after going into hospital for an operation to have the sweat glands removed from his upper lip) and, even more forcibly, against the disastrously miscalculated finale. By discovering Tricky installed in Hell, fighting an election against Satan, Roth disperses and generalizes much of the specific effectiveness of his satire—Tricky aggrandized to diabolical proportions is not the Tricky we have come to know and hate. The whole point, one had thought, was that he was a President, and thus perpetually replaceable by another Tricky, then another, for as long as Americans want to be tricked.

## (*i*) IVY COMPTON-BURNETT

### *The Last and the First* and *Dolores*

THE SYMMETRY by which the posthumous publication of Dame Ivy Compton-Burnett's final novel *The Last and the First* coincides with the reissuing, after sixty years, of her earliest book *Dolores* will delight all addicted admirers. It might not have pleased the author herself, who not only excluded *Dolores* from the canon (as do Messrs. Gollancz in referring to her last as 'the nineteenth title') but, although its original publication was apparently quite successful, published nothing for fourteen years afterwards. All the same, as Professor Burkhart says in his introduction, 'the genesis of genius attracts a natural speculation'; a dead writer forgoes the right to thwart curiosity and, as Dame Ivy herself wrote, 'Satisfied curiosity is the best thing in life. The only thing that is as good as it promises to be. Anticipation is not the best part of it.'

It is nevertheless easy to see why *Dolores* was neglected: offered to a publisher today as a first effort, it would almost certainly be turned down. So many people have commented on Dame Ivy's unique style, on her debt to classical drama and to Jane Austen, that it comes as quite a shock to find her first novel such a mixture of mood and mode, above all to find the overwhelmingly pervasive influence of George Eliot—*Dolores* is full of a heavy Victorian sense of duty, wordy and didactic discussions about Church versus Chapel, honour and self-sacrifice; even its structure strongly recalls *Middlemarch.* Dolores, a Yorkshire vicar's daughter, conceives while at Oxford an unspoken love for the eccentric elderly playwright Sigismund Claverhouse. Hoping to remain his pupil and teach, she nevertheless obeys her father's wish to come home as governess to her young stepbrother and sister, suffering the spite—a faint foretaste here of later step-relationships—of the Reverend Cleveland Hutton's selfish second wife. When freedom again offers, she realizes that Claverhouse, now going blind, has fallen in love with her insipid friend Perdita, so once more she nobly does her sacrificial duty. Perdita dies, but again Papa summons Dolores home to replace his dead wife, and again she forgoes the chance of marriage—to Claverhouse's donnish friend—in favour of her enamoured stepsister. Her final act of martyrdom—and its ironical uselessness is pointed in bitter and melodramatic tone, unpurged as in the later novels by wit—is to forsake the dying Claverhouse yet again at her father's summons, merely to hear that he is about to take a third wife; only in the final brief scene, when Dolores has become classics teacher at her old college, is there splendid evidence that already the author knew how to convey tragedy through comedy, as the coy bluestocking ladies discuss their experience of marriage proposals:

'Miss Hutton, can you meet our eyes?' said Miss Adam, not without a suggestion that this was beyond herself.

'Oh, we will acquit Miss Hutton. She is the most sensible of us all', said Miss Cliff.

In spite of its turgid style and stodgy obsession with duty, however, *Dolores* has some good comic moments—not the crudely caricatured village worthies intended as such, but the authentic Compton-Burnett sharpness of tongue, the spry querying of platitudinous attitudes by the bolder spirits of the younger generation in presence of their parents; Bertram, Dolores's somewhat shiftily amiable brother, taken to task for filial ingratitude, says, 'I should not say that affection was a strong point with fathers'; he is well matched with the aggressive Elsa, whose needling of her sanctimonious parents, though slightingly referred to by the author, is precisely the spirited sort of defiance that delights in the later novels.

It could even be said that the Elsa-Dolores type—a mixture of irreverent rebel and high-minded affection and capability—soon crystallized into the image of the Compton-Burnett ideal heroine. Certainly Hermia, the protagonist of *The Last and the First*, is such a young woman and in many ways a striking reincarnation of Dolores. She, too, is a cuckoo in the nest of an autocratic stepmother fiercely jealous of her own offspring's rights, although they appear fonder of their stepsister than of their mother: Hermia, too, longs for freedom and tries teaching as a means of escape; she has a hopeless older suitor, although he leaves her, luckier than Dolores, enough money to provide for her father's last years without sacrificing herself. Indeed, it is unthinkable that Hermia Heriot should ever play the martyr, and she looks, by the end of the book, not merely like being 'a goddess' but also a future domestic tyrant—another of the favourite cast.

One might echo the words with which Dolores seeks to cheer her despairing genius: 'This is not like the work of your prime; but then it is not the work of your prime.' Not that *The Last and the First* betrays a slackening of power—the amazing thing is that the manuscript, pieced together after her death from 'little blue exercise books', appears so very finished—a labour of devotion by Miss Cicely Greig, Miss Gollancz, Miss Elizabeth Sprigge (who vividly describes the final years) and Professor Burkhart (who contributes a brief critical appendix). The plot, not unusually, is merely a reshuffle of familiar cards. In the Big House—this time located in Somerset—Lady Heriot, second wife to the mild eighty-two-year-old Sir Robert, asserts her petty tyranny even over thirty-four-year-old Hermia (' "Did you have a fire in your room last night?" . . . "Do you eat no fat at all?" ') who decides she will become a partner in a girls' school near by. The venture fails, because Miss Murdoch, a splendid comic portrait of stupid reactionary teacher masquerading as profound scholar, blocks all change. Meanwhile, in the humbler mirror of the Heriot household, a lesser tyrant, Jocasta Grimstone, appears shattered by discovering that her pompous bachelor son Hamilton, dying suddenly, has left his fortune to Hermia. This saves her face, her family (who were preparing for 'a move to the lodge as necessitated by retrenchment' as the imposing cook describes it) and, eventually, the Grimstone dignity, for one of those undelivered letters (opened, typically, by Lady Heriot) comes to light and leads to Hermia marrying Osbert, a nicer Grimstone, first seen dressing up in his grandmother's clothes. Both he and his sister Erica, like the younger Heriots, provide scathing asides on the matriarchs:

> 'It is not a day for betraying the hidden side of yourselves,' [says Jocasta].
>
> 'Which days are the ones for that?' said Erica. 'I have never known them.'
>
> 'They say that sorrow is ennobling,' said Osbert. 'So I suppose Grannie is ennobled. That is why her standard is so high.'
>
> 'Well, it is my own, and different from yours, perhaps different from everyone's.'

It is hard not to quote many such brilliant comic exchanges, the aphoristic reversal of proverbial pomposity just as taut, and the revelation of character as precise, as Dame Ivy ever wrote. She herself said: 'I do not feel that I have any real or organic knowledge of life later than about 1910. . . . When an age is ended, you see it as it is.' It is odd to realize that 'her' age was already ended before *Dolores* appeared, that her first and last books span nearly sixty years and offer many similarities, and yet that *The Last and the First* seems by contrast so amazingly youthful, sane, and relevant to family life today; it is hard to accept that the age of Compton-Burnett has actually ended and impossible to believe it will not survive another sixty years and more.

# (*j*) JAMES PURDY

## *Jeremy's Version*

*Jeremy's Version* could be James Purdy's most ambitious work and will almost certainly be his longest to date. Subtitled 'Part One of Sleepers in Moon Crowned Valleys', it is, we learn, the first of a projected trilogy of novels to be linked by their locale—a small Mid-Western town. The title *Jeremy's Version* could (to be fanciful) stand for the best of Purdy: 'Version' is clear and direct and yet open to deceits and misunderstandings; and 'Jeremy' compounds this, a little theatrical and indulgent; at once too sweet and slightly sinister. The worst of Purdy could be sieved out of the subtitle.

The question of length is important with regard to Mr. Purdy. His short stories and novellas have been praised by distinguished authors and critics who have often referred to the effectiveness of his economy. There is nothing in *Jeremy's Version* as 'complete' as some of the short stories: nothing as compact as in some of the novellas. While protracted comparisons would be unfair—as the attempt here is so different—it might be as well to be reminded of some of his qualities earlier expressed with such brevity.

In 'Colour of Darkness', for example, we have this opening sentence: 'Sometimes he thought about his wife, but a thing had begun of late, usually after the boy went to bed, a thing which *should* have been terrifying but which was not: he could not remember now what she had looked like.' Easy as a steady breath—and yet in forty-one words he has established two major relationships, the central character, a style of life (the son is called 'the boy'), the theme and the precise nature of a puzzle which is both common experience and extremely peculiar. About 3,000 words later and the story is told without faltering, having in that space been transformed from a drawing-room comedy to a family melodrama.

Melodrama is a most favoured form of story with Mr. Purdy and nowhere better employed than in the novella '63: Dream Palace' where the 'hero' strangles his own brother after several very theatrical incidents, ending with a visit to *Othello*, after which his stage-struck companion attempts a homosexual rape on him. The story is very far-fetched but we are forced to go along with it—and not permitted to dwell on it for too long. As the language in the short story is simple, so here the operatic plot is simply told. The whole piece is no more than 20,000 words long.

*Jeremy's Version* is about 100,000 words long: the trilogy therefore could be 300,000, and here there are few restrictions on either language or plot.

*Jeremy's Version* is the saga of two families—the Ferguses and the Summerlads, both in the American Old Testament Powerful Strange Folks tradition. It tells of two mighty women, both well-connected, both dictators, enemies and opposites—Winifred Fergus, fearless old spinster and family-consumed sister to Wilders, a dissolute financier and absentee husband to Elvira, beautiful boarding-house landlady and whore: and again, like all of them, 'family-consumed'. Elvira's family is three sons, Dick, Jethro, young Rory and Matt, the 'adopted' son—and she is a lover-mother to all of them. The story is located in the Mid-West and set in about the 1920s. The action is violent, gothic, but mostly kept in the family. Elvira eventually decides to divorce Wilders, thereby lighting a long fuse. Winifred urges on her brother to defend the lawsuit for honour and revenge, and the course of events includes two possible rapes, lost fortunes, drink, fights, 'unspoken of' crimes, lurid revelations about small-town sex, scandals, climactic effects, a son's attempt to shoot his mother and a canvas of characters drawn, mostly, in blood. It is perhaps to protect himself from the assault of his own creations or creatures that Mr. Purdy uses the device of the long flashback. Jeremy is a boy of fifteen of the present day who stumbles on Matt, a survivor of the old times, and becomes his 'amanuensis'; the loving and credulous outsider, like a perfect reader, perhaps; but more like an audience.

For this book, like much of Purdy, is saturated in theatricality. The whole thing is a 'tall' story and often appears too far-stretched. Matt, who 'tells' the story, has been an actor; an ambition shared by at least three of the leading characters in the novel itself. Scenery is always described flatly, like a backcloth; most meetings are old-fashioned 'dramatic'; the characters make a deliberate Entrance or Exit or both, and the people themselves live in a welter of operatic blood, tears and sweat. (There is little toil.)

Yet Mr. Purdy forces you to go along with him. Despite the total failure of the flashback device and the boy-narrator, despite the tediously confused opening, despite the reluctance to solidify character early on which may be intended to mark a slow Act One but which appears as a churlish and unnecessary withholding of information, you are gradually drawn into the lives of these people. There is a great deal to put up with.

For they are awash in self-love, mutual love, and Mr. Purdy's love. He is, as always, at pains to say how beautiful they look: he cannot bear anyone not to look beautiful—we feel the author is more sensitive on this than his most self-adoring creations. The few who are not beautiful tend to be monstrous. His heroes and heroines in fact are a package-cliché of one area of American fiction, more usually associated with the South—Aristocratic, Beautiful, Wasteful, Passionate, Charming, Wild, Talented, Rich (or Formerly Rich), and they move in Torrid Heat or Torrential Rain drawing from the Earth and the Past and the Family both a sound and a fury which detaches them from most other mortals. But Mr. Purdy makes the cliché work for him. If we stick at the book for long enough, we care, on a personal, insistent level, about the fate of these people. As they act only on primary motives and carry out mostly primal acts, so we are teased into the primitive circle a compelling story-teller draws about him and we listen.

But is there *more* than that? For Mr. Purdy as often attracts us by the telling (as in *The Nephew*) as much as by the tale; could it be here that he has lost the graces and retained only the considerable but more common gift of the story-teller? After all, if we are prepared to read on, we will race to the end of many stories—the compulsion to finish is in one way a mark of many a genre novel. Perhaps Mr. Purdy is turning this type of American novel into a genre. And certainly there are times when the biting virgin eating her rapist raw and the same girl (in full menstrual flood) an hour later seducing a fourteen-year-old crippled boy; when crypto-homosexuality and crypto-incest and crypto-aristocratic ways sicken the plot; when those golden privileged childhoods and perfect beings of the past—when all the sperm-splattered scene appears as the empty silt-bed of a drained-out tradition.

Mr. Purdy seems to be aware of all this, and uses it, but not well enough. Jeremy, after all, is a child, and this is full of a child's fearful exaggeration and lies and fantasies. But Jeremy is not, here, convincing enough to be the author. That man is still Mr. Purdy himself, and there is a feeling that the 'encores' shouted at him after previous performances, the bouquets from John Cowper Powys and Dame Edith Sitwell, Angus Wilson and others in the past have over-intoxicated him. Sometimes in a description, or more often in an exchange with the family, we have again the best of Purdy: a fierce and deep sense of dangerous confrontation which is gripping—as few writers can be gripping. But he is eager to give us More, More! Encore!—and he raises his voice of keys up the passages or jumps to a climax and stubs that first fine accomplishment. The whole delivery has been hotted up.

Yet there is a way to see it all as the working of American legends, which have attained mythical weight, and American history of a sort which has attained common literary currency, into a grand tragicomedy. There are two other novels to come as companions to this. Perhaps one will be true tragedy, the other the real comedy. Then *Jeremy's Version* could stand between the two as a fantastic commentary.

# 19

# TROUBLED PSYCHES

## (*a*) THE END OF THE LINE

'One of the most remarkable features of the arts in this century has been the sudden, sharp rise in the casualty rate among the artists.' At least part of A. Alvarez's thesis depends not just on our accepting this proposition but also on our finding in it grounds on which to base further, and much larger, propositions—propositions to do with art as well as with the lives and deaths of artists. Twentieth-century horrors, the argument runs, have been of such scope and magnitude and have been attended by such a complete breakdown of traditional structures of belief that the artist who does not expose himself, his whole sensibility and psyche, to the full weight of those horrors will inevitably turn out to be marginal, old-fashioned or genteel. The artist who *does*, on the other hand, is running grave psychic risks—risks of misery, certainly, but also of madness and suicide.

The modern art we should value, Mr. Alvarez believes, is that art whose making we perceive to have necessitated extreme dangers of this kind—work which has manifestly 'been there' and which has miraculously returned (with or without its maker). It is no accident that Mr. Alvarez responds with fervour to that moving letter of Wilfred Owen's, written just before Owen went back to the front. The letter ends:

> But chiefly I thought of the very strange look on all the faces in that camp; an incomprehensible look, which a man will never see in England, though wars should be in England; nor can it be seen in any battle. But only in Etaples.
>
> It was not despair, or terror, it was more terrible than terror, for it was a blindfold look, and without expression, like a dead rabbit's.
>
> It will never be painted, and no actor will ever seize it. And to describe it, I think I must go back and be with them.

---

(*a*) A. Alvarez: *The Savage God: A Study of Suicide*. 249 pp. Weidenfeld and Nicolson. £3.25.

(*b*) D. W. Winnicott: *Playing and Reality*. 169 pp. Tavistock. £2.10. *Therapeutic Consultations in Child Psychiatry*. 410 pp. Hogarth Press. £4.50.

The artist as psychic hero, as lone voyager into dark, maddening terrain, as the volunteer and the elect who must 'go back and be with them' in order 'to describe it': this is the kind of artist that Mr. Alvarez is intuitively drawn to; and if one can detect behind his impulse to heroize, even melodramatize the creative effort some radical frustration with the contemporary writer's marginal and cushioned social role, this recognition serves on the whole to re-inforce rather than undermine the impact of much of what he has to say. For this book, though the larger part of it is presented as objective theorizing or literary-critical commentary, is essentially a personal testimony, an attempt to systematize private intuitions, to follow through—with as much intelligence and scholarship as can be mustered—convictions and dispositions which the author's own life—so he lets us know—has forced upon him.

Even so, the fact that Mr. Alvarez is brave enough to reveal his sources doesn't mean that we have any right to pat him on the head. *The Savage God* is divided into three main parts, each representing a different approach to the 'study of suicide'. There is the personal approach: the book opens with a long memoir of Sylvia Plath and closes with an account of the author's own suicide-attempt ten years ago. Between these two blocks of autobiography—and both over-shadowed and supported by them—comes the objective 'study'. Mr. Alvarez offers a brisk historical account of changing attitudes to suicide, as revealed in life, law and literature 'throughout the ages'; he mounts a detailed critique of the proliferating theories of modern 'suicidologists'; he argues (re-argues, really, for many of his ideas about Extremist poetry were gone into in his essay 'Beyond All This Fiddle') for the uniqueness of the modern, and particularly the con-temporary, writer's vulnerability to psychic damage.

The book's chief object, though, is to explore what one might call the 'suicidal element', to penetrate at least some distance into the existential presence of the wish, or rather the resolve, to die. Where the arguments and assertions become suspect (and they often do) it is usually because Mr. Alvarez has reached a point in his reasoning where reason isn't any use, where blank bafflement insists on taking over, where it has got to be acknowledged that the truest thing we can know about suicide is that we cannot know. It is Mr. Alvarez's ele-mentary awareness that 'suicide means different things for different people at different times' that encourages both the best and the worst things in *The Savage God.* At best, it impels him to that tentativeness, that accuracy of particular perception which informs both of his autobiographical pieces and most of his literary case-histories (the detailed studies of Chatterton and Cowper, for example). At worst, it entices him into a strained, rhetorical over-eagerness to embrace clinching summations: the kind of brilliant guesses which are seductive and permissible in a situation where—well, where it's anybody's guess.

'For Sylvia Plath', he writes, 'it [suicide] was an attempt to get herself out of a desperate corner her own poetry had boxed her into.' This apparently confident diagnosis comes in a long memoir, the chief merit of which has been its steadily respectful avoidance of anything approaching a final 'verdict' on Plath's death. In the main, this essay strikes the disinterested reader as the reverse of exploiting or sensational, and the last impression it leaves is that Mr. Alvarez is claiming to know more about it all than his direct dealings with the poet revealed to him. Indeed, a criticism of it *as a memoir* could be that it seems all the time to be leaving really important things unsaid, to be inhibited by its propriety. And perhaps it is this difficulty, together with the final and uncircuitable difficulty of knowing for sure what actually went on, that presses Mr. Alvarez into assimilating the 'case' of Sylvia Plath to a theory about the riskiness of writing poetry.

One has only to turn to the author's very fine account of his own suicide-attempt to contemplate the necessary discrepancy between the facts of these matters and the theories that outsiders might apply to them—what if Mr. Alvarez had succeeded; what would we have thought literature had got to do with it? In fact, of course, a case *could* have been made out. He himself gives us his 'explanation', but even he is only guessing and cannot remember or really account for the act itself and what immediately led up to it. No wonder he so frequently takes refuge in natty encapsulations: 'Suicide is like diving off a high board; the first time is the worst'; 'That shabby, confused, agonized crisis which is the common reality of suicide'. No wonder, either, that his favourite word is 'weird'.

Yet to have reservations about Mr. Alvarez's (albeit hesitant) impulse to establish some causal connexion between Sylvia Plath's poetry and her death doesn't mean that there might not be something in his general theory. Here, too, however, one finds him pushing himself into theoretical corners which he then has to fight his way out of. For instance, he provides us—as a kind of supporting backcloth—with a list of modern writers who have killed themselves.

> A simple point emerges—before the twentieth century it is possible to discuss cases individually, since the artists who killed themselves or were ever seriously suicidal were rare exceptions. In the twentieth century the balance suddenly shifts: the better the artist the more vulnerable he seems to be. Obviously, this is in no way a firm rule.

Obviously, since Mr. Alvarez then goes on to acknowledge that neither Yeats, Eliot, Pound, Joyce, Forster and others were in fact as seriously vulnerable as many lesser writers. And obviously, too, since Mr. Alvarez has already demonstrated in his account of Sylvia Plath that the only way to discuss cases, modern or otherwise, *is* 'individually'; how else, to go no further, can one test a theory that assumes those cases to have an important common factor? And on what does Mr. Alvarez base the assurance with which he tells us that few earlier writers were 'ever seriously suicidal'—how can we know this? They might have been more appalled and frightened by the act itself than moderns are because for them it would have had serious reverberations in the after-life, but this doesn't mean to say that they were immune to its immediate attractions. Even Wordsworth had his nervous breakdown.

But even if one accepts—as in some measure one surely must, at any rate in respect of very recent poetry like that of Mr. Alvarez's admired Robert Lowell, John Berryman, Ted Hughes and Sylvia Plath—that the modern writer is peculiarly prone to get drawn into dark interiors, one is still left with the problem of giving a value to what, in terms of art, emerges from such explorations. Mr. Alvarez is rightly cautious of seeming to over-value chaos at the cost of order and is amusingly severe in his judgment of those, from Dada downwards, who have fashionably dabbled in destructiveness. 'Control', he insists, 'is the operative word.' But there is a basic, and serious, indecisiveness here. On the one hand, Mr. Alvarez can say this:

> In a sense, the whole of twentieth century art has been dedicated to the service of this earthbound Savage God who like the rest of his kind has thrived on blood sacrifice. As with modern warfare, enormous sophistication of theory and technique has gone into producing an art which is more extreme, more violent and, finally more self-destructive than ever before.

And on the other, this:

> Twentieth century art may start with nothing but it flourishes by virtue of

its belief in itself, in the possibility of control over what seems essentially uncontrollable, in the coherence of the inchoate, and in its ability to create its own values.

It might seem that the second quotation is adequate to soothe the obvious objections to the first—objections to that 'as with modern warfare' analogy, that 'finally, more self-destructive than ever before'. The first quotation presents art as combat, as something bloody, destructive, barbaric and—one assumes—ultimately futile (its futility mocking the sophistication of its manufacture), a kind of inert enactment of the zeitgeist. The second presents art as peaceable, as coherence-seeking, value-creating and the rest. The second view, however, is offered more as a pious, blurring afterthought than as the nub of a determinedly occupied position.

Mr. Alvarez's real enthusiasm, one is forced to suspect, is for the first. And this suspicion is supported by the *way* in which he admires the poets he does admire; it *is* the extremity, the destructiveness, the pain and the damage in poets like Berryman and Hughes that appeal to him, and his response to these aspects of their poetry outweighs any objections that might be raised against their formal crudity, their linguistic self-indulgence, their cheaply wallowing glamorizations of violence and brutality. Mr. Alvarez still has enough of the moralist and the rigorous New Critic in him to *wish* to make out a case for their work in terms acceptable to his old self, but his heart is not really in it.

At the back of his attitude to poetry there seems to be a deep loss of faith in poetry, a possibly terminal scepticism about those functions and objectives—'coherence', 'control', 'ability to create its own values' (one might almost add 'life-enhancement')—which he still, however obediently, continues to acknowledge. His response to the spectacular often appears to be but a measure of his boredom, or at any rate his resignation. Or perhaps it is simply that his taste has lost contact with his training. Here again, one is pushed back to the book's personal centre—to the tone of wary, illusionless endurance that pervades the closing pages:

As for suicide. . . . It seems to me somehow as much beyond social or psychic prophylaxis as it is beyond morality, a terrible but utterly natural reaction to the strained, narrow, unnatural necessities we sometimes create for ourselves. And it is not for me. Perhaps I am no longer optimistic enough. I assume now that death, when it finally comes, will probably be nastier than suicide, and certainly a great deal less convenient.

The hint here that suicide is in some way a convenient escape-route for the over-optimistic is not one that Mr. Alvarez would think of following up in his more theoretical pages. But his belief that suicide lies beyond the reach of 'social and psychic prophylaxis' does stand at the centre of those pages, giving edge to an effective polemic against the aridities of statisticians and sociologists.

The one fault is that he tends to stray into over-emphasis now and then, as when he writes (having quoted Swedish suicide statistics to show that enlightened social welfare 'makes more or less no difference to the suicide rate'):

> It seems to me that even the most elegant and convincing sociological theories are short-circuited by this simple observation that suicide is a human characteristic, like sex, which not even the most perfect society will erase.

One can only answer that those who believe social conditions can be responsible for suicides (and one must keep in mind, as Mr. Alvarez himself makes a point of doing elsewhere in the book, the predicament of the suicidal—those who do not actually do it but spend their lives on the brink of doing it) are not talking about 'erasing' suicide but simply of mitigating it, or indeed (in his own words) of 'lengthening the odds'. Mr. Alvarez himself two pages later sympathetically analyses the suicide of one Fanny (who kills herself after being taunted and bullied by male colleagues on a building site) in terms not too remote from the sociological:

> She is no longer young and is presumably unattractive—had she been otherwise the men on the site would surely have treated her more gently despite union principles. She is so poor that she not only works as a manual labourer, she also accepts less than the already derisory wages (derisory since the period is the Great Depression). She can't even afford fuel to heat her room at night. It is a question, in short, of a poverty so grinding that it erodes her identity; being a woman didn't save her from labouring like a man; it didn't save her from being despised by the men she laboured with and getting less pay; it didn't finally save her from being beaten up as though she really were a man. When she seemed to have touched bottom, the punch forced her down still further. After that, there was nothing left and nowhere to go except death.

By and large, Mr. Alvarez is prepared to give credence to much of what the theorists have to say, to take advantage of statistics when they seem genuinely helpful, and to base much of his own theorizing in the terms and concepts of Freudian and post-Freudian analysis. In the end, though, he wishes to preserve a proper guardedness, an intensity of baffled concentration on that pure and private moment in which, as he puts it, 'the suicide creates his own society'. It is a courageous, ultimately impossible objective and Mr. Alvarez's attempt is impressively imaginative and humane. It is probable that, although not much more will be learnt, a lot more will be felt about suicide as a result of *The Savage God* than could be hoped for from a dozen academic treatises.

## (*b*) THERAPY WITHOUT MYSTERY

MOST PSYCHOANALYTICAL WRITING is meant for a restricted circle and it has been hard for the thinking public to find a middle way between esoteric papers and vulgarizations. D. W. Winnicott's posthumous book *Playing and Reality* fits into this gap and does so without concessions in either direction; not only does it condense and clarify his own contribution but it also introduces a new approach in psychoanalysis to a wider public. Winnicott's approach, while in tune with the historical development of psychoanalysis, nevertheless lays its stress differently. In short, his concern is with normality; with the role of psychoanalysis in considering the quality of ordinary life; with the new possibilities of prevention within the range of average human experience; with the normal ups and downs of life and the normal conflicts which have, for each culture, natural ways of being handled.

But how can the public assess such claims of 'a new approach'? The excursions made by psychoanalysts into neighbouring territory have often been disquieting: sometimes stimulating, often bewildering. A current example is the enthusiasm of young neo-Marxists and existentialists for the political application of Wilhelm Reich's theories of sexual freedom or for works by R. D. Laing and David Cooper which invoke psychoanalysis but are often in fact a form of sociology. Winnicott's contribution is quite different; he sees that psychoanalysis must be clinically based to remain a discipline and that in relating to other disciplines it must avoid going off at a tangent. The upshot of Winnicott's work is that psychoanalysis can establish its relation to ethics, education, morals, medicine, the law, religion and the arts in a way acceptable to specialists in those fields.

*Playing and Reality* achieves this cross-fertilizing without loss of professional identity, and in this it reflects Winnicott's working life. As well as being a psychoanalyst, Winnicott also had a pediatric appointment. In this, he applied his psychoanalytic knowledge within the limits of a busy out-patient clinic and did so, as is normal with out-patient doctors, in open forum. Thus parents and children could observe and learn his skills, as could social workers, probation officers, and the legion of child-care officers, hostel wardens and the like who have found Winnicott's work immediately relevant. A large new professional public was thus affected by awareness of the reality of the unconscious and the nature of its everyday operations.

In these interviews Winnicott reached the child's unconscious through a drawing technique (which, with characteristic understatement, he called 'a game': 'squiggles'). Through the squiggles he was often able, after one or more interviews only, to help a child to insights which then offered parents the need and chance to make different responses within the family; some of these drawings are shown in *Therapeutic Consultations in Child Psychiatry*, a permanent clinical record of paradigmatic consultations.

In addition to its therapeutic function, this technique had two other advantages in that Winnicott simultaneously reduced the number of professional child psychiatrists required and educated the public. The technique and its operation involved a whole philosophy, which goes far beyond a merely medical or social-work context. First, by dealing openly with 'private' matters, Winnicott insisted on the universality and normality of conflict. Then, whenever he was successful, he demonstrated the uniqueness and the potential contribution of individuals—which is what life for each of us is all about. His method was also new in that it brought to public notice, on an agreed and actual case, topics which are controversial and alarming if approached from the standpoint of general theory. In this way Winnicott solved the abiding problem of psychiatry and psycho-analysis: which is that to ordinary people the content and subject-matter of the disciplines are recondite, even repulsive (though less so than used to be the case).

Winnicott was the first to overcome this difficulty of acceptance by such means. First, children are aware of much that is unconscious for adults, and invoke and refer to such matters openly and of their own initiative; secondly, Winnicott's method is acceptable: no adult who is present feels personally at risk. But while this application of psychoanalysis in the public services is important in itself, what is new and especially interesting in *Playing and Reality* is Winnicott's understanding of the roots of creativity. Psychoanalysts have been disappointingly reductionist and evaluative in respect of creativity. When they have not ignored it they have seen creativity in a negative way; as a tombstone above drive impulses inscribed 'Here lie wishes now put to "better" uses'. This has seemed to outsiders to be a mechanistic and materialist reduction, a debasing of spontaneous impulse and a determinism ignoring the positive force of qualities which have their own autonomous life and which we all value in quite different ways.

*Playing and Reality* is centred on the theory of the origins and meaning of that play which begins in the early weeks of life with what Winnicott named the transitional object: 'the earliest not-me possession'. Such objects are the teddy-bear or the old blanket which, from very early weeks, infants use to bridge the gap between inner and outer experience. Transitional objects are, at one and the same time, a symbol and a plaything, and they belong, for the baby's imaginative life, both to the baby and to the outer world. Winnicott says that he introduced the term to name both the thing played with and the phenomena deriving from its use. He uses it

> for designation of the intermediate area of experience, between the thumb and the Teddy bear, between the oral eroticism [pleasure in the need for food and sucking] and true object relationship, between primary creative activity and projection of what has been introjected, between primary unawareness of indebtedness and acknowledgment of indebtedness.

Winnicott, then, is seeing in the infant (and *infans* means unable to speak) the pre-verbal imaginative life at its origin in each individual and as it continues, concealed in the shared experience of culture: 'the intense experiencing that belongs to the arts and to the religious impulse in everybody and to imaginative living and to creative scientific work'. An unusual feature of Winnicott's approach is his stress on the creative side of wishes; the *defensive problems* these provoke, which are so much the subject of psychoanalytic therapy and writing, he takes for granted.

Essential to his argument is that there is a paradox, a humility, in these experiences and that this paradox must remain and not be resolved. The paradox concerns who provided what. It is common both to the phenomena of early infancy and derivations from them at all ages. To dissect this is to destroy the omnipotent pleasure which goes with creativity: the unique pleasure we have, both as infants and all our lives, in creating our own part and our own use of the common heritage in an open-ended imaginative playing with possibilities.

Winnicott describes the need for resolution of this paradox as defensive and unhelpful. He is thinking of those precipitated solutions or systems which people develop to resolve uncertainty as being a destructive element in personality: 'a defence organisation which in the adult one can encounter as a false organisation'. This false organization, whether it remains within the personality or is projected and realized in the world, is invented in order to protect the vulnerable core of being. A personal, internal organization may, by projection, be elaborated into a system operating in the world as a structure; an administrative apparatus. Hypomania (defensive over-activity) can lead people to build but it can also lead them to destroy. Ideological movements to ban capital punishment, or, say, the Gay Liberation Front may equally be, in varying degrees, both realistic or serving a false, self-defensive function in any of us, and social forces can help by compelling such organizations to relate to facts, to be objective and so reduce their element of personal 'ism' or fanaticism.

Here, then, is a theoretical justification not only of the open mind, but also of the open society, which makes *Playing and Reality* important over a wide field. This theme, developed throughout the book, is set out expressly in two chapters: 'The Location of Cultural Experience', that is, its location within ourselves; and 'The Place Where We Live'—again, within ourselves and through the surrounding culture, which is 'paradoxically' both highly personal and general at the same time. Winnicott points out: 'We spend most of our time neither in behaviour nor in contemplation, but somewhere else.' And:

> In the vast literature that has been influenced by Freud there can be found a tendency to dwell either on a person's life as it relates to love objects or else on the inner life of the individual. The written words of psychoanalytic literature do not seem to tell us what we want to know . . . we have used the concepts of inner and outer and we want a third concept. Where are we when we are doing what in fact we do a great deal of our time, namely enjoying ourselves?

He answers: 'Creative apperception more than anything else . . . makes the individual feel that life is worth living': i.e., it is what we do in our own quite personal fashion that makes life worth living. Again, referring to the impossibility of 'diagnosing' individuals:

People may be leading satisfactory lives and may do work that is even of exceptional value and yet may be schizoid or schizophrenic. They may be ill in a psychiatric sense because of weak reality sense. To balance this one would have to state that there are others who are so firmly anchored in objectively perceived reality that they are ill in the opposite direction of being out of touch with the subjective world and with the creative approach to fact.

The use made by the individual of his experience of life, his subjective responses to the course of his own development, applies also to the effect of environment in society. Freud's death-instinct devalues the force of environment and individual experience and Winnicott says that in placing weight on an inherited death-instinct 'both Freud and Klein jumped over an obstacle . . . and took refuge in heredity', so avoiding 'the full implication of (personal) dependence and so of the environmental factor'. The inherited death-instinct would thus be a scientism; a learned-seeming hypothesis of predestination (original sin in new words). This stress on environment is the new element which Winnicott, more than most, has brought to psychoanalysis. Melanie Klein and the Hartmann School represent approaches which stress, in their different ways, the same isolated aspect of individual ontology as is found in Freud. Freud in fact left open the issue about the transmission of acquired characteristics but, as a man of his time, when he thought about it he did so in terms of inheritance.

Today many would believe that the infant is taught from birth by the mother's value systems and the wisdom she has acquired from culture. It is hard for anyone without the closest contact with infants—who has not brought them up or shared such upbringing—to believe in this earliest teaching by the mother. Especially so since this is an *unconscious* transmission of assumptions, of what the mother takes for granted. Human infants, from the very start, are acutely sensitive to cues. They are like the chicks of the domestic fowl who, from the sixth to the sixteenth hour after hatching, follow whatever moves in their environment and become, in the ethologist's term, 'imprinted' with its characteristics. In this way they will take to a striped moving target and, once imprinted, lastingly ignore one marked with squares or different colours. If this imprinting happens in the early hours of life in chicks and other animal young, it might illuminate the development of the human infant. That this early imprinting is relatively irreversible in chicks, and ducks and other creatures, is also important. Konrad Lorenz's experiments, in which he imprinted goslings with a dog kennel as a source of food, led to ganders making their sexual overtures to the dog kennel when they grew up.

The question of reversibility is important. Many suppose that because a quality has been taught—has been acquired after birth and not inherited—it should be alterable. Sometimes this can be the case, but some acquired characteristics in humans may be like animal imprinting and very hard to modify, and then prevention in infancy—normal upbringing so to speak—would be the antidote. For example, it is Winnicott's conviction that the earliest experiences are a basis laid in infancy of our sense of the real as adults. Writing of the increasing problem of alienation and depersonalization, in which people are able to act correctly but feel reality as remote and meaningless, he says:

> individuals live creatively and feel that life is worth living or . . . they cannot live creatively and are doubtful about the value of living. *This variable in human beings is directly related to the quality and quantity of environmental provision at the beginning or in the early phases of each baby's living experience*. . . . At this point where creativity either comes into being or does not come into being (or alternatively is lost) the theoretician must take the environment into account, and no statement that concerns the individual as an isolate can touch this central problem of the course of creativity.

The fact is that today nearly all infants survive, even those who have such adverse experiences as to show psychotic reactions very early on—some cases of autism may be of this kind. The problem then is not about survival but about the quality of the survivor. It may be that many who survive and do not find life worth living have, thanks to antibiotics and medical skills, the full machinery for life but lack the soul or sense of human quality which Winnicott, and many others, too, these days believe is directly related to the quality of early mothering.

What is valuable above all in the writings of Winnicott is his stress on the lifelong dependence of human beings on the real environment; the fact that a great deal has to be put into children by adults if they are to come to anything; that development is not automatic. In the case of the infant and the child the realities of culture are transmitted in the first five years by the unspoken assumptions—the reversal of the usual parental attitude into 'do what I *do* and not what I *say*'—that lie behind the habits of the caring family-group, starting with the mothering figure. This is widely known through H. J. Guntrip and John Bowlby's writings both on infant care and on the link between ethology and human development. Interest in the family, however, leads to an unfashionable concern for the contribution of the mothering process in infants and at school and all through life: for the importance of emulation and example—indoctrination in fact—in older children and adults.

What, then, has been the impact of Winnicott's ideas on formal psychiatry, on prevention and social policy and on public awareness? During the past decade the public has learnt the size of the mental health problem and has become more aware of the prevalence of all grades of psychological disturbance and its effects: that as many young go to university as will at some time in their lives go to a mental hospital; that half the hospital beds in Britain are for mental disorders, and so on. Paradoxically, this new public awareness is in great part due to the success of psychiatry. Psychiatry has continued largely to rely on a vague constitutional aetiology; to say, i.e., that it does not know how the conditions arise but that psychiatrists do know something about symptom control and have largely substituted pharmacological walls for bricks and mortar. This has been a great political gain and a great factor in awakening public interest.

Paradoxically, the success of psychiatry in control has led to an interest in aetiology and consequently in conflict. From this stems the widespread wish for a more systematic public and cultural understanding of conflict in its normal and abnormal forms. Now that any family at all may contain, say, a drug addict, conventional good manners no longer require us to pretend that only certain wayward groups contain alcoholics, perversion, violence, hallucinations or thieving; psychoanalysis has become interesting again both to the thinking public and to psychiatrists.

Winnicott's role in this ecumenical process has, over thirty years, been an important one. By working with non-analysts he has helped them better to do the healing as well as the preventive job that parents, neighbours and all sorts of social groups have always done unacknowledged. He has shown the importance of what all ordinary people have always known. In doing so he has cut out the mystification and the doctrinaire pronouncements. He has not blinded us with science but has expressed, albeit in unfamiliar language, what will surely soon be seen as common sense.

group discussion with [illegible] troubling times. This is [illegible] J. D. [illegible] and John Bowlby's [illegible] tions and as the [illegible] and human development theories of the human [illegible] for the examination of the [illegible]

What, then, has been the impact of Winnicott's [illegible] During the past decade [illegible] mental health [illegible] has become [illegible] young [illegible] mental hospital [illegible] second [illegible] Psychiatry has continued largely to rely on [illegible] classification [illegible] something about [illegible] a great deal of [illegible] interest.

Paradoxically the [illegible] the [illegible] with its [illegible] and natural understanding [illegible] its nature and [illegible] no longer [illegible] thinking [illegible] psychoanalysis.

Winnicott's role [illegible] important [illegible] worked with [illegible] the doctor [illegible] be seen as common sense.

# INDEX

This index, in addition to referring to articles and reviews in the present volume, also shows other major reviews of the year which have appeared in the *T.L.S.*

Date references and page numbers *in italic* are to articles and reviews in the *T.L.S.* not reprinted in this volume. Page numbers in parentheses are given only where the reference is not immediately obvious from the article.